MANAGING THE GLOBAL

Human Security and Global Governance

Series Editor: Majid Tehranian

Published and forthcoming:

1. Worlds Apart: Human Security and Global Governance
   Edited by Majid Tehranian

2. Asian Peace: Security and Governance in the Asia-Pacific Region
   Edited by Majid Tehranian

3. Nuclear Disarmament: Obstacles to Banishing the Bomb
   Edited by Jozef Goldblat

4. Not by Bread Alone: Food Security and Governance in Africa
   Edited by Adelane Ogunrinade, Ruth Oniang'o and Julian May

5. Managing the Global: Globalization, Employment and Quality of Life
   Edited by Donald Lamberton

6. Globalization, Migration and Cultural Security
   Edited by Jonathan Friedman and Shalini Randeria

MANAGING THE GLOBAL

GLOBALIZATION, EMPLOYMENT AND QUALITY OF LIFE

Edited by

Donald Lamberton

I.B.Tauris *Publishers*
LONDON • NEW YORK
in association with
The Toda Institute for Global Peace and Policy Research

Published in 2002 by I.B.Tauris & Co Ltd
6 Salem Road, London W2 4BU
175 Fifth Avenue, New York NY 10010
www.ibtauris.com
in association with the Toda Institute for Global Peace and Policy Research

In the United States and Canada distributed by St. Martin's Press
175 Fifth Avenue, New York NY 10010

ISBN 1 86064 706 5

A full CIP record for this book is available from the British Library
A full CIP record for this book is available from the Library of Congress

Library of Congress catalog card: available

Typeset in Baskerville 11/12pt by The Midlands Book Typesetting Co, Loughborough
Printed and bound in Great Britain by MPG Books Ltd, Bodmin, Cornwall

Contents

Contributors

Walden Bello is Professor of Sociology and Public Administration at the University of the Philippines and co-director of Focus on the Global South at the University of Bangkok. He is Contributing Editor to *The Nation* newspaper (Bangkok); Senior Fellow and former Executive Director of the Institute for Food and Development Policy (Food First); member of the Board of Directors of Transnational Institute (Amsterdam); Board member of Oxfam America and Greenpeace International; member of the Editorial Board of *Third World Quarterly*. He is author and co-author of many books, including *Challenging the Mainstream: APEC and the Asia-Pacific Development Debate* (1995); *Dark Victor: The United States, Structural Adjustment, and Global Poverty* (1994); *People and Power in the Pacific: The Struggle for the Post-Cold War Order* (1992); *A Siamese Tragedy: Development and Disintegration in Modern Thailand* (1998). He has recently focused on the Asian Financial Crises and has written extensively in a number of publications such as *The Far Eastern Economic Review* and *The National* (New York).

Brian Easton is a Professorial Research Fellow at the Central Institute of Technology and holds research and teaching positions in four New Zealand universities in economics, New Zealand studies, and public policy. His most recent books have been *The Commercialisation of New Zealand* and *Stormy Seas: The Post-war New Zealand Economy*. He is a regular public commentator and is the *NZ Listener*'s regular economic columnist.

Hazel Henderson is an independent futurist and lecturer, author of *Building a Win-Win World* and five other books, a worldwide syndicated columnist and a consultant on sustainable development. She is a member of several editorial boards, including *Futures Research Quarterly*, *World Business Academy Perspectives*, *The State of the Future Report*, *E/The Environmental Magazine* (USA), *Resurgence and Futures* (UK), and *World Paper*. She is a Fellow of the World Business Academy and serves on the Global Commission to Fund the United Nations. She also serves on the boards of Worldwatch Institute, World Futures Studies Federation (Australia and Philippines), Calvert Social Investment Fund, Cousteau Society, Council on Economic Priorities, The New Economics Foundation (UK), and WETV (Ottawa, Canada). The first version of her Country Futures Indicators (CFI©), an alternative to the Gross National Product (GNP)—is a co-venture with Calvert Group, Inc.: the Calvert-Henderson Quality-of-life Indicators.

She has been Regent's Lecturer at the University of California, Santa Barbara; held the Horace Albright Chair in Conservation at the University of California, Berkeley; and advised the US Office of Technology Assessment and the National Science Foundation from 1974 to 1980. She is an active member of the National Press Club (Washington DC), the Social Venture Network, and the World Futures Society (USA). She shared the 1996 Global Citizen Award with novelist A. Perez Esquivel of Argentina.

Wayne Hudson is Professor of History and Philosophy in the School of Humanities at Griffith University and Director of the Asian Links Programme of the Key Centre for Ethics, Law, Justice and Governance. His most recent book is *Rethinking Australian Citizenship* (2000), edited with John Kane. Professor Hudson is especially interested in global education and global citizenship.

Donald M. Lamberton is Visiting Fellow, Graduate Program in Public Policy, Asia Pacific School of Economics and Management, Australian National University, Canberra, Australia; and Adjunct Professor, Faculty of Communications, University of Canberra, Australia. He is Coordinating Editor, *Information Economics and Policy*; General Editor, *Prometheus*; and a member of the editorial boards of *Economics of Innovation and New Technology*, *Human Systems Management*, and *Futures Research Quarterly*. Formerly Professor of Economics at Case Western Reserve University, USA, 1969–72 and the University of Queensland, Australia, 1973–89, he has held visiting appointments at various universities, including Oxford, Stanford, UCLA and Pittsburgh, and research centres, including East-West Center, Honolulu and Technical Change Centre, London. He served as a member of Australian Government committees of inquiry and as consultant to international agencies, including OECD, UNESCO, UNCTC and ITU. He is currently a member of the board of the International Telecommunications Society. His recent books include *Communication & Trade* (1998), *The New Research Frontiers of Communications Policy* (1997), *The Economics of Communication and Information* (1996), and *Beyond Competition: The Future of Telecommunications* (1995).

Stuart Macdonald is Professor of Information and Organization at the Sheffield University Management School, University of Sheffield (UK). His books include *Information for Innovation: Managing Change from* *an Information Perspective* (1998), *Technology and the Tyranny of Export Controls: Whisper Who Dares* (1990) and (with Ernest Braun) *Revolution in Miniature: The History and Impact of Semiconductor Electronics* (1982). He was also editor or co-editor of *The Trouble with Technology: Explorations in the Process of Technological Change* (1982) and *Informal Information Flow* (Special Issue of *International Journal of Technology Management*, 1996). He is European Editor of *Prometheus* and a member of the Editorial Board of *Information Economics and Policy*.

Jane Marceau joined the University of Western Sydney Macarthur in mid-1996 as Pro-Vice-Chancellor (Research) and Professor of Management. She is also Director of the Australian Expert Group in Industry Studies, a research centre of UWS Macarthur. Before this she was Professor of Public Policy at the Australian National University. In 1993 she was seconded to design and create the ANU's flagship MBA Program, Managing Business in Australia. Before joining the ANU she was a Project Director at the OECD and spent many years living and working in Paris and the UK, where she also taught at INSEAD, at the University of Paris X and at Manchester Business School. Over recent years her research has increasingly focused on industry, technology, research and science policy. She has participated in a multi-country project on industrial policies for small industrial OECD nations. In Australia she has carried out research into technological change in the automotive, clothing and electronics industries and into the employment potential of small manufacturing firms. She is currently undertaking projects on innovation in the biomedical, construction and TCF industries. She has become increasingly interested in the structure of advanced innovative economies and the question of the importance of particular industrial structures to the success of strategies for growth. Her recent publications include *The High Road or the Low Road? Alternatives for Australia's Future: A Report on Australia's Industries* (1997).

Akira Onishi is Vice-President of Soka University, Tokyo and Professor and Dean of the Graduate School of Engineering. He has made a great contribution to global modeling and global model simulations and is the original designer of the FUGI (Futures of Global Independence Planning). Previously he was Dean of the Department of Economics at Soka University and Chief Economist of the Japanese Economic Research Centre. In 1991 he was awarded the First Supreme Article Award from the Japanese Association of Administration and Planning.

Michael Pusey is Professor of Sociology, University of New South Wales and Fellow of the Academy of Social Sciences of Australia (FASSA). He worked at Harvard University as a Senior Teaching Fellow and later as a high school teacher, a senior public servant, and as a consultant to several governments on education and public service reform. He is author of five books including *Dynamics of Bureaucracy* (1975), *Control and Knowledge* (1980), and *Jürgen Habermas* (1987). His work on 'economic rationalism' and the impacts of economic change on Australian society has produced over 100 radio and television interviews and a similar number of articles and references in the metropolitan press. His book, *Economic Rationalism in Canberra* (1991), first coined the term 'economic rationalism' and launched the continuing debate over the social and economic costs of neo-liberal, free market, economic reform and restructuring in Australia. Professor Pusey, at the time of the conference on which this book is based, was mid-way through his Australian Research Council (ARC) funded 'Middle Australia Project', on the impact of economic reform on the Australian middle class. He had embarked on a further ARC project on standards of living and quality of life in Australia.

Bharati Ray is a member of the Indian Parliament, Rajya Sabha (Upper House). She was Professor of History, Calcutta University and served as Pro-Vice Chancellor (Academic Affairs) there from 1988 to 1995. She was the Founder Director of the Women's Studies Research Centre, Calcutta University. Currently, she is Honorary Professor of History and Founder member of the Peace Studies Research Group, Calcutta University. Her publications include *Hyderabad and British Paramountcy* (1988); (ed.) *From the Seams of History: Essays on Indian Women* (1995); (ed. jointly) *From Independence Towards Freedom: Indian Women Since 1947* (1999); (ed.) *Women and Politics: France, India and Russia* (1999); *Sakhawat Hossain and Women of Colonial Bengal* (forthcoming). She is the editor of *The Journal of Women's Studies*, Calcutta.

Stuart Rees is Professor of Social Work and Director of the Centre for Peace and Conflict Studies at the University of Sydney. He has worked in community development and social work in Britain, in Canada, in the War on Poverty programs in the USA and with Save the Children in India and Sri Lanka. He has taught at leading universities in the UK (Aberdeen and Southampton), in Canada (Toronto and Wilfrid Laurier) and in the USA (University of

California at Berkeley, University of Texas). His publications include over 100 journal articles on valuations of health and welfare services and the attributes of peace negotiations and humanitarianism in social policy. He is the author and co-author of nine books, including *A Brutal Game* (1986), *Achieving Power* (1991), *Beyond the Market* (1993), *The Human Costs of Managerialism* (1995) and *Human Rights, Corporate Responsibility* (2000). Professor Rees' awards include a Simon Fellowship at the University of Manchester, a Humanities Fellowship at the City University of Hong Kong and, in 1998, Japan's Soka University's Award of Highest Honor for 'Contributions to World Peace'. For four years he was an elected Fellow of the Senate of the University of Sydney. He is currently council member of the Toda Research Institute into Global Governance and Human Security and a member of the Aboriginal Reconciliation Council of New South Wales.

Graham Riches is Professor and Director, School of Social Work and Family Studies, University of British Columbia. He has previously chaired the Social Work Program at the University of Northern British Columbia (1995–1998) and been head of the Department of Social Work and Community Welfare at James Cook University of Northern Queensland, Australia. His previous academic posts had been at the University of Hong Kong and the University of Regina where he had directed the Social Administration Research Unit. He has an MA from the University of Cambridge and a postgraduate Diploma of Social Administration from the London School of Economics. His publications include *Food Banks and the Welfare Crisis* (1986), (ed. jointly) *Unemployment and Welfare: Social Policy and the Work of Social Work* (1990), and *First World Hunger and Welfare Politics* (1997). He was a founding editor of the *Canadian Review of Social Policy*. His research interests include: hunger, poverty and food security; social security and welfare reform; unemployment and social work practice; critical community work; structural social work education; comparative social policy; ideology and social welfare.

James N. Rosenau is Professor of International Affairs and Professor of Political Science at the George Washington University. A former President of the International Studies Association, his scholarship and teaching focuses on the dynamics of world politics and the overlap between domestic and foreign affairs. He has held numerous teaching and research positions in leading universities in the USA (Princeton University, Columbia University) and in many other countries, including the University of Belgrade and the Jawaharlal Nehru University, India. He is the author of over 140 articles and more than 30 books, most recently *Turbulence in World Politics: A Theory of Change and Continuity* (1990), *The United Nations in a Turbulent World* (1992), *International Political Economy: Understanding Global Disorder* (1995), and *Reversing Relations with Former Adversaries: US Foreign Policy after the Cold War* (1998).

Edna Ross is an independent consultant and researcher. Areas of research, policy analysis and advocacy have included social policy areas such as employment, home-based care, community development and poverty in Australia. More recently, her work has focused on development related issues—the social and environmental impacts of trade liberalization, challenges to development posed by globalization, and issues of participation, transparency and governance of multilateral institutions such as the World Bank and the World Trade Organization. She has worked with universities, parliamentarians and non-government organizations, was the director of advocacy and public policy of the Australian Council for Overseas Aid and is a member of the Australian National Consultative Committee on Peace and Disarmament.

Frank Stilwell is Associate Professor in the School of Economics and Political Science at the University of Sydney. He is coordinating editor of the *Journal of Australian Political Economy* and author of eight books, including *The Accord and Beyond*, *Understanding Cities and Regions*, *Reshaping Australia*, and *Economic Inequality*.

Majid Tehranian has a doctorate in Political Economy from Harvard, is Professor of International Communication at the University of Hawaii, and Director of the Toda Institute for Global Peace and Policy Research. His latest books are *Technologies of Power: Information Machines and Democratic Prospects* (1990), *Restructuring for World Peace: At the Threshold of the 21st Century* (1992), *Global Communication and World Politics: Domination, Development and Discourse* (1999), *Worlds Apart: Human Security and Global Governance* (1999), and *Asian Peace: Security and Governance in the Asia Pacific Region* (1999). Since 1996, he has been directing an international collaborative project on Human Security and Global Governance.

Preface

This is the fifth volume in the Toda Institute Book Series on Human Security and Global Governance (HUGG). Since its establishment in 1996, in collaboration with other peace and policy research institutes, the Toda Institute for Global Peace and Policy Research has engaged a growing number of prominent peace and policy scholars in the project. The studies have been focused on how governance of human security can be improved at local, national, regional and global levels.

The objectives of the project are fourfold:

1. To focus on how the international community is managing or mismanaging human security problems.
2. To empower the voices that are largely conspicuous by their absence in the international discourse on security and governance.
3. To employ a dialogical method at small international conferences during which peace and policy scholars from different cultural and epistemic communities can engage each other in a frank and creative problem-solving mode.
4. To promote resolution of protracted conflicts while drawing attention to the root causes of violence in international and domestic life.

Each volume stands on its own and together, the series offers students of international affairs a deeper understanding of the role of global governance in enhancing or constraining human security and international peace. The first volume reviewed the past discourses and practices in human security and global governance while identifying the main challenges ahead. The second focused on problems of human security and governance in the Asia-Pacific region. The third took up the challenge of nuclear disarmament in the context of proliferation of weapons of mass destruction, including biological and chemical weapons as well as increasing small arms trade. The fourth volume took up the issue of food security and regional cooperation in Africa. The present volume focuses on social and economic insecurities resulting from globalization, unemployment and declining quality of life in certain world regions and population sectors. Future volumes will focus on migration, identity, and cultural security, peace and security in West Asia, and democratizing global governance.

In the year 2000, the project entered a new phase with a series of international conferences on Dialog of Civilizations: A New Peace Agenda for a New Millennium. The first one took place on February 11–13 2000, in Okinawa, Japan, focusing on the normative foundations of a new global civilization that is being born out of the contributions of all past and present human civilizations, including indigenous belief systems, Hinduism, Buddhism, Confucianism, Judaism, Christianity, Islam and Secular Humanism. The second meeting took place in Moscow in June 2001, focusing on East (Confederation of Independent States) and West (NATO) relations. The third conference is planned for June 2002 to take place in Beijing, focusing on North (more developed countries) and South (less developed countries) relations. The three volumes emerging out of this phase will together provide an agenda for peace building in the 21st century.

In keeping with the Toda Institute's motto, "Dialog of Civilizations for World Citizenship," the purpose of the HUGG Project is to foster an inter-civilizational dialog on the most pressing issues facing the world. Like other conceptual categories such as culture, ethnicity or nationality, "civilization" is admittedly a fuzzy concept, but we have found it to be a useful metaphor for approaching the current normative conflicts in the world. A dialog of civilizations on "human security" and "global governance" thus raises perplexing normative questions such as those of efficiency versus equity, individual rights versus social responsibilities, equality versus hierarchy, libertarianism versus communitarianism.

The two concepts of human security and global governance also stand at micro and macro polarities. Whereas human security is concerned primarily with individual welfare conditions, global governance focuses on generalized rules and institutions of international regimes. To juxtapose these two concepts into a single sweep may be considered too thematically ambitious and methodologically impossible. However, the dislocating pressures of globalization, including the problems of a nuclear holocaust, a polluted world, global poverty, violence, and dislocations of life and labor are paving the way for common normative grounds. Threats to basic human security such as proliferation of weapons of mass destruction (WMD), famines, ethnic cleansing, and human-rights violations have already prompted United Nations interventions, albeit awkwardly and haphazardly. The central question is how the international community can rid itself of WMD while building the technological, social, economic, political and cultural foundations for a new humane global civilization?

Under the able editorship of Don Lamberton, this volume provides excellent diagnoses, prognoses and therapies of the current globalization processes and their impact on employment and quality of life. A cursory review of the chapters demonstrates that we live in an increasingly complex world. Various pundits have characterized our own era by such catchphrases as the "global village" (Marshall McLuhan), "post-industrial" (Daniel Bell), "information society" (Marc Porat), "end of history" (Francis Fukuyama) and "clash of civilizations" (Samuel Huntington).

"Globalization" is currently the most fashionable of such catchphrases. However, as the essays in this volume show, our own era can be equally as well characterized as the "age" of regionalization, nationalization, localization, or fragmentation. If we change our perspective from spatial to temporal categories, our era can be equally as well characterized as the "beginning of history" in which over two-thirds of humanity are for the first time clamoring to be recognized as subjects rather than objects of history. There is also a powerful current toward dialog rather than clash among civilizations. The UN conferences of the past two decades have provided useful forums for world dialog. The Toda Institute's international conferences have also been focused on developing an ecumenical consensus on global ethics and norms with respect to such issues as the nuclear race, food and cultural security, and global governance. As for the label of "global village" that has been so uncritically adopted as a slogan by the mass media, we must remember that over one-half of humanity has never made a phone call. The global village is clearly not global.

The essays in this volume focus on the impact of globalization as a trend among others on employment and quality of life. Globalization is the most visible trend to those who travel internationally. No one can escape the presence of *McDonalds*, *Coca-Cola*, *Hilton*, *CNN*, and *MTV* around the world's major international airports and metropolitan centers. However, as we dig more deeply into the lives of ordinary people, other trends begin to manifest themselves. Globalization appears to be both uniting and dividing, integrating and fragmenting, the world in new and mosaic patterns. In a book entitled *Jihad vs. McWorld: How Globalism and Tribalism Are Reshaping the World*, Benjamin Barber has captured the complexity of this process.

Globalization and tribalization seem to be two sides of the same coin. The following essays dig more deeply into why this is so. Pancapitalism, as both Michael Pusey (see chapter 8) and I (Tehranian 1999) have referred to it, is a novel phenomenon. Since the widespread application of information technologies in the 1980s and 1990s to the processes of production, distribution and financial transactions, capitalism has clearly expanded its global reach and penetration. The opening of China to world markets in the 1980s and the fall of the Soviet Union in 1991 have brought two other world giants within the domain of global capitalism. Pancapitalism can be thus considered a label that captures the significance of the transformation of capitalism from its national and regional to global proportions.

As an emerging mode of production and regulation, pancapitalism is creating demand for four distinctly different types of labor: *manual, intellectual, managerial* and *refugee* labor. By computerizing, informatizing, automating or robotizing production processes, pancapitalism is doing away with millions of manual jobs. Yet it is at the same time creating new manual jobs. The pancapitalist regime needs at least two distinctly different kinds of cheap manual labor. It has transferred industries and demand for labor from high to low-waged areas of the world. But it has also created demand for guest workers, house servants and entertainers in the high-waged countries. Export processing zones in the newly industrializing countries (NICs) depend heavily on specially trained labor for routine and repetitive tasks. Pancapitalism also has created a class of newly rich countries and individuals in need of domestic service. Because they are cheap and malleable, young women frequently supply both types of manual labor. Hence, feminization of labor and migration. As Castles and Miller (1998, p. 150) have noted, about 1.5 million Asian women were working abroad by the mid-1990s, and in many migratory movements they outnumbered men. Two-thirds of Indonesian migrants from 1984 to 1994 were women. About one-half of Philippine overseas contract workers (OCWs) in 1994 were female. Most migrant women are concentrated in jobs regarded as 'typically female': domestic workers, entertainers, prostitutes, restaurant and hotel staff, and assembly-line workers in clothing and electronics. According to a report by the US Central Intelligence Agency (2000), as many as 50,000 women and children from Asia, Latin America, and Eastern Europe are brought to the USA under false pretences each year and forced to work as prostitutes, abused laborers or servants.

Transfer of billions of dollars of petrodollars to the Persian Gulf oil exporters in the 1970s and 1980s also created a high demand for manual and intellectual labor in the region's thinly-populated countries. This, in turn, led to a flood of migration from East, West and

South Asia to that region. By 1985, there were 3.2 million Asian workers in the Gulf States, of whom 2 million were in Saudi Arabia. While most of the "guest workers" in Germany and the Persian Gulf region are men employed in a variety of construction and industrial jobs, women also represent significant numbers working as servants, nurses and concubines.

The second type of demand for labor generated by pancapitalism takes place at the opposite end of the labor market, that is to satisfy the need for highly skilled, intellectual labor. In contrast to national capitalism that focused on manufacturing, pancapitalism is critically dependent on knowledge, intellect workers and financial service industries. The internationalization of production and finance is leading to increasing mobility of intellectual labor. An ILO's official has aptly termed Western Europe's growing number of professional workers the "highly invisible" migrants (Castles and Miller 1998, pp. 167–8). He has estimated that they comprise one-quarter of legally resident aliens living in the EC and include 2 million citizens of European Free Trade Association (EFTA) states, which have since joined with the EC to create the world's most populous free trade zone, the European Economic Area. The remainder of the EC's highly invisible migrants mostly consists of Americans, Canadians and Japanese. Although "guest workers" such as Turks in Germany are often stereotypically seen as blue-collar workers, they also include surprising numbers of professionals and entrepreneurs.

The third category of labor migration under the pancapitalist regime consists of managers of transnational corporations (TNCs) inter-governmental organizations (IGOs), and non-governmental organizations (NGOs). Through joint ventures, mergers and acquisitions, the global corporation is increasingly multi-ethnic in its labor and managerial staff. A growing number of such managers stay for long periods of time in their "host" countries, marry natives and develop multi-cultural families.

The fourth type of labor may be labeled refugee labor. It consists of victims of revolutions, civil wars and ethnic cleansing forced to migrate. Such migrants may or may not appear in the UNHCR's statistics of refugees. The refugee migrants may be considered an unintended consequence of militarized regimes and insurgencies supported by the Western or Sino-Russian blocs. In Eastern Europe, Asia, Africa and Latin America, the client regimes have had sooner or later to succumb to social and political upheavals such as those in Cuba, Vietnam, Cambodia, Iran, Afghanistan, the Philippines, Indonesia and communist countries in Eastern Europe. This in turn has resulted in waves of political migrations into Western Europe and North America. Civil wars such as those in Somalia and Ethiopia also are in part legacies of the Cold War era in which different sides were supported and armed by the Soviet and Western camps. Colonial policies of divide and rule in Congo and Rwanda contributed to the postcolonial civil wars. The breakups of the Soviet Union and Yugoslavia have led to civil wars in Tajikistan, Chechnya, Bosnia and Kosovo and outpouring of millions of refugees.

What about the impact of pancapitalism on quality of life? If we take the *UNDP's Human Development Reports* as our guidepost, rapid economic growth under the auspices of pancapitalism does not necessarily spell out improved quality of life for the bulk of population. This is so at least in the short run during which those tied into the corporate and government networks prosper while those without such ties lose jobs and ground. Neoliberal pundits argue that in the long run pancapitalism will trickle down its benefits more equally. That may be true, but as John Maynard Keynes reminded us, in the long run we are all dead. The short run counts for those whose loss of jobs and livelihood spells out hardship and sometime destitution.

The 1999 edition of the *Human Development Report* reveals (pp. 134–7) that countries with higher rates of economic growth do not show an equal improvement in their Human Development Index (HDI). To measure human development, HDI is constructed as an index of life expectancy, adult literacy and educational enrolment. Some high-income countries show a loss in their human development rankings. These include Switzerland, Luxembourg, Singapore, Hong Kong, Brunei, Kuwait, Qatar, Venezuela, Mexico, Malaysia, Mauritius, Oman and Turkey. Measured as purchasing power parity in US dollars, real per capita income rank minus HDI gives all of these countries a negative score indicating that their quality of life is less than their per capita income.

What can be said about development policies to maximize human security? As Frank Stilwell argues in this volume (chapter 3), the basic options may be reduced to three: going for growth, upgrading human capital, or prioritizing equity and environment. In real life, of course, it takes political will to make such strategic choices on matters that affect the vital interests of a complex variety of pressure groups. History of economic development, however, shows that countries prosper in the long run that do not neglect investment in human capital while investing in physical capital. Development ultimately means human development. Globalization from above led by transnational corporations currently shows a shift of emphasis from equity to efficiency, sustainability to growth, and social welfare to corporate welfare. Co-optation of the state by the TNCs though campaign financing, tax evasion through offshore tax havens, decline of regulatory regimes and demise of the national welfare systems constitute some of the disturbing signs. The trends do not augur well for a peaceful 21st century. Democratic rather than hegemonic globalization suggests a more promising road. This volume provides ample warnings and proposals to meet the challenges ahead.

Majid Tehranian
Director, Toda Institute for Global Peace and Policy Research
Honolulu, Hawaii

References

Castles, Stephen and Miller, Mark J. 1998. *The Age of Migration: International Population Movements in the Modern World.* New York: The Guilford Press.

Tehranian, Majid. 1999. *Global Communication and World Politics: Domination, Development, Discourse.* Boulder: Lynne Rienner Publishers.

United Nations Development Program (UNDP). *Human Development Report.* New York: Oxford University Press, annual reviews since 1990.

United States Central Intelligence Agency. 2000. *International Trafficking in Women in the United States: A Contemporary Manifestation of Slavery.* Washington, DC: CIA.

Part One

CHAPTER 1

New World Disorder?

Donald Lamberton

Globalization is a potent mix of true and false perceptions, aspirations and fears of many people in diverse economic and social circumstances. For some, their broad view of the changing world process is dominated by thoughts of 'one society,' peace and sustainable well being; for others, the emphasis is on economic development, expanding world trade, and unrestricted capital movement. For either perspective, globalization is in crucial ways an economic concept that reflects the seeking of economies of scale and scope, economic development, profit, and power through largely unfettered markets, aided and abetted increasingly by government at national and international levels (*The Economist*, 2000c). We need, therefore, to look closely at the economic reasoning underlying claims of benefits and costs and to question the relevance of mainstream economics and its policy counterpart to central aspects of this all-embracing process, especially its widely assumed inevitability. In so doing, we must avoid the artificial separation of the economic from the social, because all action involves objectives, choices and resources and is therefore economic.

I have adopted the title of Kenneth Jowitt's book (1992) for my introduction to these essays on globalization, employment and the quality of life because the general debate about globalization proclaims an element of newness and his title carries connotations of disequilibrium, unknowledge and a variety of problematics.[1] G.L.S. Shackle would have argued that such circumstances imply 'freedom for imagination and conjecture' (1972, p.18), these in turn enabling the creation of theory. For Shackle, 'Theory serves deep needs of the human spirit: it subordinates nature to man, imposes a beautiful simplicity on the unbearable multiplicity of fact, gives comfort in the face of the unknown and unexperienced, stops the teasing of mystery and doubt which, though salutary and life-preserving, is uncomfortable, so that by theory we seek to sort out the justified from the unjustified fear'. (1967, pp. 288–9).

When the theory builds upon observed and reasonably stable frequencies, we see reliable information, technology and science created and used through processes that have contributed mightily to economic and social development. Lionel Robbins wrote: 'In the last analysis the difference between the economic potential of the Stone Age and the 20th century is a difference of range of relevant techniques and information' (1968, p. 83). When, however, unwarranted importance attaches to the hopes or fears, strong contrary evidence is recognized, or the theory 'fails to support the interests of our own particular portion of humanity,' (Shackle 1967, p. 288), expectations are revised and the outcomes can seem much less beneficial.

This is a theme picked up by some economic theorists in recent times, e.g., by Romer (1990), but in a broader sense it is the central proposition fuelling much of the new/information/knowledge-based economy ideas—and e-commerce rhetoric. The newness lies in a supposedly much reduced cost of information (comparable to lowered transport cost in the Industrial Revolution), a heightened information intensity of economic activity, and the computerization, even industrialization of information activities.

There are very direct implications for economic theory which had taken 'on a character belonging to the manipulable, calculable, external world of things, not the world of the conscious mind in its eternal station on the edge of the void of time, the conscious mind whose being consists precisely in the endless gaining of knowledge' (Shackle 1972, p. 3). To the extent that there is a new dimension to world circumstances and it can be identified in the plethora of images conjured up by such labels as the 'information revolution,' the death of distance, the online economy, the digital society, cyberspace and globalization, there should be little about the irrelevance of much economic theory to the big problems of information, knowledge[2] and coordination to occasion surprise. Mainstream theory could never be comfortable with 'unknowledge' and would seem inevitably to lead us astray in a world where the bulk of our resources are devoted to learning, innovation and adapting to change (Carter 1996). Just as the opening up of territory and the new powers over natural forces that came with steam power and electrification had provided opportunities for entrepreneurs—and for governments—in the past, so this new emphasis has been greeted hopefully by those who seek to gain: the new information and communication industries that appear to be a key component of future world business and are already a major influence upon world government.

There was an understandable tendency to cling to traditional theory, especially when it supported the alleged superiority and dominance of the market as a form of organization and thereby protected established interests. To do so was in effect an insurance policy for those directly engaged in those information and communication activities. But it was also supported, again understandably, by those who made up the social and political infrastructure. Such infrastructure was not as directly exposed to market pressures. There was a time lag that was reinforced by the profoundly important tendency to organizational obsolescence or lock-in, which was itself a consequence of the combination of economic characteristics of information itself. As Kenneth Arrow reasoned:

> The combination of uncertainty, indivisibility, and capital intensity associated with information channels and their use imply (a) that the actual structure and behavior of an organization may depend heavily upon random events, in other words on history, and (b) the very pursuit of efficiency may lead to rigidity and unresponsiveness to further change (Arrow 1974, p. 49).

While the importance newly assigned to information activities—at least since 1962 when Fritz Machlup's pioneering book was published—has become a major, even the principal challenge to mainstream economics, information problems of one kind or another are at the heart of the tensions within the economics discipline (Boyle 1992, p. 1444, n.73); they are general and all pervasive (Vines and Stevenson 1991, ch.1). We need, however, to keep in mind that the real economics failure lay in ignoring 'unknowledge' and so neglecting what people know and learn and 'what they do know that isn't so'.[3] The role of unknowledge was no doubt just as real long ago when Ricardo was drafting his additional chapter 'On Machinery' to fill a gap in his *Principles of Political Economy and Taxation* (1971). And the information/organization nexus was still a matter of great importance when the architects of the modern theory of rational expectations turned the clock back with their hypothesis based on decision-makers being well-informed and making good use of their information.[4] Here then is further evidence of economic reasoning buttressing dominant ideas and the organizations that embrace them. Of course, there is always the threat of obsolescence with large, undetected costs, both private and social, with loss of both jobs and profits. From that perspective, the delayed adjustments are no doubt evidence that the market works, but there remain doubts about the social desirability of the processes.

Globalization is one, perhaps currently the most important, of these dominant ideas. It shares with—to use an ill-advised word—its companion 'driver', technology, the illusions of newness and inevitability. While technology, especially information technology, is seen as a driver of globalization, it is argued also that technology can be a source of diversity because IT, for example, has great enabling potential. Time will tell whether this assessment is justified. So far, there seem to be grounds for believing that major indivisibilities in the form of information and organizational structures will be found in the information economy—the Information Age equivalent of the big machines and big factories of the Industrial Age (Lamberton 1997a). The looming rush to alliances and mergers in the world's communications, media, and airline industries (*The Economist*, 1997; 2000b; 2000d) does not suggest bigness has gone out of fashion. As Stiglitz, former Chief Economist at the World Bank, points out: 'knowledge, almost by definition, gives rise to a form of increasing returns to scale which may undermine competition' (Stiglitz 1999, p. 7).

If globalization means that diversity in goods, services, culture, language and institutions is to be stamped out, should not this expectation lead us to ask fundamental questions: Are not differences the basis of trade? Is the global village to be a place of enervating sameness? Is the modeling of the world economy we are witnessing a projection of domestic smoothing out of local differences onto the world stage?

One of the major problems with the thrust of recent economic analysis is illustrated by the manner in which Romer and many others have responded to the Information Revolution. While conceding its importance, they have nevertheless gone down a wrong road. They have attempted to modernize their analysis by admitting the importance of knowledge but have insisted that it can then be positioned and analysed as an additional variable, K for Knowledge, in the old production function analytical framework. They wish to remain in the 'manipulable, calculable, external world of things', failing to appreciate that the technologies they seek to summarize in the production function are, and remain, products of that 'endless gaining of knowledge'.

There are dimensions of the role of knowledge that cannot be depicted in this fashion and it is not possible to use the production function approach as a basis for the dominant perspective from which the globalized world is to be viewed. Development may have the potential to be freedom (Sen 1999), but in what may prove to be a long interim—if that is what it turns out to be—the prospect is either sinking or swimming in a global state (Sobel 1999, ch.5). It is important therefore to clarify some of the underlying reasoning that supports the claims for the benefits and inevitability of globalization; claims that stem from the supposed consequences of a combination of the competitive process, trade and development and, ultimately, globalization.

A heavy emphasis has been placed on capital flow (without comparable attention to movement of labor) and international cooperation to modify legal relations, especially those governing the rights of investors and of the owners or controllers of intellectual property. From this perspective true globalization means that capital would flow in a roughly uniform way into all developing regions, being attracted by comparative advantage: 'there should be no pockets of stagnant growth where disciplined work forces and/or abundant natural resources are under-utilized' (Johnston 1991, p. 1). At present some areas receive more economic attention than others, so world markets are not global according to this test: 'examination of the flow of capital, trade relationships, and income levels reveals strong regional patterns of development. Thus *regionalization* frequently appears to be a better description of world market evolution than globalization' (Johnston 1991, p. xi. See also *The Economist*, 2000f).

This involves much, much more than the flows of investment funds. It would appear that this test of globalization might apply to areas similarly endowed. Over and above the complex mix of money capital, disciplined/trained workers, monopoly business situations (see Parente and Prescott 1999), and known and imagined natural resources, there are organizations and institutions, accumulated knowledge, language and cultural traditions, along with varying degrees of political stability and social cohesiveness (Lamberton 1993). There are different patterns of external ties. Can these be ignored so easily? Together they constitute the social capabilities of the nation concerned; they are its organizational capital. So few areas will, therefore, be similarly endowed. Investors are looking for profit and would be unwise to ignore the lack of such capabilities.

Information, communication and coordination aspects dominate in the integration process (Lamberton 2000). If the information resource is treated as shorthand for the information stocks and flows, the capability of handling that resource, and the institutional channels that have been created to enable its handling, there is reason to think, first, that an existing distribution of information resources may confer a comparative advantage on a regional bloc, just as it can on a nation; and, second, that regional bloc activity may achieve further advantage through specialization in information activities. Madden (1999) has used international telephone traffic data as the base metric to consider movements toward or away from situations of bilateral reciprocity, multilateralism and market diversification. His findings for Asia-Pacific communications patterns were that China has begun to develop stronger communication links with Asian partners, while India and Pakistan remain outside the mainstream of Asia-Pacific communications developments, and have some way to go to achieve the degree of regional assimilation of China. Overall, the path of Asian integration is generally increasing.[5]

Some of the resources needed to achieve such advantage are not readily amenable to WTO leveling of the playing field. Consider the case of culture. If by culture we mean the living historical product of group problem-solving, it is a public and private sector form of organizational capital that will not be captured in the plans of international bodies for investment and yet can confer advantage. Perhaps the sharing of such organizational capital can be a source of sufficient benefits to make regional integration more attractive than the shared but uncertain benefits on a level, or not so level, playing field peopled by players of very different size and capability. It is an easy step to assume that all these other considerations will adapt to central economic pressures. The reality may be slow processes of change. For example, the search for optimality should, so many believe, have favoured a universal language—after all, 'the usual g.e.t. economics tends to predict convergence' (Arrow 1987, p. 213). But history shows the record of romance languages was not one of convergence; rather 'one language... became many languages' (Arrow 1987, p. 212. See also Pelikan 1969; Snow 1998; *The Economist*, 2000e).

This suggests that some history lessons are needed. Is it true that the appropriate international division of labor and the realization of a country's comparative advantage are best achieved by free market forces? Penrose asserts that 'neither appeals to history nor experience demonstrate its truth in a dynamic world... Where did the government not play, in collaboration with local business and other elites, a very powerful role?' (1992, p. 238–9). Not one, says Penrose, got it right by relying on the free play of market forces, abandoning subsidies, and being freely open to imports and foreign investment.

Leafing the pages of history, she contends what was true of the British economy and North America holds for the non-European countries that have successfully industrialized today. Where then is the experience that justifies what she calls 'the repeated insistence' of the IMF and the World Bank that developing countries should practice this economic liberalism? One of her most telling points relates to the Bank's assertion that while industrial countries have restricted trade to promote industry, their objectives 'could have been obtained in other [unspecified] ways'. The Bank asks that the standard of demonstrability be applied to justify departures from liberal style policy, but it does not attempt to apply that standard to its own theorizing.

It would seem that other lessons from history are being ignored—lessons that bear upon the assumed inevitability. O'Rourke and Williamson (1999) have examined the experience of 'the first great globalization': the period 1840–1914 'was in its way a far more dramatic occurrence than the integration of world markets that has been taking place since 1945. Transport costs and trade barriers fell faster; international capital flows as a share of national output were far larger; and cross-border migration was far greater' (*The Economist* 2000a). There was increasing international trade. A World Bank report acknowledges these seemingly good times: 'a period of considerable global economic integration supported by relatively liberal economic policies,' when migration was less restricted than today. (1996, p. 21). But the Bank did not go on to tackle the question: Why is globalization inevitable today when the process was cut short after 1914? This is a big question deserving close attention. The study by O'Rourke and Williamson points to a mix of influences that worked against continuing international economic integration: a political backlash, war, reaction against trade with closure of agricultural markets, protection of infant manufacturing industries, abandonment of migration. In short, the main message, as stated by *The Economist* reviewer, is that 'globalization can sow the seeds of its own destruction'. Perhaps events at Seattle and Davos were indications of that possibility (*The Economist*, 1999a, 1999b).

Underlying all these issues are two basic theoretical problems, both of which are tending to become more complex and more directly relevant in this Information Age. First, there is the theoretical support advanced for private enterprise. The best short critique (Nelson 1981, p. 60) of that doctrine makes the following points: 'the standard welfare economics arguments propose not that private enterprise is better than any other organizational solution; only that if certain assumptions are met, "it can't be beat"' (Nelson 1981, p. 94). In practice, the support rests on implicit beliefs about the superiority of private enterprise in respect of administrative parsimony, responsiveness and innovativeness (Nelson 1981, 59–77). The contrasts beween reality and the assumed conditions combine with the informational and organizational dimensions of the Information Age economy to mount a major challenge to private enterprise doctrine. As Stiglitz has argued cogently: 'the critical failing in the standard neoclassical model... [is]... in its assumptions concerning information... [S]light perturbations in the standard information assumptions drastically changed all the major results of standard neoclassical theory. The theory was simply not robust at all' (1994, p. x).

The second theoretical problem is a very old one: how to draw the boundary between the economy and its infrastructure.[6] Recognition that, for example, knowledge, a patent system, business organization, and culture as well as roads, water supply, airports and telecommunications are all part of infrastructure undermines the seeming neatness of a production function, no matter how elaborate its subscript and superscript adornments. If technology is useful knowledge, the assumption of a given technology is difficult to work with in relation to human organization directed to 'the endless gaining of knowledge' (Lamberton 1997b). As the pattern of investment shifts in favour of knowledge and intangible assets generally (Webster 1999), theory is less applicable—and official statistics cover less of what they are supposed to cover.

There are risks that policies are misdirected and resources wasted; and that concerted action to deal with problems bearing upon economic efficiency goes unattended. Even when the right objective seems to have been identified, actions may be inappropriate. Funding allocations may prove to be much less important than organizational and institutional innovation—and this may well mean a greater rather than lesser role for government: 'A Global Labour Office capable of looking the World Trade Organization in the eye, for instance, could set standards protecting those interests as strongly as those insisted upon by international agencies for "transparency" in accounting, "fair" competition and the like' (Toulmin 1999, p. 905). As Hazel Henderson argues in this volume, other sectors of life have to follow the multinational corporation onto the global stage.

Encouraging statements issue from the IMF and the World Bank. On February 16 2000, Bank President Wolfensohn told the Tenth Ministerial Meeting of the UN Conference on Trade and Development (UNCTAD): 'Globalization must have a "human face" and help improve the daily lives of the 1.3 billion people worldwide who live on less than $1 a day... Globalization is here to stay. Thus, the challenge to us all is to harness the positive aspects of globalization in the cause of development and poverty reduction, and to offset its less positive aspects for those adversely affected. We need globalization that promotes social equity and works for the poor. At the same time, we very much believe in growth as a key to reducing poverty and we also believe in sound micro and macro economic policies.' And in January 2000 IMF Managing Director Michel Camdessus pledged cooperation and association with the poverty reduction strategies developed in individual African countries. Noting that the new Poverty Reduction and Growth Facility replaced the Enhanced Structural Adjustment Facility, he went on to state that the objectives of the new PRGF would be poverty reduction, debt reduction and stability, marking, he added, a 'profound shift' in the IMF's way of doing business (IMF 2000, p. 17). These are good words but time will tell whether the ways of achieving these objectives to be used by these two key institutions and the priorities they will pursue reflect the concerns in the chapters of this book.

A distressing feature of the current situation is the widespread adoption of the focus on business activities in the shaping of standards and the interventions by global agencies. In the words of Tony Judt:

> We live today in a world where the 'sovereign state' is hemmed in by an evergrowing body of international laws, regulations, treaties, and unions. 'Globalization,' if it means anything, means that the national state has been forced to abandon many of the economic and fiscal instruments that once defined its claim to autonomy. If a sovereign state can't make multinational companies conform to its tax laws, can't ignore international regulations on air traffic safety or food manufacture, and can't block the cross-border flow of money and goods without facing the wrath of various international agencies and banking authorities, why are we so quick to acknowledge its right to rape and murder its citizens? (Judt 1999, p. 16).

A small step that could help change this state of affairs bears on the recruitment policies of those global agencies. Who takes note of the contrasting analyses justifying their prescriptions for development? An ILO report, *Facing the Technological Challenge*, saw the conditions of availability and assimilation of technology as crucial to growth and argued, first, that externalities, e.g., technical education, are pervasive, and, second, that these externalities cannot be accommodated in an economy of undisciplined, private firms. Economist John Enos queried the contrast: why do World Bank employees ['most of whom are economists'] oppose the creation of the national (or regional) organization needed to secure accommodation of the externalities whereas the ILO approach [shaped by employees from 'diverse disciplines'] supports such an initiative? His answer was a challenging one: 'the matters that the employees of the IMF and the World Bank avoid are the very vexatious matters that economic theorists abstract from, matters such as technology, psychology, culture, wars, legal systems. These matters undermine the theory, and trouble those whose intellectual foundations are built on the theory; but they do not trouble those of diverse backgrounds. In consideration of the manifold matters that affect economic development, diversity is strength. *Vivent les differences!*' (Enos 1997, p. 810).

Part One of this volume contains the three invited papers presented at the conference held at the University of Sydney, Australia, jointly sponsored by the Toda Institute for Global Peace and Policy Research and the Centre for Peace and Conflict Studies. Around these the rest of the presentations and discussions were organized. Walden Bello opens with a spirited and at times caustic assessment of the various groups involved in the Asian financial crisis as the pre-eminent example of the downside of globalization. Frank Stilwell focusses on the employment implications of globalization, giving attention to structural and technological change. In terms of strategic responses, he envisages three scenarios: Going For Growth; Upgrading Human Capital; and Prioritizing Equity and Environment. His personal forecast—at least for the more economically advanced nations—is a muddling through, which leaves the big question of political will. He concludes with the question: Have we the collective inclination and capacity for effective governance to address the challenges currently posed to employment and the quality of life?

It is not possible to summarize in a few words the broad sweep of Hazel Henderson's chapter. She acknowledges the complex relationships between today's globalization of finance, technology, and trade and issues of employment, social safety nets and quality of life. She advocates multidisciplinary systemic approaches. Globe-girdling technological hardware has created an interdependent world and we still need to write the software to manage our global affairs in the transition from the Industrial Age to the Information Age, let alone guide us towards the Solar Age, where deepening knowledge of nature and ourselves becomes the key factor of production.

With such a broad sketch of the problems of globalization laid out in Part One, it was a difficult task to order the separate contributions of the other participants—contributions prepared over the following months in light of the conference discussions. In the event the sequence adopted was to begin Part Two with issues of definition and work into interconnected but more specific issues. What is globalization? Do we need a new lexicon? Can we develop a curriculum to learn from globalization? Is life getting better or worse? What are the constraints on the welfare state? Why are wealthy countries disregarding the human right to food? What are the costs of globalization failures? Does global modeling suggest a quality of life crisis? Are managers the saviors of the global society? Who gets the benefit from internationalized R&D?

Noting that no single coherent account of what globalization means has emerged, Wayne Hudson argues that it is important to appreciate the plurality of different concerns passing under the term, not only in order to understand what particular authors are really talking about, but in order to grasp how different topics and concerns may or may not be related. He distinguishes major patterns, each of which is often (singly or in concert) called globalization. These range widely, including the emergence of global currency markets, competitive pressures on corporations to become global, and the intensification of global cultural flows, communications and migration. He catalogues major common claims: capital, goods and services move freely throughout the world; the role of the nation-state in shaping national policies has reduced; and migration patterns have shifted from South to North. He concludes with the advice that globalization currently covers different problematics, and that we would do well, both in theory and in practice, to distinguish them.

James Rosenau argues that the dynamics of economic globalization, new technologies, and evolving global norms are clashing with equally powerful localizing dynamics. The new conditions that have evolved in recent decades cannot be explained by a single source. Technological dynamics are major stimulants, but so is the breakdown of trust, the shrinking of distances, the globalization of economies, the explosive proliferation of organizations, the information revolution, the fragmentation of groups and the integration of regions, the surge of democratic practices and the spread of fundamentalism, the cessation of intense enmities and the revival of historic animosities—all of which in turn provoke further reactions that add to the complexity. A new lexicon is needed to address, for example, the mushrooming tensions between the fragmenting consequences of conflict and the integrative effects of cooperation. Rosenau proposes "fragmegration," a term that juxtaposes the process of fragmentation and integration occurring within and among organizations, communities, countries and transnational systems such that it is virtually impossible not to treat them as interactive and causally linked. Questions arise. Who shall be the parties to the new social contracts if the state can no longer be the only collective agent who strikes a bargain with individuals? Is there a core set of values on which all the contracts can be founded?

Rees' starting point is clear: 'globalization means the use of financial capital to turn the world into one very competitive market.' As such it can be viewed as a threat or turned into a promise. The outcome depends on what can be learned from current experiences. To this end he presents Learning from Globalization: A Curriculum. The initial steps are to overcome fatalism, to identify causes beyond people's control so they need no longer blame themselves, and then pose choices. The market is not the only solution. There are ways between the opposites—left or right, socialism versus capitalism, government intervention or markets—instead of veering to an extreme of economic and social policies and the ideological basis of political allegiances. Escaping the constraints of polarized ideas requires using criteria which resonate with people's experiences: full employment, family life, friendship, intellectual growth, self reliance and self esteem rather than GNP.

The losers from financial globalization, e.g., the poor in developing countries, need to develop political clout if they are to be heard. But the chances of indigenous voices being heard are lessened by the ideology that business corporations have to control land and mineral resources in order to compete. An important victory for new voices was the postponing of MAI—and Third World debt reduction holds promise.

Such steps require the development of an ethical political economy—nationally and internationally—making the public better prepared to advocate democracy in many forms and never again be overawed by corporate agendas. To secure this state of affairs, the obstacles to learning have to be identified.

The central questions for Michael Pusey are: Is life getting better or worse? How should the judgments be made? Confining his attention to 'first world' or so-called developed countries, he seeks to identify the impacts of globalization on well being and quality of life. He explores the problems of evaluation involved. For Pusey, globalization can be seen as a reconfiguration of the international political economy that is attempting to integrate pancapitalism around the interests of some 40,000 transnational corporations currently operating in over 100 countries. This definition identifies the structural aspects of a process that is everywhere de-traditionalizing settled ways of life, undermining established authority, and producing a hitherto undreamed of interaction of ethnicities, religions, world views and local and national cultures. While key institutions like the World Bank, the IMF, WTO and OECD are held responsible, the process is driven by a neoliberal economic rationalism which assumes: (a) that markets offer, at least in principle, the most reliable means of setting values on all goods, and (b) that economies and markets can always, in principle, deliver better outcomes than states, governments and the law. What are the pluses and minuses? For these first world countries, Pusey sees cultural impacts that are mainly positive and structural impacts that are mainly negative. A global commons is needed but how would it be organized? Pusey's answer is that the creative energies of NGOs and of other citizen, community and regional organizations will not be enough to restrain or control corporate power without strong and effective governments. In searching for balancing forces, Pusey calls attention to the diversity of capitalism in the contemporary world.

Bharati Ray looks at quality of life issues in an Indian setting and from the women's standpoint. The Indian ideal encompasses both the physical and mental states of existence. The goal relates to basic needs—food, shelter, drinking water, access to health care and education, right to employment—but also to psychological security—peace, happy family life, tolerance for others and togetherness. Quality of life, therefore, is determined by a person's capability of achieving the goal.

What are the effects of globalization on the economy and society of a developing country like India? It brings structural change in circumstances of unequal competition. Crucial questions are: How does it affect the teeming indigent masses who form the majority of Indian people? Does structural change serve the interests of women, especially poor women? Should there be safety nets provided by the State and international agencies to counteract adverse effects?

- Women are being marginalized in economic activities;
- With the advent of consumerism, women who are regarded as the preservers and upholders of tradition are worse off socially and losers of the traditional position in the family;

- Male unemployment has increased men's frustration, tension and fear of job insecurity and women pay the social cost. Family violence has increased, rape has become an everyday event, and dowry deaths are escalating;
- The economy is unable to bear the burden of necessary health care and education expenses.

Whose responsibility is it to provide means to satisfy these needs? The State, according to Bharati Ray, must not shy away from intervention to provide basic education and healthcare, to guarantee employment, and adopt poverty alleviation policies—with the civil society being an active partner. This requires that women be empowered politically and economically: through high quality basic education, access to credit, and opportunities to get training in technology while still preserving traditional skills. Protection against violence and political participation are essential. The most important step is for women to organize themselves.

Brian Easton challenges the common view that international competitive pressures are so strong that they will drive every country down to the lowest common denominator of a pure market economy, with a minimum of government intervention. He acknowledges that there appear to be severe limitations to a tax system being able to raise taxes on capital, or to have a progressive structure, and that these point towards limited government spending and a restricted welfare state. However, the bleakness is moderated because: (a) factors and individuals are not perfectly mobile; and (b) where there are enforced international standards, signatory countries are prevented from undercutting one another. International standards are mainly developed for human rights rather than economic rights. Such economic standards as exist promote mobility of products and investment. So a nation open to the globalized world has some control over its social and cultural policy but less than it had in the past.

Graham Riches identifies two significant obstacles in the way of advancing the quality of life of the world's most vulnerable people, the poor and the socially excluded. These are the increasing commodification of human life and nature and the power exerted by global markets over democratic life and decision-making. He questions how far the economic and social rights of citizenship, e.g., to employment, adequate incomes and a decent social wage, can be advanced on a global basis, when the world's wealthiest countries are adopting food and welfare policies which neglect basic human needs and fail to respect, let alone advance, the human right to food.

Edna Ross argues that continued failure to address the social and environmental costs of the deregulation of trade, investment and financial flows is likely to result in a backlash against global integration, international cooperation and international institutions. The potential benefits of globalization will be lost as will the potential for greater international cooperation, at precisely the time when such cooperation is essential. The backlash will also result in a rejection of international institutions, essential for developing and implementing collaborative strategies to address global problems.

What is required, however, goes beyond identifying strategies for regulating financial flows and other aspects of the global economy. There is need to review the objectives of economic policies and how we measure success. The trend of the last twenty or so years, of having economic rather than social objectives, has led to ordinary peoples' growing disenchantment with politics, cynicism about and alienation from the political process.

Akira Onishi provides an introduction to the FUGI (Futures of Global Interdependence) global model which classifies the world into some 200 countries and 80 regional groupings, where the countries and regions are globally interdependent through international trade, financial flows and information flows. There are eight major subsystems: Population; Foods; Energy; Environment (ecosystem); Development; Peace and security; Human rights; and Human healthcare. Innovative software allows large-scale integrated global modeling which seeks to track the consequences of the opening of markets, intensified private foreign direct investment, and technological progress and infrastructure investment in the 21st century information society. A crucial finding is that the future path of the global economy is in some ways unstable because of increasing international per capita income disparity.

Stuart Macdonald puts developments in management under the microscope and suggests that it is a weak element in the achievement of the business success that underlies the assumed benefits of globalization. He explores the world of management method and particularly the role of method in reducing the perceived uncertainty of the manager. He then considers the manager's ability to deal with uncertainty in the context of innovation. Examples are provided of policy and programs to capture the information critical for innovation, and the similarity of these and the corporate practice advocated by management method is explored. Speculation is provided on the link between these approaches to innovation and the external advice on which managers have come to rely for their method.

Much strategy and policy is now framed in terms of systems in which the managers play the part of technical experts. Even innovation, that most fundamental and uncertain of organizational requirements, is now regarded as a process like any other part of production; and information, that most fundamental and nebulous of organizational resources, as something to be managed like any other resource. An important contribution to this process is said to be management method, which offers the manager a companionship of expertise and an illusion of certainty. As Macdonald emphasises, 'In the efficient organization, questioning is both wasteful of resources and disruptive ... Rather than reconciling themselves to living with uncertainty, managers are provided with the comfortable delusion that method will eliminate uncertainty.' We might well ask whether such managers have the capabilities to play the crucial role assigned them by the proponents of the global business system?

In the concluding chapter, Jane Marceau examines some current trends in the internationalization of R&D, another vital element in the success attributed to globalization. She asks questions about the potential to assist developing countries in their quest for economic growth. For several decades now, developing countries have hosted manufacturing plants owned and operated by multinationals from the developed world. The internationalization of production has led to many debates about whether the presence of transnational corporations permits technology transfer such that the host nations can use them to improve their skills and economic chances. Her focus is not on manufacturing plants but on R&D laboratories and the conduct of R&D in specific overseas countries by foreign-owned transnational corporations.

Can developing countries trap the benefits of the overseas-funded R&D performed inside their borders? Marceau argues that it is what happens inside national borders that largely determines the success of national economic endeavor. It is still within the national arena, for example, that policies for research, for training, for the protection of intellectual property, for access to finance for development and so on are decided and local business skills developed. It is not clear, therefore, that TNC investments in R&D facilities in developing countries are an unmixed blessing. The outcomes will clearly depend on the skills with which policy-makers can ensure that there is maximum transfer of technology at minimum cost and that local industry can be brought to a level where it can absorb the new opportunities potentially available—and this is difficult in nations as strapped for capital as most developing countries are today.

Notes

1. I am ready to 'forego monocausality in favor of recognizing the complexity of the world' (Kindleberger 1994, p. 1224).
2. I am indebted to Fritz Machlup for his insightful remark that knowledge is information of indefinite tenure (Machlup 1982).
3. As Kenneth Boulding drew to our attention, quoting the classic Will Rogers *bon mot* (1966, p. 21).
4. See Lucas 1972; Maddock 1984—and take warning from Arrow's injunction: 'once you go down that route, you are led to rational expectations and all the rest of that devil's trap' (1987, p. 231). In these days with such emphasis on the enabling power of the computer which serves to model so much, it is helpful to recall that Karl Pearson more than a century ago resorted to a central telephone exchange as a metaphor for the brain (1892, pp. 42–3).
5. Such regionalization plays tricks with the widely used global integration index, i.e., the overall ratio of trade to GDP.
6. See Lamberton 1995. Marx and Engels had trouble with this. They grappled with 'all the interactions, the innumerable intersecting forces giving rise to the "historical event"'. Engels explained: 'Marx and I are ourselves partly to blame for the fact that younger writers sometimes lay more stress on the economic side than is due to it. We had to emphasize this main principle in opposition to our adversaries, who denied it, and we had not always the time, the place or the opportunity to allow the other elements involved in the interaction to come into their rights' (Engels, quoted by Venable 1945, p. 31).

CHAPTER 2

Globalization and the Asian Financial Crisis: The Movie

Walden Bello

First of all, let me thank the Toda Institute and the Center for Peace Studies for giving me the honour of heading the list of contributors. I told our hosts that the IMF's Michel Camdessus or the World Bank's James Wolfensohn would probably be a better choice for this task, but they insisted on saddling you with a crazy Filipino. So you know to whom to complain.

Ever since I was asked to contribute a paper on Globalization: Issues of Interdependence, there was one thing I was sure of: that I would not give you another theoretical treatise. I was not quite sure what to do at first, but then I realized that what I really should address is what is happening to us in East Asia, which is, after all, the pre-eminent example of the downside of globalization. And instead of an academic paper, I thought that I should write a screenplay, since this form would stand a better chance of capturing the complexities and nuances of globalization than a theoretical treatise. I told myself after seeing Steven Spielberg's *Saving Private Ryan*, a rather disappointing film on American soldiers in Normandy during the Second World War, that surely I could manage something better on the Asian financial crisis. So today I will give you the script for a movie that is tentatively titled *Globalization and the Asian Financial Crisis: The Movie—Heroes, Villains, and Accomplices.* I am, incidentally, thinking of selling the rights to Oliver Stone, who directed *Platoon* and *JFK*, and insisting that he cast Australia's very own Mel Gibson as George Soros.

But let me be clear, first of all, there are no heroes. The Japanese could have played the role of knights in shining armour in early 1999, when they had the chance to reverse the descent into depression via the proposed Asian Monetary Fund (AMF)—a mechanism capitalized to the tune of $100 billion that was designed to defend the region's currencies from speculative attacks. But, in typical fashion, they shelved their proposal when Washington opposed it. Though the AMF was resurrected as the Miyazawa Plan that would give the troubled Asian economies $30 billion in financial aid, it was too little and too late.

Villain of the Piece: Crony Capitalists or Foreign Speculative Investors?

For our movie, there are a number of candidates for the role of principal villain. Taking our cue from the western press, let us take the practices and institutions that are usually presented to the public as the villains of the piece—that is, aside from Prime Minister Mohamad Mahathir of Malaysia, who has become the US media's favorite whipping boy—at the same time, it must be noted, that they are in the process of elevating Philippine President Joseph Estrada to Asia's new hero.

Let me quote a person that has come to be the chief screenwriter of one version of the crisis, US Treasury Secretary Robert Rubin. In assigning the blame for the financial crisis, Rubin assigned pride of place to lack of information on the part of investors. In a speech he gave at the Brookings Institution in April 1999, Rubin said:

> [T]here are obstacles to getting good information about economic and financial matters. One is the temptation—in the private sector and in government—to avoid disclosing problems. But sooner or later, as we have seen in Asia, the problems will make themselves known... In many cases, lack of data meant that no one had a true understanding of this build-up or of these economies' vulnerabilities (Rubin 1998a).

This lack of transparency on the part of financial institutions went hand-in-hand with distorted incentives, lack of supervision, and the absence of so-called prudential regulation. All this is, in turn, part of a witches' brew of unsound and corrupt practices known as crony capitalism, which Larry Summers, the famous economist who is Rubin's undersecretary, says is 'at the heart of the crisis' (Summers 1998). Interestingly, it might be pointed out, Summers and others picked up a term—crony capitalism—that we Filipinos coined during the Marcos period.

Before going on, one might also briefly note here that this is a massive reversal of the view that held sway at the World Bank when Summers, who now plays the Sundance Kid to Rubin's Butch

Cassidy on CNN, was that institution's chief economist in the late 1980s and early 1990s. For those of us who are too young to remember what the orthodoxy was then, let me cite the Bank's famous *East Asian Miracle* published in 1993:

> In each HPAE [high performing Asian economy], a technocratic elite insulated to a degree from excessive political pressure supervised macro-economic management. The insulation mechanisms ranged from legislation, such as balanced budget laws in Indonesia, Singapore, and Thailand, to custom and practice in Japan and Korea. All protected essentially conservative macroeconomic policies by limiting the scope for politicians and interest groups to derail those policies (World Bank 1993, pp. 348–49).

To repeat, economic policy-making by Asian technocrats was largely insulated from political and business pressures, and this was a large part of the explanation for the so-called Asian miracle. Every mortal is, of course, entitled to an about-face. But the problem with the latest intellectual fashion from the Summers' salon is that the practices of crony capitalism were very much part of economic life in the three decades that East Asian countries led the world in the rate of growth of GNP. If, indeed, crony capitalism was the chief cause of the Asian collapse, why did it not bring it about much, much sooner? How could economies dominated by these practices of rent-seeking that supposedly suffocate the dynamism of the market—including Japan and South Korea—even take off in the first place?

Moreover, crony capitalism has, recently, become so elastic in its connotations—which range from corruption to any kind of government activism in economic policy-making—as to become useless as an explanatory construct. It is one thing to say that corruption has pervaded relations between government and business in East Asia. It has, as it has in Italy or in the USA, where it is legalized through such mechanisms as political action committees (PACs) that make politicians' electoral fortunes dependent on favorable treatment of corporate interests. It is quite another thing to say that corruption and its companions, lack of regulation and lack of transparency, constitute the principal reason for the downfall of the East Asian economies.

Now, in the light of the developments since the financial crisis, criticizing the crony capitalist thesis might strike those of you who have followed these events closely as flogging a dead horse. It is, but this dead horse deserves to be beaten and buried because it has a way of resurrecting periodically in Dracula fashion. Nevertheless, after the Russian crash and the later collapse and bail-out of the hedge fund Long-Term Capital by the US Federal Reserve, there is now little doubt that the central cause of the financial crisis was the quick, massive flow of speculative capital and bank capital into East Asia in the early 1990s and its even more massive and even swifter exit in 1997.

And there seems to be little doubt as well that the multilateral institutions, in particular the International Monetary Fund, played a key facilitating role by pressing the Asian governments incessantly to liberalize their capital accounts, in order precisely to encourage massive foreign capital inflows into their economies in the belief that foreign capital was the strategic factor in development. Indeed, one can say that the IMF has been the cutting edge of globalization in the region, since it is financial liberalization that is the cutting edge of the integration of these national economies into the global economy.

Now, Northern speculative funds came to Asia not because they were conned by crafty and dishonest Asian financial operators. Don't get me wrong, there are many, many dishonest financial operators in Asia, including, for instance, the Filippino finance minister, who heads a bank that benefited immensely from these inward speculative flows. But that these western investors were conned or fooled? Come on. No, speculative investors came into Asia because they saw the opportunities to gain greater margins of profit on financial investments than were available in the northern money centers in the early 1990s, owing to the much higher interest rates, the low stock prices, and—not to be underestimated—the incredible hype created around the so-called Asian economic miracle.

The fact is, money was very eager to get into Asian capital markets in the early 1990s, and whether or not the information was available, investors and fund managers were quite non-discriminating in their moves into these markets. As Rubin himself admitted in a speech at Chulalongkorn University in June 1998:

> One of the things that has most struck us about the Asian crisis, is that after the problems began to develop and we spoke to the institutions that had extended credit or invested in the region, so often we found these institutions had engaged in relatively little analysis and relatively little weighting of the risks that were appropriate to the decisions (Rubin 1998b).

The fund managers were going to see what they wanted to see. Not only did many not assess their investments and local partners or borrowers, but they actually made their moves mainly by keeping an eagle eye on the moves of other investors—especially those with great reputations for canny investing like George Soros or Long-Term Capital's John Merriwether. But if there was little room or desire for serious analysis of markets in the entry phase, there was even less in the exit phase, as the rush of investment leaders communicated panic to one and all.

Indeed, in the first months of the crisis, Stanley Fischer, the American Deputy Managing Director of the IMF, was attributing the crisis not to politicians or to lack of transparency or to crony capitalism but to the investors' herd behavior: '[M]arkets are not always right,' he said. 'Sometimes inflows are excessive, and sometimes they may be sustained too long. Markets tend to react late; but they tend to react fast, sometimes excessively' (Fischer 1997).

Bangkok, for instance, was a debtor's rather than a creditor's market in the early 1990s, with so many foreign banks and funds falling over themselves to lend to Thai enterprises, banks and finance companies, and they were willing to forego the rigorous checks on borrowers that western banks and financial institutions are supposedly famous for. The bad—indeed, shady—financial history of the Thai finance companies was not a secret (Pakorn Vichyanond 1994). In the 1970s and 1980s, many finance companies resorted to questionable business practices to raise capital, including widespread speculation and manipulation of stock prices, leading to the closure of some of them. Any neophyte in Bangkok's financial club knew this history. Yet, the finance companies were flush with foreign cash, often urged on to them by foreign lenders unwilling to forego what could turn out to be a goldmine.

Throughout Asia, American Chambers of Commerce, foreign correspondents' clubs and expatriate circles were replete with stories of rigged bids, double—sometimes triple—accounting, false statistics, cronyism in high places, but everyone accepted that these were the risks of doing business in Asia... you had to live with them if you were going to have your share of the bonanza. In the end, what really served as the ultimate collateral or guarantee for the investments foreign operators made in Asian enterprises and banks was the six to ten percent growth rates, which they expected to continue far into the future. Now you might end up with some duds, but if you spread your investments around in this region of limitless growth, you were likely to come out a winner.

Supporting Cast

This brings up the role of strategic expectations and the role of certain players and institutions that encouraged and maintained those expectations. In other words, there was a whole set of actors that played a supporting but critical role, and the speculative investors were operating in a context where they were locked into mutually reinforcing psychology of permanent boom with these other players.

A key player here is much of the business press. Business publications proliferated in the region from the mid-1980s. But proliferation alone is not adequate to convey the dynamics of the business press, since there was also a process of monopolization at work. The Asian prosperity started attracting the big players from the West, and among the more momentous deals were the purchases of the famous *Far Eastern Economic Review* by Dow Jones, of *Asiaweek* by Times-Warner, and of Star Television in Hong Kong by Rupert Murdoch. CNN, another Time-Warner subsidiary, and CNBC also moved in, with much of their programming devoted to business news. These news agents became critical interpreters of the news in Asia to investors located all over the world and served as a vital supplement to the electronic linkages that made real-time transactions possible among the key stock exchanges of Singapore, Hong Kong, Tokyo, Osaka, New York, London and Frankfurt.[1]

Now, for the most part, these publications and media, whether they were independent or part of the big chains, highlighted the boom, glorified the high growth rates, and reported uncritically on so-called success stories, mainly because their own success as publications was tied to the perpetuation of the psychology of boom. A number of reporters writing critical stories on questionable business practices, alarming developments, or failed enterprises complained that they could not place their stories, or that their editors told them to accentuate the positive.

Parachute journalism—a phrase applied to writers who flew in, became instant experts on the Vietnam War or the Philippines under Marcos, then left after filing their big stories—became a practice as well in economic journalism in the 1990s, with *Fortune*, *Business Week*, *Newsweek*, and *Time* setting the pace. It was parachute journalist Dorinda Elliot of the *Newsweek* staff, for instance, who, more than anybody else sanctified the Philippines' status as Asia's newest tiger during the Subic APEC Summit of November 1996—a status that lasted less than eight months, until the collapse of the peso in July 1997.

Many of these business publications, in turn, developed an unwholesome reliance on a character type that proliferated in the region in the early 1990s, the investment adviser or strategist—an expert connected with the research arms of banks, investment houses, brokerage houses, mutual funds and hedge funds. Indeed, in many instances, notes Philip Bowring, former editor of *Far Eastern Economic Review*, economic journalism degenerated into just stringing along quotes from different investment authorities (Bowring 1998).

Interestingly enough, many of these people were expatriates, some of them refugees from the collapse of stock markets in New York and London in the late 1980s. Some of them were Generation X or pre-Generation X types who had been too young to participate in the junk bond frenzy in Wall Street in the Reagan years but discovered similar highs in the East. Many of these people were as young as Nick Leeson, the 26 year old broker who brought down the venerable Baring Brothers, but to the reporters in the business press, their advice on going underweight or overweight in certain countries or taking short or long positions in dollars or moving into equities and out of bonds and vice versa was dispensed to readers as gospel truth. Now, this is not to say that all of these actors dispensed uniformly optimistic advice to investors playing the region. It did mean, however, that they could not afford to paint too pessimistic a picture of any country in the region since, after all, their bread and butter came from bringing global capital into Asia.

Let me give you an example of how one of these expat experts—who was widely cited in *The Economist*, *Far Eastern Economic Review*, *Financial Times*, Reuters, and the *Asian Wall Street Journal* as the last word on the Asian investment scene—assessed Thailand in December 1996, when it was becoming clear to the rest of us mortals in Bangkok that the economy was in real deep trouble:

> We believe that current pessimism about the Thai economy is based on a number of key misconceptions. We do not believe any of the following:
> - Thailand is entering a recession.
> - Investment is collapsing.
> - Export growth is collapsing.
> - The Bank of Thailand has lost control.
> - Current account deficit is unsustainable.
> - Thailand faces a debt crisis.
> - There is a chance that the baht will devalue.
> - Economic prospects for 1997: expect a rebound (Saker 1996).

Now, the reason that I quote Neil Saker of Singapore's SocGen Crosby Securities is that he is one of the best examples of the way markets operate in our part of the world. One would have expected that after such a massive misreading of the situation, he would have been run out of Asia by irate investors. But lo and behold, Saker was able to transform himself from the prophet of permanent boom into the prophet of doom after the financial collapse of 1997, this time issuing statements about how investors would be wise to go underweight in their investments in the region for a long time to come. More recently, in 1998, he again reinvented himself, this time as the prophet of the Asian recovery, advising investors to go overweight in Thailand and Singapore, which so happened to move into recession on the day he issued his recommendation (Reuters 1998). And, worse, he continues to be quoted just as frequently in the *Financial Times*, the *Far Eastern Economic Review*, *Asiaweek*, and the *Asian Wall Street Journal.* The market has such a short memory that it rewards charlatans instead of punishing them.

Academics: Bystanders or Accomplices?

But to lay the blame only on the business press and the investment advisers for the creation of an atmosphere of inflated expectations would not be fair. For the academic world played a key role. Indeed, it was economists and political scientists in the West who, when seeking to explain the high growth rates of the Asian countries from the 1960s on, formulated the interrelated propositions that an economic miracle had come about in Asia, that high growth was likely to mark the region in the foreseeable future, and that Asia would be the engine of the world economy far into the 21st century. What is even more amazing is that there was a remarkable consensus between the left and the right in the academic world that Asian growth was exceptional—though for diametrically opposite reasons. The right insisted that it was because of free markets, the left because of the role of the interventionist state.[2]

Writing on why and how the Tigers evolved and why Asia would be the center of the world economy in the coming century became big business, and here the most thriving business was in those books that sought to equip Uncle Sam with insights on how to deal with those formidable Asians, like James Fallows' *Looking at the Sun.* Not to be left out of the boom, the security experts sought to cash in on the Asian miracle mania by writing on how Asian prosperity could produce either peace or war, with the most crass pop analysts writing on 'the coming war with Japan,' 'the coming war with China,' or, like Harvard's Samuel Huntington, on the long twilight struggle against the 'Islamic Confucian Connection'.

But whether they liked Asia or saw it as a threat, most academics and policy analysts believed in the long Asian boom. Now, how Australia's academic institutions fit into all this, I will leave up to you to discuss and debate. Let me just get the ball rolling by saying that some units of the famous Australian National University played a not insignificant role, since they functioned as the ideological and analytical spearheads of the Labor Government's frenzied drive to integrate Australia into Asia in the early and mid-1990s via the Asia Pacific Economic Cooperation (APEC).

The few of us who dissented from this consensus were attacked by both sides. Our critique of the increasing stresses of the newly industrialized countries (NIC) growth model on account of collateral damage in the form of environmental devastation, the subjugation of agriculture to industry, the growing income disparities, and the growing technological dependency that was behind the creation of structurally determined trade deficits was dismissed by the right as well as the academic liberals (center) as a case of sour grapes. Indeed, I still remember how in 1994, during a debate at the Australian National University, Hal Hill, a prominent Australian specialist on Indonesia, did not meet the substance of my arguments but chose, in a distinctively un-Australian patronizing fashion, to attribute my pessimism to my supposedly looking at the NICs' experience through the prism of the failed Philippine development experience.

But we were also dismissed by the academic left, who saw us as adhering to old-fashioned dependency theory or to obsolete variants of Marxism. Indeed, the most savage criticisms sometimes came from the left. To cite one example, a reviewer of my book, *Dragons in Distress*, in a progressive journal said that our prediction in 1990 that Korea's problem in a few years' time would not be how to enter the First World but how to avoid being hurled back into the Third World was simply laughable. I wish I could give you the name, but I have forgotten the reference.

In any event, the World Bank stepped in to serve as arbiter between the left and right interpretations in the early 1990s and found merit on both sides of the argument—though more merits, it said, resided on the right than on the left. But what is particularly significant for our purposes here is that the Bank declared that, despite slight deviations here and there, the Asian Tigers had the economic fundamentals right and were thus geared to enter a period of even greater prosperity. Since the World Bank is the equivalent in development circles of the papacy in the Roman Catholic Church, the World Bank's report, *The East Asian Miracle*, (World Bank, 1993), became a kind of bible, not only in the academic world but in financial and corporate circles, and the rush into Asia of speculative capital in the next few years must certainly be at least partly tied to its thesis of Asian exceptionalism, to Asia as the land of the never ending bonanza.

Let me, at this point, recapitulate my main points:

1. Crony capitalist practices pervaded Asian capitalism, but they were definitely not the cause of the financial collapse.
2. Northern finance capital was not conned into investing in the region by dishonest Asian banks and enterprises that concealed the actual state of their finances. Although they cooked their books, they fooled nobody.
3. Portfolio investors and banks moved vast quantities in and out of the region, often without any real effort to arrive at an assessment of local conditions and borrowers and largely as a result of herd behavior.
4. The fundamentals of borrowers were often ignored in favor of what many investors and lenders saw as the real collateral or guarantee that they would eventually get a high rate of return from their investments, which was the eight to ten percent growth rate of the country and that was expected to extend far into the future. Now with such a perspective, you should expect to end up with some bad eggs among your debtors, but if you spread your investment around in this region of everlasting prosperity, you were likely to come out ahead in the end.
5. Also playing a critical role as accomplices in the Asian financial crisis were three institutional actors: the business press, the investment analysts, and, last but not least, the majority of academic specialists on the East Asian economies and political systems.

Let me reiterate that a global network of investors, journalists, investment analysts and academics were locked into a psychology of boom, where growth rates, expectations, analysis, advice and reporting interacted in a mutually reinforcing inflationary fashion characteristic of manic situations. Just as in the case of the Cold War lobby in the US, there was a whole set of actors that—perhaps half consciously, one must concede—developed an institutional interest in the maintenance of the illusion of a never-ending Asian bonanza so that, whether in the press, in the boardroom, or in the academy, alternative viewpoints were given short shrift.

But not to worry, many of the prophets of boom quickly adjusted and became prophets of doom or sanctimonious exponents of the crony capitalist explanation for Asia's problems. Many are coming through with their reputations intact and some are realizing that books on why Asia collapsed can be just as profitable as books on why Asia was going to be the driver of the 21st century during the boom.

But, friends, I just realized that this only brings the story to July 1997, the day the floating of the Thai baht triggered the crisis. The screenplay to the sequel, from July 1997 up till today, still needs to be written, but for this part the storyline is much clearer, with the IMF and the US Treasury, Japan and Prime Minister Mahathir serving as chief protagonists, with brief walk-on performances by China and Hong Kong, and an even briefer cameo appearance by a composite Australian character named Pauline Howard Evans.

And how will this film end? That part of the story remains to be written by the peoples of East and Southeast Asia. Let me just say in this connection that in this script for the first part, I have refrained from bringing in the silent actors in this saga—the hundreds of millions of ordinary Asians—for they were largely passive participants in this drama. They were acted on rather than acted. That may no longer be the case, judging from events in the streets of Jakarta, Kuala Lumpur and Bangkok. In the coming period, we are likely to see movements that will be motivated by resistance not only to indiscriminate financial and economic globalization but to its cultural and political aspects as well. Within the region, we are likely to see a move away from dependence on foreign financial flows and foreign markets toward economic strategies based principally on domestic financial resources and the local market. That means greater pressure on governments for redistribution of assets and income in order to create the dynamic domestic market which can serve as the engine of growth in place of the roller-coaster global economy.

Elements of the domestic alternative are already being discussed actively throughout the region. What is still unclear, though, is how these elements will hang together. The new political economy may be embedded in religious or secular discourse and language. And its coherence is likely to rest less on considerations of narrow efficiency than on a stated ethical priority given to community solidarity and security. Moreover, the new economic order is unlikely to be imposed from above in Keynesian technocratic style, but is likely to be forged in social and political struggles. For one thing is certain:

mass politics with a class edge—frozen by the superficial prosperity before the crash of 1997—is about to return to center stage in Asia. In short, to pirate a line from my favorite poet, the ending of *Asian Financial Crisis III* is likely to be a bang, not a whimper.

Notes

1. A good study of how these global, real-time linkages made money-making among those farflung stock markets possible via arbitrage can be found in Gapper and Denton, 1997.
2. On the right, see Krueger 1993; Little 1982; Hughes 1992. On the left, Wade 1990; Amsden 1989.

CHAPTER 3

Globalization, Employment and Economic Strategies

Frank Stilwell

Faced with recurrent fears of a global recession, the relationship between globalization and employment is necessarily at the forefront of our attention. Longer term economic trends and structural problems also require attention and redress, whatever the immediate global economic prospects. The prospect of achieving full employment seems to have permanently receded. Even before the intensification of financial instability in 1997–98, the number of people out of work in the OECD—the club of rich countries—was of the order of 40 million (depending on precisely how unemployment is defined). Taking account of poorer nations too, and adding in estimates for under employment as well as unemployment, the International Labour Office suggests a global total in excess of 800 million people (ILO estimates cited in Rifkin 1995, p. xv.). This constitutes a massive wastage of economic potential, quite apart from its damaging effects on the people themselves and on the revenue base from which governments can finance their expenditures.

There have also been dramatic changes in the nature of work, affecting those who do have jobs. An increasing proportion are in intermittent casual employment, competing in the secondary labor markets for jobs characterized by low wages and poor job security. The polarization of living standards between these marginalized workers and those in executive, professional and administrative positions is increasingly evident. It overlays the widening of income inequalities associated with work and non-work, posing threats to social cohesion and causing more potentially productive economic resources in many countries to be redirected into the processes of social control. As Jeremy Rifkin puts it in one of various recent books addressing the future of work: 'just outside the new high-tech global village lie a growing number of destitute and desperate human beings, many of whom are turning to a life of crime and creating a vast new criminal subculture' (Rifkin 1995, ch. 11). Not surprisingly in these circumstances, one of the few rapidly growing categories of employment in many nations is private security guards.

Labor market conditions and government policy responses vary from country to country, of course. The USA is perhaps the most striking example of how deregulated labor markets function: its proponents boast of the relatively low official unemployment rate, while its critics point to the low wages associated with the emergence of a 'working poor' and to the high incarceration rates which keep people—especially young black males—out of the workforce. European nations have more extensive social security systems and in some cases are also taking initiatives to try to redistribute the work more equitably, but unacceptably high unemployment rates persist.[1] In African, South American and Asian countries the problems of the labor markets interact with the general problems of economic underdevelopment. Massive rural–urban migration fuels the labor supply of major metropolitan areas, typically well in excess of labor demand. The old refrain 'how are you going to keep them down on the farm now that they've seen Paris' now applies equally to Seoul, Shanghai and Saigon. Chronic urban unemployment is a predictable outcome. Only in the exceptional city-states of Singapore and Hong Kong does any semblance of overall labor market balance exist. With the financial crisis of the South-east Asian nations, the petering out of the Japanese economic 'miracle' and growing nervousness about the US economy, the global employment problems are compounded; pessimistic 'animal spirits' among investors are never conducive to the restoration of the conditions for economic prosperity.

My perspective on the world is Australian. In many respects this is indeed a lucky country. It has a small population in a large land. It has abundant natural resources. Most of its people, by international standards, have a good standard of living. A tradition of egalitarianism (sitting uncomfortably alongside the influences of racism and sexism) has nurtured policies to provide a 'wage earners welfare state' (Castles 1985). Yet this is a nation which has had an official unemployment rate of eight percent or more for nearly a decade, and studies of concealed unemployment indicate an actual rate of up to twice that level (Langmore and Quiggin 1990). The nation is failing to provide employment opportunities for all its citizens. Beyond the capital cities, the problems are particularly acute and welfare dependency is correspondingly pronounced: government social security payments in some regions comprise more than one-third of total regional income (Bray and Mudd 1998). If full employment is not achievable in Australia, one might ponder, is it achievable anywhere? It is not that there is a shortage of work to be done—building better roads and railways, improving schools and hospitals, environmental repair, providing better care for children, the elderly and so forth. The social task is clear—to marry the fulfilment of these social needs with the employment of the potential workforce. But establishing the institutions for that purpose seems as elusive as ever. If this is the case within a single, relatively affluent nation like Australia, it is many times more complex on a global scale where the relationships between economic forces, social needs and ecological capacities seems to be increasingly out of control.

That is why it is so important to carefully analyse the nature of the contemporary employment problems and to explore possible solutions. Some would say the difficulty of marrying labor resources and social needs is intrinsic in the structure of capitalism. It is a system of production for profit, capable of tremendous dynamism because of the material incentives directly linked to the accumulation of capital. Simultaneously though, it is always vulnerable to criticism because of the tenuous links and recurrent tensions between such economic activity and broader social concerns—health, environment, culture, individual and community development. Certainly, the innate tendencies of the economic system towards instability, insecurity and inequality have been increasingly evident in recent years, alongside the relentless commodification of society and nature. Full employment under capitalism has always been the exception rather than the rule, as the economist J.M. Keynes emphasized more than half a century ago. In that sense, the long boom of the 1950s and 1960s was atypical. The partial withdrawal since then of the stabilizing mechanisms associated with counter-cyclical fiscal policy (a casualty of the commitment to balanced budgets), a regulated banking system and an extensive welfare state leaves us with 'capitalism in the raw'.

Of course, that is precisely the goal of the neoliberal policies which constitute the current economic orthodoxy. The assault on Keynesianism and the welfare state has been long, sustained and powerful (Crockett 1995). Deregulation of capital and labor markets, the privatization of public enterprises, the removal of restrictions on international trade and capital flows, and curtailment of social security entitlements are pervasive policies, pursued with varying degrees of vigor in different countries. Even governments formed by parties to the left of center have been drawn into this push for reform (a term whose meaning has been dramatically transformed in the process.) The more unconstrained operation of markets is the evident goal, based on the expectation that this will reinvigorate the dynamism of the economy, open up more profitable investment opportunities and thereby generate more jobs.

Globalization

That is where globalization enters the story. Its meaning and significance is much debated, as illustrated by various other chapters in this book and elsewhere (See Ohmae 1996; Hirst and Thompson 1996; and Burbach *et al.* 1997). However, some of its general features are now clear. Geographical limits on the operation of market forces, associated with nation-states, are being eroded. There has been increased interconnectedness between nations—and cities and regions within them—in terms of the organization of production, flows of trade and investment, and in the operation of financial institutions, as well as interchange (some would say homogenization) of culture. None of this is altogether novel, and certainly not uniform over different spaces and places. Indeed, to a considerable extent globalization is an ideological construct—a particular way of seeing structures thought to be necessary and/or desirable. But it is also a convenient label for a set of significant material changes on the ground.

Essentially, globalization results from the interaction of three phenomena: modern technology, consumerism and neoliberal economic policies. Modern technology has extended the potential for global reach in economic affairs. Advances in transport and communication technologies, together with the development of computer-assisted manufacturing and design, dramatically extend the capacity for global information—dissemination, production and distribution of goods and services. Consumerism, as the dominant 'religion' of the era, means that the fruits of this global production are readily saleable—indeed, thirstily sought after. It is fostered through the marketing activities of corporations worldwide, competing for market shares, and reinforcing the consumerist ethos—'I consume therefore I am'—as a by-product of those activities. Neoliberal policies implemented by nation-states remove the barriers to these production and consumption processes. In that sense globalization is a product of government policy choices, although governments commonly claim little alternative because their capacity to maintain conventional economic boundary controls is undermined. Far from being rendered redundant, as the more extreme versions of the globalization versus the nation-state perspective imply, what this means is that the modern nation-state is an integral part of shaping the globalization process (Bryan and Rafferty 1999).

The process of globalization is not without limits or contradictions. The balance between global production and consumption is a case in point. To the extent that investment in production facilities is attracted to particular localities by low-waged labor, there is a race to the bottom in living standards. Different localities engage vigorously in beggar-thy-neighbor competition. But that leaves the question of where the additional demand for the commodities produced will come from. For any one export-oriented nation this is not a problem, but if all nations are simultaneously engaged in labor cost-reduction, there is a global tendency to a crisis of economic over-production (unless the enhanced spending power of managerial and professional elites outweighs the effect of wage-cutting). Arguably this over-production tendency is what we are starting to see flow on from the financial crisis of the South-east Asian region—a global mismatch between productive capacity and the level of effective demand, resulting in growing unemployment.

A second contradiction concerns the pervasive fiscal crisis of the state. International competition also generates a race to the bottom in corporate taxation levels, as governments seek to provide the conditions to attract mobile capital. That undermines their capacity to finance substantial public expenditures. This in turn limits the employment-generating capacity (both direct and indirect) of public sectors. Neoliberal ideologies emphasizing the desirability of smaller government legitimize this outcome. The effect of both supporting ideologies is to further undermine any residual Keynesian commitments to the pursuit of full employment. Employment levels have become incidental outcomes arising from market processes.

Downsizing and Structural Change

Downsizing is the micro-managerial equivalent (within both public and private sector enterprises) of this macro-governmental neoliberalism. It has been a recurring theme in corporate strategy, as the corporations respond to these same pressures for globalized competitiveness. The pursuit of world's best practice is the characteristic justification, manifest typically as attempts to raise productivity in conjunction with increases in work intensity. This may be regarded as an extension of the principles of scientific management (pioneered by Frederick Winslow Taylor) or the increased exploitation of labor (as described by Karl Marx), according to your point of view. Working smarter or just working harder? Increasingly authoritarian relations of production, speed-ups and unpaid overtime are commonly the hallmarks of downsizing in practice. Its proponents contend that there is no alternative—that being 'lean and mean' is an inevitable outcome, even a necessary evil. A book by American political economist David Gordon (1996) effectively refutes that view, showing that the emphasis on labor cost-cutting does not apply equally to the managerial and supervisory ranks. Contrary to the lean and mean corporate rhetoric, the proportion of supervisors to supervised has risen significantly in the last two decades. As Gordon points out, this is no accident. Rather, it reflects a two-way process. More coercive labor relations require more supervisors, while payment of high managerial and supervisory salaries requires yet more austerity to be applied to the conditions of the workforce. Corporate bloat and a squeeze on workers' wages and jobs are two sides of the same coin. As general employment conditions deteriorate, the corporate sector becomes, to quote Gordon, ever more 'fat and mean'.

This analysis is useful in linking the problem of growing economic insecurity with that of growing social inequality. The pervasive tendency towards polarization in incomes and living standards, within and between nations, is now well documented. (See, for example, Wolff 1998). Executive remuneration packages and incomes from the ownership of capital have risen rapidly over the last two decades while, on the other hand, there has been a significant expansion of the secondary labor market where wage incomes are low and/or irregular. The proportion of part-time and casual jobs has risen sharply, constituting in effect a reproduction of the 'reserve army of labor'. Between the two extremes there is a shrinking middle. The trickle-down process seems ever more ineffective in redistributing economic rewards in these conditions. The two mechanisms through which that trickle-down has traditionally operated—wages and welfare—have been particular targets for the neoliberal policies. If these processes persist the result is likely to be a general tendency towards the sort of 40:30:30 society Will Hutton (1996, p. 14) describes in the UK: 40 percent of the population having reasonably secure full-time employment or self-employment, prospering from technological progress, while 30 percent are battling in the secondary labor market to retain some stake in the economy, and 30 percent are more or less permanently marginalized from the mainstream of economic life.

Technological Change

Underpinning these social transformations are dramatic changes in technology, which bear on the future of work. Economists have usually adopted the optimistic view that technological change, by increasing productivity, would add to incomes and employment in the long term. Indeed, when stagecoach makers lost their jobs many more employment opportunities did open up for workers in the emerging car industry. So it has been in many industry sectors over a long period. Somewhat schematically, one can visualize the process as one whereby successive waves of labor displacement have moved through from agriculture to manufacturing and then to service industries (Heilbroner, preface to Rifkin 1995).The International Labour Office report, *World Employment 1996/7*, emphasizes that this process is still continuing: one of its claims is that 'high current employment is largely the result of slower growth of output and productivity rather than of the labor-displacing effects of hyper-productive new technologies' (ILO 1996, p. 23). However, as Barry Jones, the Australian intellectual/politician (a rare combination) argued more than two decades ago, the process of employment growth matching output growth cannot be assumed to continue indefinitely. With the technological changes associated with computerization now taking place in the services sector, there is the obvious question 'where to next?' Jones (1982) talked of the quaternary and quinary sectors, where information-processing and personal/community services would become the new focus. Jeremy Rifkin has more recently argued the case for fostering the development of 'the third sector'—beyond public and private sector employment—where voluntary work in neighborhoods and communities becomes recognized as legitimate, and is financially supported by 'taxing a percentage of the wealth generated by the new Information Age technology' (Rifkin 1996, ch. 16). How the institutions of the labor market and the social security system are articulated in this process is crucial.

These are major challenges but the issues are not altogether novel. It is more than 70 years since Bertrand Russell (1918) advocated the introduction of a guaranteed minimum income system on the grounds that modern industry was sufficiently productive to sustain the society without all having to work: he argued that this would give creative people, for example, the opportunity to pursue their interests free from the necessity of waged toil (Russell 1918). Other visions of technology opening up liberating and/or leisured futures abound. The problem is that these visions sit uncomfortably alongside the observation of a real world in which the labor-displacing effects of technological change are remarkably uneven and socially divisive. It is as if the old order is collapsing but there is no agreement on the form of a new one to replace it.

Strategic Responses

So what is to be done? It is possible to envisage at least three scenarios:

I Go For Growth

The first scenario can be labeled 'go for growth'. It is the current orthodoxy—emphasizing the pursuit of faster economic growth as the means of generating more jobs and incomes. Ironically, the current turmoil in world financial markets and fears of a possible global recession may be tending to buttress this orthodoxy, or at least provide breathing space for it, notwithstanding the flurry of calls for some global regulation of financial flows. If the prospect of rising unemployment is the problem, the restoration of economic growth is the solution. From this perspective the principal task is to remove the obstacles to more rapid growth. Variations on the 'go for growth' theme depend on how those obstacles are interpreted. The dominant view—thoroughly in accord with prevailing neoliberal orthodoxy—emphasizes obstacles which have impeded the operation of free market forces. Such obstacles include the legacy of centralized economic planning and state-owned enterprises (as in Russia), welfarism and Keynesianism (in the mixed economies) and excessive state intervention which fosters cronyism (in Indonesia and some other developing nations, which, ironically, had been celebrated for their rapid economic growth until the recent Southeast Asian economic crisis). Deregulation of capital and labor markets are the characteristic panaceas, notwithstanding the failure of cross-sectional and time-series international comparative studies to show any clear correlation between such market liberalization and macroeconomic performance (see, for example, Parker 1998). Indeed, as the New Zealand experience discussed elsewhere in this book indicates, these policies demonstrably *don't* achieve their stated objectives, although they do produce other results, such as increased inequality, which cynics would say is the real agenda.

The other version of the 'go for growth' theme is rather more sophisticated and attractive to many who are politically left of center. It involves interventionist policies to reduce the effect of structural 'speed humps' which cause economic growth to be curtailed. Such speed humps may include balance of payments problems or inflationary tendencies. If, for example, acceleration in a nation's economic growth increases the demand for imported goods and services (in excess of the increase in sales of exports), there is a tendency towards a current account deficit. Deflationary policies, either through restrictionist monetary or fiscal measures, are the characteristic response. This is stop-go economics, with all its predictably damaging effects on sustainable employment growth. If inflationary tendencies increase whenever labor markets (or, more typically, sub-markets) tighten as a result of economic growth, similar problems arise. Various interventionist policy measures can be used to reduce the size of these speed humps. Industry and incomes policies, going well beyond what is normally acceptable in a neoliberal economic agenda, are commonly advocated in these circumstances; for an Australian example, see Burgess and Green (1997). The calls for partial re-regulation of global capital markets and for a stronger international commitment to redistribute income towards the poorer nations may be regarded as equivalent responses on an international scale, precipitated by the current global economic difficulties.

The 'go for growth' strategy has obvious appeal, both for the advanced industrial countries whose economic structures are geared to capital accumulation and for the poorer countries wanting to emulate the living standards which faster economic growth promises. However, there are at least two problems which prevent 'go for growth', in both its neoliberal and interventionist forms, being a viable long-run strategy for securing full employment and prosperity. First, growth in the volume of goods and services produced does not bring forth an equivalent number of job opportunities. This is the effect of the technological changes discussed earlier, manifest as jobless growth. Notwithstanding the ILO's view that the downturn in growth rates is a greater contributing factor in the increased unemployment than technological change, there is evidence that simply boasting aggregate growth rates provides no general solution. GNP in Spain has doubled over the past twenty years but employment has actually declined, and the official unemployment rate has hovered around twenty percent throughout the 1990s. Although this is an extreme case, the experience of jobless growth in other countries has also been evident in recent years.[2]

Second, economic growth butts up against environmental constraints. Obvious examples are global warming and the damage to the ozone layer (two separate problems that now show evidence of interacting) as well as depletion of major non-renewable energy sources and other natural resources. The ecological consequences of the People's Republic of China, for example, seeking material living standards comparable to advanced industrial nations, are potentially massive, unless it is based on intermediate technologies. There are grounds for thinking that there are social constraints on the 'go for growth' strategy too. The neoliberal variant predictably leads to growing economic inequalities: the efficiency–equity trade-off beloved of orthodox economists starts to bite with a vengeance in these circumstances. The costs of imposing social order on an increasingly unequal society absorb more of the fruits of economic growth.

Even the more pragmatic policy-interventionist variant of the 'go for growth' strategy may face social limits, notwithstanding the calls for some degree of progressive redistribution as an element in making capitalism more viable on an international scale. The principle of diminishing marginal utility, also beloved of orthodox economists, presumably applies to the growth process itself—as more and more outputs of commodities yield diminishing increments of satisfaction, their capacity to substitute for other sources of satisfaction comes increasingly into question. The enormous range of studies compiled by Robert Lane (1991) remind us that income and consumption, although essential up to a certain level, are not the key source of human wellbeing, relative to satisfying experiences of work, personal security, good interpersonal relationships and community networks. The recognition that the *homo economicus* assumed in conventional economic theory is a poor approximation to real human beings casts doubts upon the efficacy of a 'go for growth' strategy, even if the faster growth could be achieved. Qualitative as well as quantitative changes are needed if economic structures are to better serve human needs.

II Upgrading Human Capital

The second scenario is based on the human capital model. This emphasizes the importance of the skills of the workforce and, more generally, of education and training as the key contributors to a workable economic future. This is an adjunct to 'go for growth' to the extent that education and training are key sources of competitive advantage and economic dynamism. But the qualitative changes can be regarded as more than a means to the end of making more goods and services. Education and training, from this perspective, are integral to a higher quality of working life. It is a viewpoint with obvious appeal in both rich and poor countries. The emphasis on the development of human capital, particularly where it links employment with other social policy goals, has appeal in advanced industrial countries seeking to improve their competitive edge: looking for a high road to economic prosperity. It also has appeal in nations seeking to improve educational standards as an integral part of their economic and social development.

Again there are two variations on the theme. One, to twist his arguments somewhat to fit in with this typology, is that presented by William Bridges in the book *Jobshift* (1996). Bridges claims that we face a 'de-jobbed future' as 'part-time and temporary work situations' replace conventional jobs. Jobs, indeed, are seen as 'artificial limits' on how we, as a society, tackle the work that has to be done. Faced with such a future, Bridges contends, each of us will have to have particular marketplace skills—of managing ourselves as businesses ('You and Co',) and developing work-search skills as well as generic attributes of literacy, numeracy and computer capability. Bridges is not unaware of the need for broader societal change, but the emphasis is on the individualistic response to developing appropriate human capital (Bridges 1996). It is a chain of reasoning which fits neatly with neoliberal ideology. However, its effectiveness depends acutely on class position and level of economic development. For downsized corporate executives in advanced industrial nations this may indeed be a positive and effective response—repackaging themselves for re-entry to the competitive marketplace. It accords with the tendency for more professionals and technicans to be employed on short-term contracts or as consultants doing outsourced business.

For working class people unfamiliar with the entrepreneurial characteristics required, the sort of proposals put forward by Bridges are a more daunting prospect. It is an even more daunting prospect for the bulk of the population in the poorer nations, lacking the 'resources and skills for survival as global competition forces employers to mechanize and rationalize labor' (Schlemmer 1998). Of course, the day-to-day existence of many of these poorer people is often based on their capacity to make and/or sell whatever they can through the informal sector of the economy. From this point of view,

Bridges' proposals can be regarded as bringing Third World practices back into the working arrangements of the advanced industrialized nations.

The more policy-interventionist variation on the human capital model at the national scale emphasizes more investment in education and workforce training. Being a 'clever country' is seen as a source of competitive economic advantage (and just possibly a source of personal fulfilment too . . .). This can be construed as a zero-sum game—'clever countries' capturing investment in knowledge-based and high-tech industries from the not-so-clever—but there is a tantalizing possibility of an aggregate net gain. To the extent that there is a link between the development of human capital and the provision of social capital infrastructure (schools, universities, etc.) then there is a net addition to social wealth. To the extent that there is also a link between this human capital strategy and Keynesian economic policy, through the boost to effective demand generated by more investment in education, an employment-generating effect can occur. To the extent that there is a further link with interventionist industry policies—as one might expect through the integration of labor market and industry development plans—that too can contribute to employment growth (see, for example, Marceau *et al.* 1997). According to the latest book by Lester Thurow (1996), the future of advanced capitalist economies depends on these qualitative changes being effectively managed—otherwise deepening economic and social crisis beckons.

However, some of the problems facing the 'go for growth' strategy also apply with this human capital scenario. The jobless growth phenomenon is a case in point. It is deeply embedded in the nature of technological change, which a human capital strategy might be expected to further accelerate in the longer term. The environmental constraints on growth also have to be considered: indeed, it is to be hoped that higher education and greater consciousness of the need for ecological sustainability go together. So too, this scenario brings the issue of the distribution of work much more sharply into focus—how the work will be shared between those with educational attributes and skills in high demand and those who are less able to command roles as 'symbolic analysts', to use Robert Reich's (1996) term. A striking 20:80 outcome is posited by Martin and Schumann (1997), whereby only a minority of the population benefits from the high-tech/advanced human capital growth path, while the majority are marginalized and consigned to a diet of bread and circuses (or 'tittytainment' as they call it). Social and ecological sustainability are evidently key problems to be addressed if we are to go beyond the 'go for growth' and human capital models to a more comprehensive view of the future of work.

III Prioritizing Equity and Environment

The third scenario focuses on equity and environment. It emphasizes redistribution to achieve sustainability and to provide economic security as a foundation for fulfilling lives. The key words here are redistribution, sustainability, security and fulfilment. This is the essence of a humanistic policy response. The linking of equity and environment is particularly important because, as environmental activists are increasingly stressing, without an emphasis on social justice there is seldom the collective willingness to tackle environmental problems. This is the case both within nations, where economic inequalities undermine a sense of common purpose, and between nations, where inequalities of development lead to different perceptions of acceptable economy–environment trade-offs. Strategies to deal with employment and unemployment need to be set in this broader context of economic, social and ecological concerns. This is easier said than done, of course: the key question is what political–economic strategy is implied.

The relatively low-key strategy, compatible with existing capitalist institutions, involves developing incentives to promote the redistribution of working time and economic restructuring towards ecological sustainability. The working time issue is of ever greater significance. European nations, France in particular, are taking the lead in reducing the working week in order to spread the work more broadly over the population. Particular companies like Volkswagen, Hewlett-Packard and Digital Equipment have successfully implemented shorter working hours policies to prevent dramatic job losses (Rifkin 1996, p. 225). Of course, there is a recurrent problem about the necessity and acceptability of shorter hours if that means lower wages. Interestingly, surveys indicate that willingness to accept such trade-offs may be greater than generally believed: Christer Sanne (1998), for example, reports on Swedish surveys indicating that 50 to 60 percent of workers would prefer shorter hours to higher wages. Some employers and workers will inevitably resist change but there are relatively modest measures which could be more widely implemented in order to effect significant progress. Possibilities include (a) taking the benefits of productivity improvements as shorter hours rather than higher wages, (b) changed working-time arrangements such as a four-day week, and (c) allowing workers to take long periods of leave without pay with income spread over working and non-working periods (Jamieson House Employment Group, 1996). Governments can provide taxation incentives to encourage such redistribution of working time.

Similarly, in regard to the promotion of economic restructuring for ecological sustainability, there are modest steps that can operate within the framework of existing capitalist institutions. Tax reform can significantly change the pattern of incentives for both consumers and businesses. The introduction of a carbon tax, to discourage production and consumption of goods and services using non-renewable fossil fuels in their manufacture and delivery, is one such possibility. In the Australian case, it has been estimated that the introduction of a carbon tax, together with the removal of payroll taxes, could expand the number of jobs sufficiently to mop up a quarter of the total national unemployment (Hamilton *et al.* 1997). In general, ecologically sustainable patterns of production and consumption tend to be more labor-intensive. The comparison between solar energy and nuclear energy is a striking case in point.

A more radical variation on the 'equity and environment' theme would entail more fundamental challenges to the work-wages nexus and the primacy of the profit motive, thereby challenging the power structure of capitalism. Take the redistribution of work, as advocated by Andre Gorz (1985), for example. Gorz suggests that a lifetime commitment of, say, 20,000 hours from each person would be sufficient, given modern technology, to generate the goods and services needed for a reasonably affluent society. Ideally, individuals should have choice about how they organize this, whether in full-time work leading to early retirement, more continuous part-time work, or in blocks of work interspersed with periods of education, recreation or whatever. Ideally too, the income stream should be reasonably consistent over time irrespective of the pattern of work. This throws up a major challenge for capitalist institutions for which the direct nexus between work and wages has always been a central feature. My own view is that such a scheme could only be managed through a social contract managed by the state: it is incompatible with the free-market capitalist system favoured by the neoliberals who currently dominate the public policy arena. Similarly, although the rate of environmental decay in a capitalist economy can be affected by taxation and other pricing and regulatory measures, the essence of a system geared to capital accumulation is anti-ecological. Its growth orientation is incompatible with the resource constraints of a finite planet. Ecologically-sustainable capitalism is an oxymoron. No wonder that restructuring for equitable distribution of work and sustainability remains in the realm of rhetoric rather than reality.

These concerns draw attention more generally to the difficulties of implementing any policy changes of a radical reformist character. Gorz's analysis presents us with a vision of a post-capitalist society in which the relationship between work and nature, economy and social structure is transformed. Yet its achievement is inconceivable without a fundamental shift in prevailing economic structures and ideologies. There would also need to be a major cultural shift, probably involving significant changes in the role of men and women in families, in communities and social arrangements more generally. The conventional notion of breadwinner is already breaking down as both men and women juggle increasingly complex patterns of paid and non-paid work: this a commonly-cited source of personal and familial stress. Whether reducing the dominance of work—both for those who have too much of it and for those who have too little of it—would reduce stress depends on the social valuation of leisure, people's contributions to community organization and citizenship in general. Liberating *homo economicus* is an enormous social challenge.

Conclusion

What does all this mean for the future of work? My analysis has just scratched the surface of the issues raised in a rapidly growing array of books, articles and reports on various aspects of this topic. But it does indicate some key structural forces which are transforming the relationship between work, economy and society, and it points to some alternative policy responses with broader ecological and cultural implications.

In summary, the argument is that there are three interconnected forces having particularly dramatic effects in the current era—globalization, downsizing and technological change. These forces are affecting the availability of jobs; the sectoral composition of employment; the nature of working life and patterns of remuneration. The general tendency is for these changes to accentuate the underlying tendencies in the economic system to instability, insecurity and inequality—the three I's of contemporary capitalist development. These circumstances throw up major policy challenges. As I have described them, the possible strategic responses can be categorised as:

I the 'go for growth' strategy, with its two variants: (a) neoliberal and (b) policy-interventionist;

II the 'human capital' strategy, emphazing either (a) individualistic responses or (b) a leading role for the public sector;
III strategies for linking employment to 'equity and environment' objectives, either (a) through adaptation of capitalist market structures or (b) through development of post-capitalist institutions.

It is important to emphasize that these scenarios are not mutually exclusive. I (b) and II (b) are certainly compatible, and could lay some political–economic foundations for the development of III (a). To be generous, we may see this as being, in part, what the current flurry of interest in a 'third way' heralds (although cynics see that, in the hands of a politican like Tony Blair, more as a marriage of social democratic rhetoric with neoliberal policy practices). Scenarios I (b), II (b) and III (b) also have some degree of compatability, at least in regard to their emphasis on the importance of institutions beyond the market; but III (b) is ultimately at odds with the acceptance of growthmania which remains implicit in I (b).

It is also important to emphasize that the three scenarios are not predictions. Indeed my personal forecast—at least for the more economically advanced nations—would be a more incoherent muddling through, based on an increasingly ineffective neoliberal 'go for growth' approach, augmented with piecemeal attention to improvements in human capital and with some experiments in restructuring for ecological sustainability to the (limited) extent that it is compatible with short-term profitability. This is a much more messy outcome than that posited by the ideal type scenarios. Indeed, the point of setting up the scenarios is partly to make that contrast and provide a spur to action. This leaves us, as ever, with the question of political will. Have we the collective inclination and capacity for effective governance to address the challenges currently posed to employment and the quality of life? As the political economist Joan Robinson (1973) wryly noted, the answers to economic problems usually turn out to be political questions.

Notes

1. The latest percentage unemployment rates as of November 1998 included France 11.7, Germany 10.6, Britain 6.2, Sweden 6.1 and Italy 12.3. The Euro-11 average was 11.1 for the eleven nations listed in *The Economist* 14–20 November 1998.
2. As long ago as 1970 Lionel Stoleru, then French Secretary for Manual Employment, noted that some countries were 'observing, in a period of

accelerating growth, a new phenomenon: a certain increase in unemployment made its appearance, as if the acceleration of growth, instead of making it possible to draw still nearer to full employment, was itself spawning unemployment' (OECD 1977, p. 8).

CHAPTER 4

Quality of Life: Issues and Questions

Hazel Henderson

Preceding dialogs have illustrated the complex relationships between today's globalization of finance, technology and trade and issues of employment, social safety nets and quality of life. These interrelated issues call for multi-disciplinary systemic approaches. We live in an interdependent world created by our globe-girdling technological hardware and as I wrote 25 years ago (Henderson 1978), we still need to write the software to manage our global affairs. Our universities are still struggling to globalize their curricula and relax the borders between ever more fragmented disciplines. They have hardly begun to deal with the great transition from the Industrial Age to the Information Age, let alone to help guide us toward the Solar Age, where deepening knowledge of nature and ourselves becomes the key factor of production.

Such topics were addressed during my first visit to Australia in 1971, at a conference sponsored by the Royal Australian Institute of Architects. I gave a paper, "Ecologist versus Economists," later published in the Harvard Business Review (Henderson 1973). I was amazed at the awareness of global economic and ecological issues in Australia at that time. I was met at Sydney Airport and ushered to a waiting press conference with some 50 journalists replete with TV cameras, and was invited onto ABC's national morning news show two days running. Call-in viewers told of corporate environmental pollution, employment issues and how their grassroots groups were addressing these concerns.

More than 25 years later, all these issues are still unresolved—something we should ponder, since the story is similar in most countries. It is a story of rapid social and technological change, shifting populations and values, powerful interest groups entrenched in obsolete institutions and legislative processes, while emerging movements are not yet able to effect even clearly beneficial change approved by majorities in opinion polls (Kay 1998). Such is the cultural and political confusion experienced in the USA and many other countries. We should not be surprised that the enormous changes of the past 25 years, accelerated by globalization, have left whole societies and their leaders with their paradigms down. We are still operating on old metrics measuring vanished territory, using old statistical cameras focused on obsolete targets and irrelevant goals. It took 25 years for my colleagues in Germany's Green Party to become part of the ruling coalition under Chancellor Gerhard Schröder.

My first civic action, in New York City in 1964, was to get television weather reports to carry the city's still primitive air pollution index. The power of mass media helped our little group, Citizens for Clean Air, succeed in getting Detroit to clean up its cars a bit and in promoting other clean-up measures. Business groups called us 'communists' who were 'spoiling the city's business climate'. I learned that social change and paradigm shifts take decades and generations and that this is probably as it should be. Order, however dysfunctional, is preferable to most people and historically societies and cultures have changed slowly. Since Alvin Toffler's *Future Shock* (1971) the spread of highly interactive communication technologies now accelerates global change and destroys local cultures and societies even more rapidly. The good and bad news of globalization has still to be assessed.

Thus, issues of employment, social safety nets and quality of life are urgent—yet require much rethinking. Political processes are overwhelmed and issues spill into new venues: corporate annual meetings, conferences, new movements, social conflict and, if not channeled, end in alienation, apathy, xenophobic and racist scapegoating or even revolutions. I became fascinated with mapping the social landscape of which I was a part. As a newly naturalized citizen of the USA, I started the National Citizens Committee on Guaranteed Income—since it was clear that information technologies would automate many workplaces, disrupt traditional employment and life patterns, and require new forms of income to maintain purchasing power in consumer-driven societies. By the late 1960s, this jobs–automation–incomes debate was in full swing in the USA and Europe. As farming and manufacturing were automated, people were gradually absorbed into services (now 70 percent of the US economy). But this process carried uncounted social costs, disrupting lives and communities. While unemployment grew, rustbelts declined and economists moved the statistical goalposts upward to seven percent as the Non-Accelerating Inflation Rate of Unemployment (NAIRU). Governments became employers of last resort, providing 'warfare, workfare and welfare,' in Louis O. and Patricia Kelso's terms, as they promoted universal capital ownership (Kelso and Kelso 1967). The Kelso Employee Stock Ownership Plans (ESOPs) allowing workers to buy their companies' stock with borrowed money were revolutionary then. Today, Patricia Kelso and a host of disciples are spreading ESOPs in Russia, China, Europe and worldwide after their successful application in the USA. Yet today, formerly sovereign nations can no longer maintain their welfare programs, high workplace standards, benefit packages and social insurance in the face of global capital flows driven by the market logic of national competitiveness.

One thing has been learned from the tug-of-war between governments and market players that pervaded the 1990s: markets need rules. Democracies use two forms of feedback from individuals to decision-makers: prices in the market and votes to determine policies. But prices must be correct (including social and environmental costs) and votes must be uncorrupted by money. Even free market ideologues acknowledge that free markets rely on government regulations of: property rights, contracts, national and international law, accounting rules and disclosure, enforcement, police, courts and even reliable tax collection (for infrastructure, health, education and other public services). Absent from such social institutions, markets descend into anarchy, criminality, violence and the mafia. Yet *laissez-faire* beliefs that markets are self-correcting die hard.

The current global ascendancy of markets and privatizations began in Britain in 1979 with the election of Margaret Thatcher. Today the British are facing up to the realities of the need for costly regulation of now private electric, gas, water and other services where companies are accused of price gouging, over-paying top executives and cutting off poor people from such essential services. Yet Mrs Thatcher's revolution did force many needed changes, and led to millions of new home owners, entrepreneurs, and investors, while privatizing government corporations: from British Airways and British Telecom to thousands of shops which sold gas stoves and household appliances.

The see-saw experiments in restructuring relationships between the state and the market continue worldwide and are well described in Yergin and Stanislaw's *The Commanding Heights* (1998). While

France, Britain and Germany re-elected socialist governments, Chile, Argentina and Brazil continue privatizing, as shown by Brazil's recent flotation of Telebras. India and China continue opening their markets. Russia, where vouchers were issued to 144 million citizens between 1992 and 1994, now seems ready to abandon its painful experiments with global markets. In spite of the pain of unemployment and shredding safety nets, markets continue spreading. Even in Asia, where economic growth has been thrown into reverse, China's markets are growing and privatizations accelerating.

The watchword today is experimentation beyond the simple prescriptions and shock treatment seen in Russia and Eastern Europe. Much of the future struggle between governments and market players will be fought over second generation reform issues—including broader analyses and metrics of success and how regulations and social institutions interact with markets. The older ideological battles which underlay the first generation of market reforms derived from the Cold War: communism versus capitalism. Sloganeering oversimplified and confused the writings of contending economists, left right and center: from Karl Marx and Mao Zedong to Raul Prebisch, John Maynard Keynes and Friedrich von Hayek and his famous students Milton Friedman and Margaret Thatcher. Misunderstandings and policy errors arose from applications of these texts: governments should own the means of production (i.e., companies in major industries) rather than regulate corporations and markets. Markets should be free from burdensome regulatory red tape—rather than clarifying which regulations were in fact essential. The neoclassical economics textbook generalizations summed up as the Washington Consensus were purveyed worldwide by the USA, the World Bank and IMF economists in their policies, loans and structural adjustment conditionalities.

Economic textbooks theorize that the price system, driven by individual rational economic men competitively maximizing their own self-interest, is the most efficient and, therefore, preferred form of resource allocation, and ultimately should become the preeminent regime in all countries. Some equate markets with democracy. These textbooks admit that market failures can occur (due to unequally distributed power, wealth, and information) but deem them exceptions. The demise of the Soviet Union in 1991 left the Washington Consensus unchallenged.

Today, globalizing electronic markets offer a fast-forward view of what we can expect as they accelerate the dominance of the price system over diverse traditional values, cultures and institutions which form the cultural DNA codes of different societies. Today's global economic crises, exacerbated by the unfettered globalization of financial markets driven by deregulation policies, electronic trading and commerce, have eroded the powers of all nation-states. Even the most democratically elected politicians' policies are disciplined by computerized currency and bond traders in today's \$1.5 trillion daily global casino (90 percent of these flows are unrelated to trade or the real economy, i.e., they are speculative). Thus, maintaining adequate domestic macroeconomic policies, investments in infrastructure, education, research, and so forth to maintain social capital and safety nets to cushion unemployment and provide social services have fallen victim to such volatile unregulated markets and the global financial bubble. This does not mean that governments are powerless (Weiss 1998).

Yet we still see national governments and politicians ducking these responsibilities, which are often part of their electoral promises to voters. Even the most democratically elected politicians, on attaining office, too often renege on these promises and begin to cast their policies in line with the *status quo* and special interests. Money has become the curse of democratic political processes in many OECD and developing countries aspiring to become more democratic. Today in the USA, we see the spectacle of scandals and widespread corruption in campaign financing with the resulting catastrophic loss of trust in government. Only 30 percent of US adults trust their elected representatives and public officials in Washington; the same American Talk Issues survey in 1994 found that US adults actually trusted the UN more than their government in Washington.

In Europe many other scandal-ridden governments put their taxpayers' funds on the global auction block, along with their workforces and natural and environmental resources in the new global bidding war to lure (bribe) corporations, banks, and financial institutions to locate in their countries. These bidding wars broker taxpayers' funds to subsidize such new corporate facilities, often at absurd costs. For example, London-based *The Economist* reported (1997a) that in 1991 Portugal paid Auto Europa, Ford and Volkswagen \$254,000 per job created, while the state of Alabama, USA, bribed Mercedes-Benz with \$167,000 per job created. These enormous corporate subsidies might have financed micro-businesses or provided guaranteed incomes for life to many of these prospective job holders. Heads of state troop dutifully to the World Economic Forum in Davos to offer these deregulation sweeteners, subsidies, and tax breaks to corporate CEOs. They bargain away their citizens' sovereignty in the now familiar global race-to-the-bottom. Cronyism is endemic—not something recently discovered in Asia. This corporate–government collusion in OECD countries and developing countries is spreading worldwide. It is corrupting democracies and betraying their citizens, voters, employees and investors. Democracy is perverted worldwide to serve fictitious corporate 'humans' whose charters permit evading liabilities and public accountability.

Changing Economic Paradigms

Today many different hypotheses concerning the so-called New Economy of information technology in the USA can be seen within today's global context of social system transition. Other hypotheses set local, ethnic, community and nationalistic backlashes against the backdrop of globalization (Müller 1995; Huntington 1991). These New Economy and other hypotheses stem from different paradigms and interpretations, which produce conflicting forecasts of productivity, inflation, deflation, effects of the Asian meltdown, etc. Such statistical paradigms underlie GNP/GDP, Purchasing Power Parity (PPP), Consumer Price Indexes (CPIs) and new approaches to include in national accounts asset balance sheets, social and environmental capital, unpaid work and externalities. Some of this statistical work is underway, but still under-funded—from retooling GNP/GDP to account for natural and human capital and subtract social and environment costs to recalculating the CPIs. CPIs should reflect higher quality in some goods and the shift to services.

Macroeconomic policies should also account for the valuable public goods and services that add to quality of life but are unpriced (e.g., police and fire services, infrastructure, health and environmental protection agencies, etc.), without which complex technological economies cannot function. Thus, the US CPI may be overstated by as much 1.5 percent, as the US Boskin Commission says, or by more than this if the value of unpriced public services are factored in. Energy and food prices continue to be excluded from the core rate, along with depreciation of infrastructure and other national assets. *The Economist* now recommends adding financial and real estate asset inflation to CPIs (1998a). All this statistical revisioning will end up recalibrating US Federal Reserve and other central bank policies and the NAIRU, as well as the budget, social security and deficits.

Disorderly, inequitable global financial markets (on which traders and brokers thrive) have also led to tax evasion, money laundering, insider trading, bear raids and cronyism; for example, the recent US bailout of the private hedge fund Long-Term Capital Management from its over-leveraged derivative positions. Such chaotic capital markets remind us of the Mundell–Fleming model of the 1960s, which showed that nations wishing to integrate their economies and trade cannot simultaneously expect to enjoy (a) domestic economic autonomy, (b) stable exchange rates and (c) unfettered global capital flows (Mundell 1962; Fleming 1962). Now that the global casino has lost 'the mandate of heaven' and plunged millions back into poverty in Asia, the fundamental redesign of its architecture called for at the 1995 G7 Summit in Halifax, Canada is back on the agenda.

Today, the search for more comprehensive and dynamic models of our economies is also driven by globalization and electronic markets. Forecasters from many disciplines—economics, technology assessment, game theory, ecology, or chaos and complex adaptive system modeling—now agree that equilibrium models drawn from Cartesian–Newtonian worldviews of a deterministic, clockwork universe no longer cut it. In fact, the post-Cartesian scientific principles that I have been urging for more than 20 years are now almost conventional wisdom (Henderson 1981). The tightly interactive global economy is increasingly dynamic, creating a world in a hurricane of change. Nations and institutions are restructuring due to such forces. (See Figure 1 below). Such a world cannot be understood by conventional macroeconomic models assuming equilibrium. The economics textbooks' favorite 'Rational Economic Man' with his unchanging preferences, still underlies macroeconomic models and the statistics that drive most decision-making in our economies, including Australia, as wittily described by Brian Toohey in *Tumbling Dice* (1994).

Yet humans are neither guinea pigs nor atoms. Contrary to observation, Rational Economic Man never learns or grows or changes his preferences for maximizing his material self-interest in competition with others. Psychologists would say that this model represents humanity's primitive reptilian brain. Robert Lucas won a Nobel Memorial Prize for promoting the 'Man's' higher forebrain functions and his rational expectations. But if they fully discount all government actions and market information, this leaves us with only nihilism. In the face of new global conditions—pollution, growing gaps between the rich and poor, spreading deserts, burning rain forests, and ozone depletion—Rational Economic Man waits for the market to act while Pareto optimality (which assumes that information, wealth, and

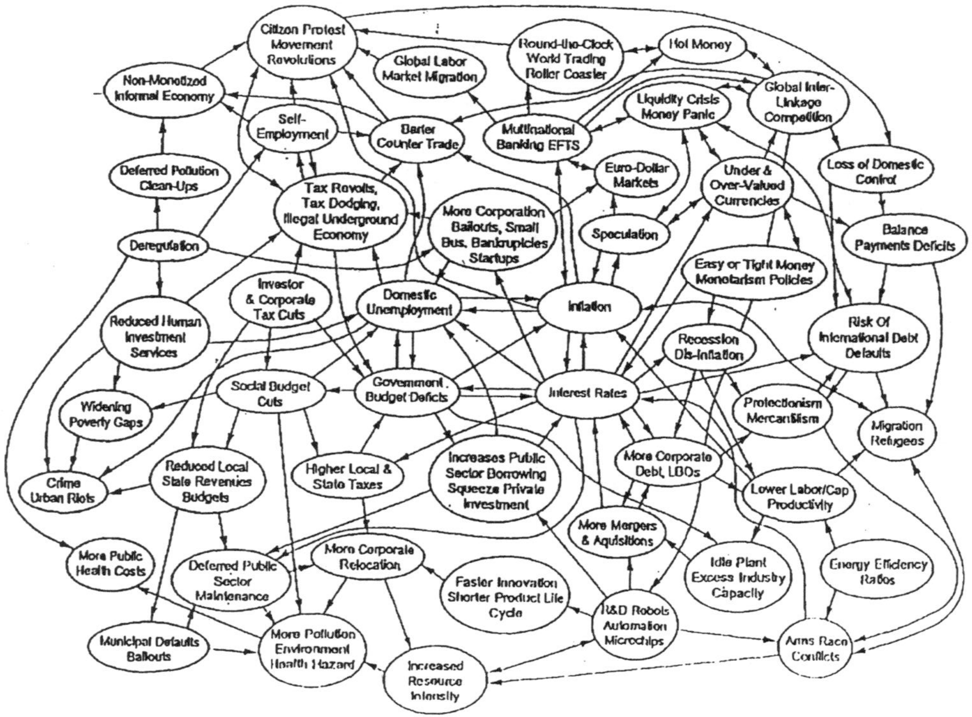

Figure 1. System view of global 'Vicious Circle' economy (fast feedback loops) © 1980/91 Hazel Henderson

power are given) still rules its collective decision-making. Technology is also assumed to be a parameter in most economic models—rather than as futurists see it, the driving variable of the still-evolving Industrial Revolution, now well into its post-industrial, information technology dominated phase. Economics professors acknowledge these unrealistic assumptions, yet still keep on teaching with them.

Thus, futurists contend that most economic models in the public and private sector are still backing us into the future looking into the rear view mirror. Human agents are still seen as either the guinea pigs in the computer models of fashionable social simulators or as the golf balls or atoms of traditional Newtonian physics. This objective view (which does make the math easier!) assumes that all human actions in society are irrelevant, statistically damped out by the Law of Large Numbers. Even powerful producers in many computer models are assumed to have no impact on the structure of the economy. On the contrary, some economists and most futurists acknowledge that financial markets are influenced by large institutions—from governments to global corporations and institutional investors—increasingly interwoven global real time networks, where over-shoots and herd behavior are amplified. Thus, game theory, chaos models and psychology become sharper tools for examining how markets are affected by the interactions of mutual expectations of players. Unfortunately, the Artificial Society models of mathematical economists often program their simulated human agents with the same competitive, self-maximizing, economic behavior, and, unsurprisingly, recreate poverty gaps and trade wars (e.g., Epstein and Axtell 1996). The now defrocked *quants* and rocket scientists whose computer models calculate the prices of derivatives allow a 20–40 percent risk factor due to their own models, but still lead to huge losses. The red-faced Nobel Committee which awarded the 1997 economic prize to the two partners of the ill-fated Long-Term Capital Management hedge fund, awarded the 1998 prize to Amartya Sen, who studies poverty and moral issues.

Of course, one or two innovative economists (borrowing models from systems and game theory and from chaos and complex adaptive systems studies) have moved beyond this Industrial Age, Cartesian–Newtonian worldview. For example, the Santa Fe Institute's W. Brian Arthur (1990) uses fifty-year-old cybernetic, feed-back driven systems models to illustrate that in network markets there are increasing (not diminishing) returns to scale and path-dependency in innovation (i.e., initial conditions will amplify in non-linear systems).[1] This phenomenon underlies Microsoft's market domination.

Buddhists call this 'laying down a path in walking.' Stanford University's Paul Romer reminds his fellow economists of what futurists have known for decades: that technology must be incorporated as a key variable in all macroeconomic models (1990). Others include Michael Rothschild (1990) who envisions economies as ecosystems in terms long familiar to futurists and ecologists, echoing my *Creating Alternative Futures: The End of Economics* (1978). Clearly, interdisciplinary dialogs between all these worldviews would create sharper analytical tools.

All this underlies today's pop debate in the financial press about the nature of the New Economy and the explosive US stock market rises and volatility, as well as whether US Federal Reserve Board Chairman Alan Greenspan's new view of the statistical lag in measuring productivity is correct. *Business Week* has frequently editorialized that globalization, and the increasing competition it brings, does discipline even the biggest firm's pricing—just as it does wages—echoing calls for dumping the Phillips Curve (Phillips 1958), as I have urged since 1978. Even Phillips didn't believe in the Phillips Curve. All this has shifted the NAIRU into lower territory so that interest rates can be reduced and sustainable economic growth can proceed in a new virtuous cycle. All this sounds great and it is half right, as a market flow model, i.e., the conventional monetarist bathtub model of the national economy as a hydraulic system. In the UK, Roger Bootle makes a similar case in his *The Death of Inflation* (1996) but with a longer timescale interpretation beyond simple monetarism and a more radical conclusion: that OECD economies face a future of deflation. Certainly the deflationary effect of the Asian meltdown has not yet been fully felt in the world economy. Indeed, the US and European stock markets have been pumped up with billions in flight capital seeking safer havens. A fast feedback loop is created by the herd behavior of asset managers who follow asset allocation theory and feel obliged to buy the big indexes: Dow Jones, Standard and Poor's, and London's FTSE100. This herd behavior effect is reinforced in the USA by the 'prudent man rule', which prevents asset managers from straying far beyond such blue chip stocks—thereby bidding up the big indexes. I call it 'the prudent lemming rule'.

Beyond these expanded economic models, the less examined other half of the story relates to assets (stocks of built, natural, and human capital) as well as liabilities, debt, and other aspects of restructuring outside much market data and models. Here, the gloomier view of the $1.5 trillion daily global casino emerges, with its

$50 trillion in outstanding derivatives positions where individuals hedge their own risks by adding to systemic risks. Today's tidal waves of hot money and speculation challenge central bankers charged with the now impossible job of managing national economies and currencies. They still foolishly play at the same casino table with highly leveraged, profit-maximizing currency traders, who arbitrage interest rates and national government policies alike (Henderson and Kay 1996). The central bankers, under pressure from banks and financial interests, have stripped themselves of other macroeconomic tools: adjusting bank reserve ratios and stock brokers' margin requirements, as well as capital and currency controls. They now must rely on interest rates alone to cool inflation and financial bubbles. US and European central bankers are now afraid to use interest rates to cool their economies – not only because this throws the real economies of Main Street into recession and unemployment but also because it pricks asset bubbles too drastically and could cause further global deflation. Thus, central bankers today are left with jaw-boning stock markets about irrational exuberance. Even *The Economist* is revisiting the issue of unregulated capital flows (1998b). A currency exchange fee of 0.05 percent is now back on the agenda of many governments. Russia has few options to restoring state control of some areas of its economy—an unfortunate but understandable backlash to the human misery of its economic meltdown.

Marginal reforms will not be enough. The G7's $90 billion line of credit pledged to the IMF on 30 October to help countries with 'sound economies' to 'ward off the global economic crisis' (i.e., currency speculators) was more orthodox and designed to please financial markets. Stock markets rallied worldwide at the prospect of yet more public funds to buttress private markets. The world's taxpayers are aware of the moral hazard involved in bailing out reckless investors. So far, timid debates among G7, G10, G22 leaders, have not led to coordinated interest rate cuts or promised reform of the IMF. Another global deflation is still imminent; and the dangers of political extremism grow, as they did during the Great Depression and led to World War Two. In addition, the mountains of unrepayable debt of the poorest countries must, at last, be written off. Currency exchange will need to be taxed, as James Tobin (1978) and Lawrence Summers (Summers and Summers 1989) have recommended. To do this the central banks will need to implement the proposals for a public utility foreign exchange so that they can audit all trades and monitor fraud, money laundering, speculation, etc. and impose fees and fines (Henderson and Kay 1996). Rhetoric from the G7 of a 'new roadmap for a new century' to include increased global financial regulation and codes of conduct for hedge funds and other market players, must show results. Germany and France wanted tight controls on international capital flows (a key source of instability) but this was opposed by the USA and the UK, according to London's *Financial Times* (1998).

More than ever, new multidisciplinary metrics to measure quality of life must supplement current GNP/GDP systems of national accounts (UNSNAs), which must be corrected to account for social and human capital and ecological assets and unpaid work. Most urgent is the inclusion of an asset budget in such national accounts, so as to properly account for infrastructure and other public investments. Such huge investments have been expensed in GNP/GDP, leading to massive budget deficits and overstating of inflation. The USA followed the lead of New Zealand and Switzerland in 1996 in creating such an asset account for its infrastructure, leading to its FY1999 budget surplus. With even *The Economist* (1998c) calling for Japan to start printing money, i.e. monetizing its debt, it would surely make more sense to properly account for much of its debt as public assets. Meanwhile, Japan's ruling LDP was forced to accept opposition parties' conditions that use of taxpayers' funds to bailout banks must entail strict public oversight.

It is now imperative for the common good that national accounts in all countries and the United Nations System of National Accounts (UNSNA) include caring unpaid work to maintain family and community life. These changes have been recommended by an ethical minority of economists: e.g., K.W. Kapp (1950); E.J. Mishan (1974); K.E. Boulding (1968); B. Ward and R. Dubos (1972), as well as myself, since the UNSNA was set up in the 1950s after being designed originally to maximize war production in the United Kingdom during World War Two. In 1995 the United Nations Human Development Program (UNDP) produced an estimate of $16 trillion of such unpaid caring volunteer work simply missing from 1995 global GDP of $24 trillion (UNDP 1995)—illustrating the enormity of this omission. I have estimated such unpaid work (parenting, caring for old and sick family members, growing food for family and community needs, maintaining households, volunteering in community service, do-it-yourself home and community construction and repair projects) as some 50 percent of all production in OECD countries and some 60–65 percent in developing countries—depending on the size of their traditional village-based and indigenous economies (Henderson 1971b. See Figure 2 below). The

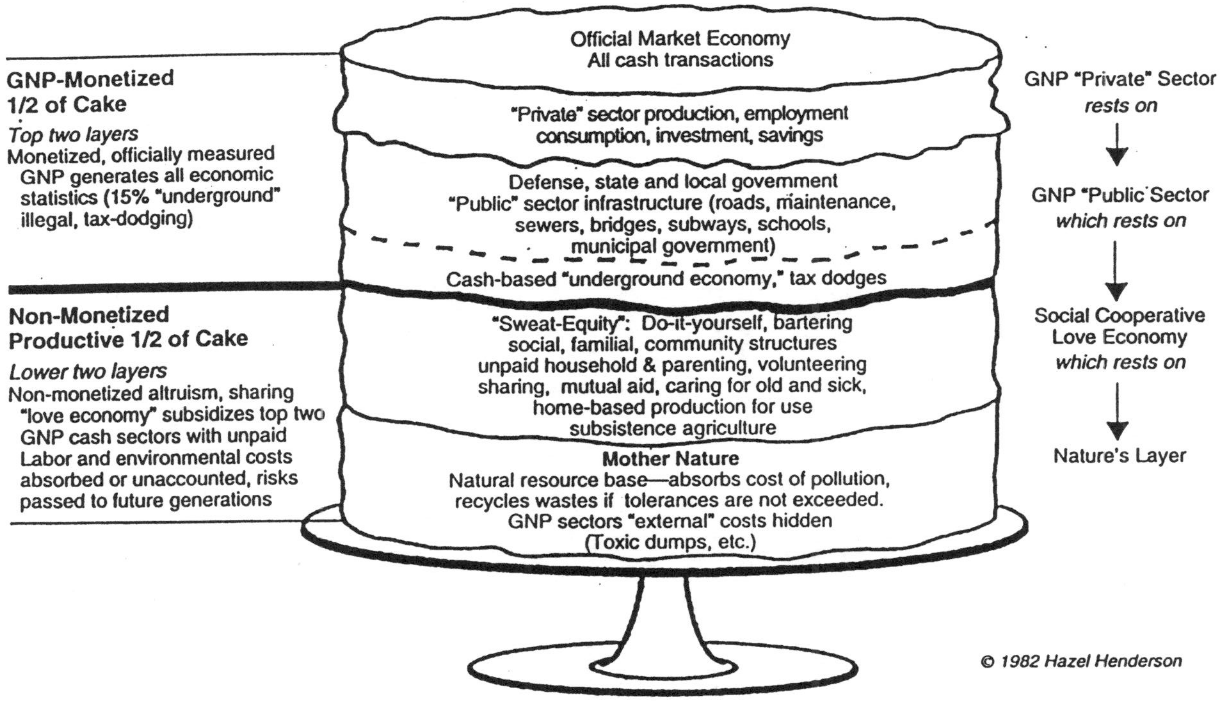

Figure 2. Total productive system of an industrial society (layer cake with icing)

environmentalists' critique of the UNSNA has been the most insistent and many green GDP alternatives have been proposed, such as the PQLI (Physical Quality of Life Index) by David Morris and the ISEW (Index of Sustainable Economic Welfare) of Herman Daly and John Cobb now calculated in many versions in OECD countries including the UK, Sweden, USA (See Henderson 1981; Daly and Cobb 1989) and my own Country Futures Indicators (See Figure 3 below), the first version of which is the Calvert–Henderson Quality of Life Indicators for the USA (see *www.calvertgroup.org* and Figure 4).

Taming the Global Casino

The reasons for the urgency of these efforts to overhaul the UNSNA are now growing more obvious. Steering national policies via the GNP-growth formula has proved disastrous, socially and environmentally, allowing enormous backlogs of social and environmental costs to be swept under the accounting rug. These costs of cannibalizing a country's social and human capital, institutions, family and community life as well as polluting and depleting environmental resources are now all too visible. The Asian economic meltdown showed that dashes for GNP-growth via slave wages and environmental destruction are unsustainable, as is today's deregulated global financial casino (Henderson 1998).

We measure according to our dominant cultural view of what is valuable. When GNP/GDP accounts were set up in World War Two, bombs, bullets and war production were the goal, while the value of children, a healthy educated citizenry, infrastructure, social safety nets and the environment were all set at zero. This statistical viewpoint is still perpetuated, not only by bureaucratic inertia but by the sectors, interest groups and politically powerful forces amplified by such a system of national accounts. Military budgets remain off-limits while social safety nets, health, education, environment and even repairs to infrastructure are pushed down national budget priority lists.

A subtle disintermediation has occurred, slowly devaluing employment, caring work, parenting, social services and safety nets while overvaluing finance itself, i.e., paper asset shuffling. The financial services sectors grew ninefold—out of all proportion to the real economies of Main Street they were designed to track and serve (Dembinski and Schoenenberger 1998). This same sort of disintermediation has also devalued the commodities sector and natural resources. One could simply make more money by holding and

Re-formulated GNP to Correct Errors and Provide More information:

- PURCHASING POWER PARITY (PPP) corrects for currency fluctuations
- 'INCOME DISTRIBUTION Is the poverty gap widening or narrowing?
- COMMUNITY BASED ACCOUNTING to compliment current enterprise-basis
- INFORMAL, HOUSEHOLD SECTOR PRODUCTION measures all hours worked (paid and unpaid)
- DEDUCT SOCIAL AND ENVIRONMENTAL COSTS a 'net accounting avoids double counting'
- ACCOUNT FOR DEPLETION OF NON-RENEWABLE RESOURCES analogous to a capital consumption deflator
- ENERGY INPUT/GDP RATIO measures energy efficiency, recycling
- MILITARY CIVILIAN BUDGET RATIO measures effectiveness of governments
- CAPITAL ASSET ACCOUNT FOR BUILT INFRASTRUCTURE AND PUBLIC RESOURCES (Many economists agreed this is needed. Some include environment as a resource.)

Complementary Indicators of Progress Toward Society's Goals:

- POPULATION birth rates, crowding, age distribution
- EDUCATION literacy levels, school dropout and repetition rates
- HEALTH Infant mortality, low birth weight, weight/height/age
- NUTRITION e.g., calories per day, protein/carbohydrates ratio, etc.
- BASIC SERVICES e.g., access to clean water, etc.
- SHELTER housing availability/quality, homelessness, etc.
- PUBLIC SAFETY crime
- CHILD DEVELOPMENT World Health Organization, UNESCO, etc.
- POLITICAL PARTICIPATION AND DEMOCRATIC PROCESS e.g., Amnesty International data, money-influence in elections, electoral participation rates
- STATUS OF MINORITY AND ETHNIC POPULATIONS AND WOMEN e.g., Human rights data
- AIR AND WATER QUALITY AND ENVIRONMENTAL POLLUTION LEVELS air pollution in urban areas
- ENVIRONMENTAL RESOURCE DEPLETION hectares of land, forests lost annually
- BIO DIVERSITY AND SPECIES LOSS e.g., Canada's environmental indicators
- CULTURE, RECREATIONAL RESOURCES e.g., Jacksonville, Florida

Figure 3. Country Futures Indicators™ (beyond money-denominated, per capita averaged growth of GNP) © 1989 Hazel Henderson

Calvert-Henderson Quality of life Indicators

To overhaul GNP/GDP.
- EMPLOYMENT: Unemployment (including discouraged and demographic breakouts); Net job growth.
- INCOMES: Per capita in Dollars (plus "standard of living" purchasing power); Poverty gap (richest–poorest quintiles); Unpaid work (hours worked, paid and unpaid).
- POPULATION: Growth rate—Demographics.
- CAPITAL ASSETS/INFRASTRUCTURE/PUBLIC SERVICES (including natural resources and depletion rates and measuring "net worth" as in corporate balance sheets).
- MILITARY/CIVILIAN BUDGET RATIO (measuring international competitiveness).
- ENERGY/EFFICIENCY RATIO (measuring international competitiveness).

Quality of Life Criteria:
- EDUCATION/HUMAN CAPITAL: Literacy; Percentage of preschoolers in Headstart; Patents ganted.
- HUMAN RIGHTS/POLITICAL PARTICIPATION: Status of minorities/women; Voter registration; PAC money per voter.
- HEALTH: Infant mortality; Life expectancy; Percentage of Americans with no access to care.
- PUBLIC SAFETY: Violent crimes per 10,000 population.
- SHELTER: Homelessness; Affordability of housing.
- ENVIRONMENT: Urban air pollution; Water systems (EPA standards).
- CULTURE/RECREATION: Urban parks per capita; Federal and State $s spent on the Arts.

Figure 4. Calvert-Henderson Quality of Life Indicators

trading financial assets. Many critics like myself pointed out over the past 25 years that this overblown finance sector was a bubble and when it deflated, as it did on 19 October, 1987, Main Street and the world's traditional resource and human capital based economies of the world would actually benefit (UTNE Reader 1997).

Even though cyber-libertarians and electronic currency traders do not like earthbound constraints, the laws of thermodynamics still operate. One cannot fill a car's gas tank with a virtual gallon of petrol or drive across the flow of services of a bridge. All this was pointed out by Nicholas Georgescu-Roegen, whom I have regarded as the much sought-after 'new Keynes,' in his *The Entropy Law and the*

Economic Process (1971; see review, Henderson 1971a). Although improvements in communications and materials sciences have since led to a profound dematerializing of OECD economies, today's debates involve the extent to which this process, which Buckminster Fuller called 'ephemeralization,' can continue substituting knowledge and communications for natural resources. Here is where social and human capital and investments in people and social infrastructure are key. Societies cannot continue dematerializing their economies without investing in maintaining such social architecture and human capital for further advances in research (Lamberton 1971). Knowledge, human capital, trust, cohesive values and sound management of the planet's biodiversity and natural resources are now the key factors of production.

Biodiversity is another newly perceived global common resource now under constant attack. The recognition of biodiversity as the basic information code of all living organisms—a resource far richer than coal or oil—has caused today's stampede of chemical and pharmaceutical companies into the last indigenously occupied rainforests and other unexploited biomes. The rush to expropriate wild plant species and genomes guarded by indigenous people for centuries has led to enormous inequities and manipulation of Western patent laws to justify such wholesale biopiracy. This has led to consideration of culture as a common resource along with the value of maintaining cultural diversity, that rich storehouse of human cultural DNA codes: information, values, ethics, customs, languages, art and the range of human behavioral repertoires that over the ages have helped humans adapt and survive in many different ecological niches. In my *Creating Alternative Futures* (1978) I called for assembling databanks of such human cultural DNA codes to help assess which behaviors had proved survival-enhancing in facing ecological stresses. Certainly we will need the widest repertoire from competition to cooperation, sharing and creativity, if we are to survive the planetary challenges our past behaviors have produced.

Currently, economists still bestride the policy process and offer concepts for managing global commons based on extending property rights. They bring along their obsolete models of Pareto optimality, which assumes away unequal distribution of wealth, power and information. Economists propose to enclose the last commons as property regimes for economic efficiency while omitting the truth that all such schemes are essentially political allocations of resources. Futurists and systems theorists see them as closed systems requiring win–win rules (See Figure 5 below). Today, economists are busy

	Economists	Futurists/Systems
	Markets Private Sector... • Individual decisions • Competition • Invisible hand	Open Systems • Divisible resources • Win-lose rules • (Adam Smith's rules)
	Commons Public sector ... • Property of all • Monopoly under regulation • Consortia	Closed Systems • Indivisible resources • Win-win rules • Cooperation • Agreements

Note: One must remember that all such schematizations are, at best, approximations and often culturally arbitrary.

Figure 5. Differing models of markets and commons

calculating the price of rainforests, biodiversity, watersheds, etc. using opinion surveys of Willingness to Pay (WTP) to preserve such commons. This forces ordinary citizens to bid for such resources (of no direct benefit to them) against commercial developers who would directly benefit. Such absurd WTP-derived contingency prices are hopelessly inaccurate and drastically undervalue common resources. Only calculating replacement costs would suffice but these resources are often irreplaceable. So the task is beyond money equivalents and the skills of economists and requires interdisciplinary teams and multiple metrics (e.g., Calvert–Henderson QOL Indicators).

Meanwhile the UNSNA still overvalues the goods and artifacts of the receding industrial era, while many OECD economies are approaching the USA's 70 percent level of services. Such services still do not include those of the Love Economy, eroding daily through neglect, in broken families, community breakdown, drugs, inner city decay, and spreading epidemics such as tuberculosis, once thought contained. Statisticians in the USA are at work overhauling the categories of GNP/GDP, which still are dominated by widgets and goods, to include software, services, knowledge industries and intellectual capital. But the conceptual confusion continues as we proceed further into the Age of Light (See Figure 6) based on deeper knowledge of nature, ourselves and powered by renewable resources and solar energy (Henderson 1991, p. 261–72).

Emerging Lightwave Technologies (Phototronics)

- Fiber optics ... communications cabling, voice, data, etc.
- Optical scanners ... supermarkets, banks, on-line computer systems
- Lasers ... laser surgery, laser printers, laser phonographs turntables, laser bottles to see atoms, laser propulsion, Star Wars laser weapons systems, laser art
- Holography ... computer assisted design (CAD), computer assisted manufacturing (CAM), computer integrated manufacturing (CM), art
- Solar technologies ... passive solar heating and cooling, Trombe walls, solar-thermal energy conversion, ocean thermal, tidal and wave power, bio-energy conversion, hydroponics, aquaculture, solar reflector 'power towers', photochemical conversion (artificial and natural photosynthesis), photovoltaics, solar cell arrays for powering satellites, space based solar collectors, solar sails for deep space voyages
- Optical computers ... use light pulses instead of electrical impulses—pushing toward the speed of light
- Multiprocessors, parallel computers and neural net computers ... very fast architecture allows simultaneous, rather than sequential processing, speech and voice recognition, language and artificial intelligence (AI) applications
- Imaging technologies ... TV images, liquid crystal screens, magnetic imaging diagnostics
- Biotechnologies ... gene splicing, designing, molecular engineering, medical diagnostics, immunology, tissue culture, cloning, plant hybridization and 're-designing', and bio-remediation
- Gene machines ... which automate the synthetic asssembly of genes
- DNA sequences ... which 'speed read' the DNA code in cells
- Tagging and tracking chemicals and genes ... using luciferase, etc.
- Nano technologies ... molecular 'machines' to assemble, repair molecules, in many diverse ways (e.g. theories of Eric Drexler in *Engines of Creation*, 1986)

Photons (sunlight) falling on the earth supply enough energy in 10 minutes to put our entire five billion population in orbit!

Figure 6. The Age of Light © 1987 Hazel Henderson

For example, the egregious error mentioned earlier in GNP/GDP is the lack of asset accounts for investments in infrastructure and human capital. These investments should be carried and expensed over their useful life, often 50–100 years. GNP/GDP are cash flow statements of money-denominated transactions, with such longer-term investments (infrastructure, education, infant health, etc.) treated as consumption and written off each year. Try running a corporation that way if a costly productive facility could not be amortized over its useful life. The recent example cited, when in 1996 the USA added an infrastructure asset account to its GDP, illustrates the enormous implications and real world effects of such errors in UNSNAs. This statistical correction reduced the US budget deficit by approximately $100 billion per year, by accounting for some infrastructure assets, but still not education or other investments in human or social capital (e.g., science, R&D etc.). The USA's budget surplus was also achieved by some $100 billion reduction in its still-bloated military expenditures. This budget surplus, claimed as the result of superior economic management (certainly improved accounting) attracted billions in flight capital from other jittery markets after Asia's meltdown went global, and to seek safe havens in the US stock and bond markets. Furthermore, if all other countries simply made the same recalculations to their own GDPs, all would soon show similar budget surpluses. The question is, why don't they? Surely, such sensible corrections to all national accounts are preferable to the moral hazards of putting taxpayers at further risk of, as *Business Week* proposed in its editorial, 'a global write-down of debt' (1998).

European Union member countries (with an average of eleven percent unemployment) have cut their domestic safety nets to attain the Maastricht criteria which included three percent or less of budget deficits. Some years ago, I urged that the Commission's policy staff might check their member nations' GDPs for asset accounts to see if infrastructure investments were missing. This might have saved painful budget cuts and the ensuing political unrest and strikes, particularly in France. The introduction of the euro in January 1999 constrained domestic economic policies further, exacerbated by the growth and stability pact. Further straitjacketing of fiscal policies will force deregulation and cuts in employment security and benefits for employees in the eleven Euro countries and promote labor mobility between them (i.e., more economic migration with its social costs unaccounted).

Likewise, in the current global economic crisis, a great proportion of public debt in Japan, Korea and other Asian countries, as well as in Europe and Latin America, could be reduced, along with unemployment, by such accounting corrections. It must be emphasized that such asset accounts in GDP should also include investments in education, health, child development and in R&D to maintain a society's knowledge base and general quality of life. The World Bank's new Wealth Index, introduced in 1995, moves in the right direction, but still has little effect on operations. Instead of making such needed corrections in national accounts, the G7 called on governments to make their currency reserves, fiscal and monetary policies more transparent via an international code of conduct. This will be a step forward only if their proposals for similar codes of conduct can be forced on private banks, TNCs and international speculators. Similarly, accounting firms are grappling with intellectual capital and goodwill in corporate balance sheets. All these overhauls represent the biggest advance in accounting since the invention of double-entry bookkeeping.

Before we can steer our economic policies back toward the common good, quality of life and sound environmental management, we must complete this accounting revolution. The current globalization of bubble finance and the global economic crises it has exacerbated suggests the need for a crash program to correct all countries' GNP/GDP accounts—a prerequisite for all the other reforms of the global financial architecture now so urgently needed. These cannot come soon enough if we are to save safety nets, human and social capital, the Love Economy and the environment from obsolete economics and faulty accounting.

Even ex-President Clinton has called for a rewriting of these old economic prescriptions to deal with today's globalized finance and markets. During his term of office he pointed out that 'poor and vulnerable people affected by these global markets should not have to be sacrificed to economic theories.' Clinton wants to see reforms at the IMF, which has been blamed for making the Asian crises worse, but he is short on specifics. The 3 October, 1998 meeting in Washington of central bankers and finance ministers to 'promote global growth, write down debt, replenish the IMF and continue opening markets' discussed such familiar nostrums. The IMF's new $90 billion standby rescue fund includes $30 billion for Brazil's Real and other countries targeted by speculators, which only whets their appetites by increasing opportunities for arbitrage. In 1997, when the Asian currencies began melting down, Japan proposed leading an Asian IMF bailout, which might have contained the ensuing contagion, but the USA opposed this sensible proposal.

The G7 also proposed new rules for monitoring international capital flows, but passed on Clinton's earlier proposal to open the WTO to scrutiny by consumers, employees and citizens adversely affected by narrow trade pacts, and to consider the environment. At least, the G7 called on the World Bank for a 'new welfare fund to alleviate economic suffering among the most vulnerable people in the emerging economies.' Most of the G7 proposals echo their Background Paper issued at the Halifax Summit in 1995, including opening up the secretive IMF to external review (Henderson 1996a, ch. 13).

What is needed, however, is nothing short of a new Bretton Woods. Times have changed since this international conference which, in 1944, created the first global economic architecture. The Bretton Woods gathering set up multilateral rules and agencies, including the World Bank and the IMF, which served the world economy until 1971, when Richard Nixon unilaterally pulled the plug by slamming shut the US gold window (removing the gold standard). Since then, the world has lurched from crisis to crisis, through a rollercoaster of global recessions, currency gyration and many *ad hoc* arrangements for floating currencies, capital movement controls and convertibility rules.

Back in 1995, at the UN Summit on Social Development at Copenhagen a set of proposals emerged in the report of the Global Commission to Fund the United Nations (See Henderson *et al.* 1995). We called for:

> A very small (0.05 percent) tax on all currency trades, first discussed at Bretton Woods in 1944 with later versions proposed by US economists James Tobin and Lawrence Summers, now Under Secretary of the Treasury. Such a tax would not hurt real, long-term investors, but would bite speculators who move money across borders often hundreds of times a day.
>
> A global version of the US Securities and Exchange Commission (SEC) to harmonize regulations of securities and currency markets. Such an international supervisory body would curb today's unregulated global casino of insider trading, fraud, money laundering and capital flight. Today, speculators' bear raids attack perceived weak currencies such as those in 1993 which drove the British pound down and out of the European Monetary Union (EMU).
>
> The proposal mentioned earlier that the world's major central banks get together and set up their own public utility currency exchange. Thus they could compete with today's money center banks and speculators and properly oversee their currencies to protect their domestic purposes, just as they oversee their sovereign bonds.

The new Bretton Woods conference should be convened by the United Nations and include all countries in designing cooperative new rules needed to tame the global casino. The world needs reformed financial institutions. But they will also need to be based on new accounting systems that can better monitor long-term investments, ecological assets, human and social capital and properly account for the loving services provided unpaid and voluntarily in the caring sectors of all economies. The extent of the paradigmatic error underlying the globalization of markets and market economics, involves its exclusive focus on competition. Such win–lose, zero sum paradigms exist also in nation states, since the Treaty of Westphalia in 1648.

In the past, domestic macroeconomic management and democratic governance was shielded from such international conflicts as much as possible. Today, the enthroning of market economics, via the US–World Bank–IMF Washington Consensus, has led to opening up nations' economies, privatization, free trade, convertible currencies and export-led GNP growth. Thus national politicians have been pulled into this global competitiveness race-to-the-bottom, cutting regulations, safety nets, and social and environmental protection and placing their societies on the global auction block of daily capital markets. Even the World Bank has issued a 1998 report, *Beyond the Washington Consensus* (Burki and Perry 1998), acknowledging the crucial importance of regulations, contract law, social institutions, infrastructure and values. As these global competitive markets spin out of control, even the wounded players demand that governments bail them out, i.e., cooperative behavior is needed to balance competition, as in all ecosystems. All other social sciences except market economics have covered the full repertoire of human behavior (See Figure 7 below). Thus today we can see at every level from

CONFLICT ◄— COMPETITION	COOPERATION —► SHARING
◄—— GAME THEORY ——►	
◄—— PSYCHOLOGY ——►	
◄—— SOCIOLOGY ——►	
◄—— ANTHROPOLOGY ——►	
◄—— INFORMATION/DECISION/THEORY ——►	
◄—— SYSTEMS THEORY ——►	
◄— MARKETS ECONOMICS —►	

Figure 7. Repertoire of human behavior

local to global, cooperation must now be recognized and rewarded as essential to the functioning of all human societies.[2]

The extent to which the world's banks have mismanaged the global economy is only now becoming visible. Short-sighted, imprudent, badly supervised banking systems, as well as deregulated and virtually unregulated financial markets, changing technology and globalization have been at the heart of these problems (*The Economist* 1997c). The BIS rule on eight percent reserve capital requirements, promulgated in 1988, has also proved inadequate.[3] All this costs the world's taxpayers, employees, small businesses and investors dearly. The world's poorest citizens remain the most tragic victims of maldesigned, malfunctioning financial systems and the debacles caused by the false promises of a generation of economists. Add to all this the formidable technical and political challenges posed by the start of the European Monetary Union and the launching of the Euro on January 1, 1999, and the simultaneous effects on banks of the multibillion dollar costs of upgrading their computer programs to handle the Year 2000 (Y2K)) problem. We pray that it will not take such catastrophic learning experiences for current decision-makers to rethink and reshape the global economy into the win–win game that it can become. Necessary but not sufficient is the cancellation of the debt of the most indebted countries, perhaps using US Chapter 9 Municipal Bankruptcy Law as proposed by the Vienna-based Kreisky Forum (Henderson 1996a, ch. 13).

Failed macroeconomic abstractions are giving way to the new view in many disciplines (from game theory, psychology, political science, anthropology and ecology) that human beings are fundamental actors driving evolving economies and societies, as well as corporations and financial market institutions (Loye 1998) and a spate of recent books on corporations as living organisms. Are we only pawns in society, as neoclassical economics insists? US Assistant Treasury Secretary Larry Summers still believes so in a recent interview reported in *WIRED*. Yet are we not also powerful visualizers—of innovations, new technologies, new cities and architecture, new design principles, new disciplines such as risk analysis, technology assessment and futures research, new social arrangements such as insurance, pensions, mutual funds, as well as economic sanctions and treaties instead of wars?

Can we not redesign malfunctioning central banks and misguided government macroeconomic policies to close the gap between the rich and poor? Of course we can and we must, since the pain they inflict on real people and real economies is so evident. This will require building strong citizenship skills and civic societies in all countries and cleaning up cronyism and collusion in our corrupted democracies in Asia and elsewhere. The social sciences have provided the now misused tools of random public opinion surveys, enabling the location of consensus on policies among millions of voters, as effectively as in the local town meetings of yore (Kay 1998). We humans have always been instigators of powerful movements for social change toward universal human rights, democracy, environmentalism, feminism, ethical responsibility for future generations, and socially responsible investing. The UN itself, with its 50 years of global standard-setting, is itself a powerful social innovation. So are business codes of conduct and such NGO inventions as the Costa Rica-based Earth Council's Earth Charter.

Changing Values and the Emerging Global Civic Society

Since the Calvert Social Investment Funds were founded in 1982, I have listened, as a member of its Advisory Council, to debates on Wall Street. They range from Milton Friedman's followers, who say the only moral behavior for fiduciaries and corporate managers is to maximize their investors' rates of return (whether from tobacco or land mine companies), to the emerging socially responsible investment view that investors have many complex goals and investment objectives. They seek competitive returns and more. Happily, as documented by research and practitioners, investors can have competitive returns and hold portfolios that reflect their broader social goals and values (Guerard 1996). Such social value investors are currently changing the economics of the tobacco industry and, as indicated by the 1997 Social Investment Forum in Washington DC, account for $1.1 trillion in managed assets in the USA alone.

Civic groups are proliferating in all countries, providing a third force to check governments and corporations and make them more transparent and accountable. An example of the growing values schism between global corporations and financial players versus citizens and their democratically elected politicians was the firestorm of protest and derailing of the OECD's MAI. Citizen watchdog groups correctly labeled the MAI a new Bill of Rights for global investors and corporations. Now, the same financial special interests are trying to slip a new form of MAI into the IMF charter to prevent countries from imposing capital controls and local government from setting environmental and workplace standards. We all know that rights bring balancing responsibilities. Investors are often individual human beings, not corporations, and millions of them in today's globalized economy are very conscious of their responsibilities e.g., not to invest in companies manufacturing addictive drugs like tobacco and alcohol; those producing landmines and other weapons; those whose products and processes pollute our environment; those who exploit employees or refuse to respect their human rights; or those who do business in countries that oppress their own citizens. These conscientious human investors' ranks are growing in many OECD countries, but still represent a ten percent active, creative minority. Through their ownership of such ethical and green mutual funds, they helped to end apartheid in South Africa. They raise public concern about child labor, slave wages, the dumping of toxic and radioactive waste in the world's oceans, pollution of the atmosphere. They and their portfolio managers often join with labor unions and civic groups, taking their responsibilities to their fellow humans seriously (Henderson 1996b). These creative 'contrarians' illustrate the full repertoire of human behavior—beyond conformity to existing rules and economic ideologies of global competition and win–lose games, to the broader, cooperative strategies of win–win coalitions for future generations and sustainable development (see Figure 7).

Alas, most investors are not human beings, but legal fictions, corporations whose paper charters, granted by governments, limit their and their officials' liabilities. Worse, these charters allow them all the rights of natural persons. These corporate and financial entities have grown over the years to wield enormous power over their nations' elected and governmental officials. Citizens in most OECD countries organized such government protection from corporate irresponsibility and voters have passed overwhelmingly such national laws and regulations. The joint statement sent to the OECD by a coalition of 565 citizen groups in 68 countries called MAI 'a damaging agreement which should not proceed in its current form—if at all.' Many of MAI's provisions would run counter to already ratified UN protocols on biodiversity and climate change, as well as the 50 years of UN treaties and standards on human and employee rights and environmental protection. Citizens must now be vigilant in preventing MAI being sneaked in under the IMF. Meanwhile, *The Economist's* Clive Crook tells us that governments are not in retreat—but getting bigger—citing percentages of nations' GNPs spent by governments. These overall figures do not tell us how much of this government spending is steered by financial and corporate interests into the billions of annual subsidies they enjoy—along with their other legislative priorities, such as the MAI. Indeed, many governments have become corporate cash cows—a point I made in *Creating Alternative Futures* in 1978—while some have sunk into 'kleptocracies'.

Today's politics must be seen in the context of global struggles—human employees, citizens, voters, consumers, farmers and investors versus faceless megacorporations, banks and financial institutions. Ambitions of the global private players for their MAI should be subordinated to the urgent need to regulate investments and create a Global Securities and Exchange Commission to hold investors, traders, brokers and all market players to the highest ethical principles and enforceable standards for human rights, labor and environmental protection. Private sector players must accept the legitimacy in many countries of the rights of voters, unions and civic organizations winning local and national standards to protect their health, safety, wellbeing and safety nets that their taxes support. Corporations which downsize or move offshore to find less democratic but more economically liberal and business-friendly nations or go in search of politicians willing to further deregulate will reap the results: adverse publicity, further mistrust of voters, employees, customers and investors. Our elected political leaders and business lobbies can no longer hide behind the supposed exigencies of global competitiveness (*The Economist*, 1997a). Some may say such practices are time-honored backroom politics of all elites. But today we live in a new Age of Truth: a global information society where such practices are now attacked as cronyism, lack of transparency, and corruption.

Grassroots global coalitions are still pressing the WTO, which is largely a creature of global corporations and financial groups. These special interests manoeuvred their respective national governments through earlier GATT rounds, supported by the constant drumbeat of their in-house neoclassical economists and academic consultants hailing free trade as good for everyone—the ultimate win–win. The WTO has moved somewhat toward transparency and lip service to labor and environmental issues since the meeting I attended in Geneva in December 1995, arranged by Mikhail Gorbachev with some top WTO officials. At that meeting, Deputy Director General Hoda stated that WTO did not have to interact with NGOs—and was a purely intergovernmental body. By March 1997, when I spoke at the Geneva Conference on Policing the Global Economy, co-hosted by the Global Legislators for a Balanced Environment (GLOBE) and the Bellerive Foundation, Director General Renato Ruggiero reported on WTO's as yet toothless Committee on Trade and Environment, but stressed that WTO has 'no competence in labor and environmental issues'. The

500 parliamentarians, ambassadors, and civic leaders present deplored such disingenuousness, noting, of course, that every ruling the WTO makes is a *de facto* environmental ruling and affects labor as well. Most concluded that the WTO is still dangerously beyond democratic control. At the same meeting, World Economic Forum President Klaus Schwab's presentation of the Forum as a benevolent group of 1,000 global corporations devoted to sustainable human development was greeted with derision, since many present saw the Davos Culture as a threat to their own visions of sustainable human development (Prince Saddrudin Aga Khan *et al.* 1998).

WTO rulemaking often divides consumers, unions and activist NGOs around eco-labels and social clauses, labor standards, etc., seeking to tie them up in endless legalistic wrangling over minutiae. Yet OECD markets are moving so rapidly toward such cleaner, greener, more socially responsible business practices, standards and codes of conduct that such WTO divide-and-conquer strategies cannot succeed for long. Instead, developing countries are better served by promoting industrial leapfrog strategies to reposition themselves for 21st century Information/Solar Age markets than accepting transnational corporate cast-off technologies and building in obsolescence. Many countries and NGOs are actively exploring such leapfrog scenarios. An example of what can be achieved by small village producers is the Purolator Air Filter, made with hand-made paper by India's Development Alternatives-linked producers, which meets ISO 14000 standards. Aid agencies and development banks should be actively helping such developing countries to design these leapfrog technological sectors, shifting from industrial fossil-fueled metal bashing and concrete pouring to high-tech, information and renewable energy infrastructure and manufacturing facilities. The Clean Development Mechanism, which Brazil offered at the United Nations Climate Conference in Kyoto, December 1997, together with other such initiatives, can move developing country production toward both sustainability and equity.

We need to move more rapidly toward capitalizing the clean, greener, more energy-efficient technologies that can address sustainable human development, equity and climate change in fundamental ways, beyond end-of-the-pipe and other palliative approaches, such as emissions trading (See Figure 8 below). So why cannot US voters persuade the US Congress of all this and push the Administration further toward the Solar Age? Again, the answer is in the corruption of the US political system by lobbying, campaign contributions and mass media campaigns by the fossil-fuel, auto and other related

Obsolescent Sectors (Unsustainable, entropic)

- Industries, companies based on heavy use of non-renewable energy and materials
- Bureaucratic, large, less flexible
- Non-recyclable products, packaging
- Military contracting
- Products involving toxic, non-biodegradables, polluting materials, throwaway items
- Planned obsolescence
- Chemical pesticides, inorganic fertilizers
- Heavy farm equipment
- Polluting, inefficient capital equipment, process machinery, processing systems
- Extractive industries with low value added
- Fossil fuels, nuclear power generation
- High tech hospital based medical care
- Highly processed foods
- Advertising encouraging waste and polluting practices
- Shopping center developers
- Speculative real estate development
- Large, fuel-inefficient vehicles
- Mono-culture farming
- Hardwood and tropical forest products

Emerging Sectors (Sustainable, low entropy)

- Industries, companies based on efficient use of energy and materials and human skills
- Entrepreneurial, small, flexible
- Recyclable products, re-manufacturing
- Conservation, innovation
- Fuel efficient motors, cars, mass transit
- Solar, renewable energy systems
- Communications, information, services
- Infrastructure, education, training
- Space communications satellites
- Peacekeeping, surveillance of treaties
- Efficient capital equipment
- Restorative industries, reforestation, desert greening, water quality management
- Health promotion and disease prevention
- Organic agriculture, low till systems
- Integrated pest management
- Pollution control, clean up and prevention
- Natural foods
- Waste recycling and reuse
- Community design and planning
- 'Caring' sector

Source: Hazel Hendrson, *Paradigms in Progress*, 1991.

© 1989/91 Hazel Henderson

Figure 8. Restructuring industrial economies

industries of the receding Industrial Age. Unfortunately, such lobbying has created enormous subsidies to these fossil-fuel industrial sectors to the tune of between $750 billion to $1 trillion annually worldwide in the energy, transportation, agricultural and construction sectors. Agenda 21 in Rio in 1992 estimated that the shift to sustainable economies would cost roughly $650 billion. Thus, we see that if governments would simply stop subsidizing unsustainable development, progress would be much faster. Many individual investors like myself, as well as the budding trade associations of the renewables and socially responsible business and investment sectors, which represent about ten percent of OECD economies, work hard to raise global standards to protect the environment, human rights and workers. Only if we can raise this ethical floor under the global playing field can we hope to succeed in the long run.

All of these global standards-setting mechanisms, including ISO 14001, SA 8000 and others, as well as eco-labels and the newer human rights labels, not to mention user fees, taxation and fines, are also important mechanisms for the shift to sustainability. Indeed, it will take an array of such policy mechanisms. Social and environmental auditing of corporations is vital. National governments need to shift tax codes around the world from incomes and payrolls onto resource depletion, waste and pollution if we are to make the progress we seek on climate change and sustainability. Germany's new coalition government has announced that it will begin shifting taxes from payrolls and incomes to natural resource use as I have promoted (Henderson 1990, p. 19). Fullcost pricing, lifecycle costing, and internalizing social and environmental costs into capital asset pricing models (CAPMs) as well can reduce environmental destruction, irrational investments (particularly in the energy sector) and redirect much of today's entropic world trade. When thermodynamic and economic models of efficiency are aligned, we see that local and provincial efficiencies of scale are correct, as I emphasized in *The Politics of the Solar Age* (1981). But with all such policy tools, equity must be key if we are to address the needs of the two billion people still below the poverty line. Equity is especially important in emissions allowances, quotas and all trading mechanisms.

Thus, any pollution emissions trading regimes that are set up at the global level should incorporate the important lessons learned from the US experience. For example, if the US had really wanted to set up a vigorous public market for such emissions trading, it could have awarded an initial allocation to every man, woman, and child on a *per capita* basis as a right to the air as a public commons, while auctioning such rights to polluting profit-making corporations. This could have created a deeper market and additional equity benefits and allowed millions of poorer citizens who are exemplary low energy consumers to sell their quotas to affluent energy over-consumers. As we consider a global trading regime for CO2, an equitable distribution of any emissions quotas should be made on a *per capita* basis, so as to treat developing countries equitably. The new UN trading facility under UNCTAD may assure this.

The New Attention Economy

We in OECD countries are well into a new era of the Information Age. We are transiting to the Age of Knowledge, where scarce human time and attention, as well as living ecosystems, are recognized as more valuable than money. At the same time, we live in mediocracies where a few media moguls now control the attention of billions of people—for better or worse—which has changed politics forever. We are already living in the new Attention Economy (Henderson 1996a, Chapter 5; See Figure 9 below) a term since picked up by Arthur Andersen and *WIRED*. Attention deficit is not a disease. We now live in Attention Deficit societies where each of us is bombarded with information overload from advertisers, media, politicians, teachers, health providers, not to mention junk e-mail. The good news is that this is forcing us to go inside ourselves and ask some pretty basic questions: What do I want to pay attention to? Who am I and what do I want written on my tombstone? Such basic defensive reactions will define the growing sectors of our

- As information-based economies shift to services
- Time and attention become as valuable as money

NEW TRADE-OFFS:
- People seek new challenges, experiences, personal growth, and quality of life
- Many opt for less income and urban stress—more time with friends and family, community-involvement, hobbies
- Traditional material goods (even cars, PCs, VCRs) become commodities
- Services grow as % of GNP (opera, movie tickets, music, leisure, sports, events, education, crafts, etc.)

© 1989 Hazel Henderson

Figure 9. The new 'attention economy'

Attention Economies and their inexorable shift from material goods (measured by traditional GNP/GDP *per capita*) to services and more intangible factors in living standards, measured by new scorecards such as my Country Futures Indicators (CFI). As our economies dematerialize, it will be harder for governments to hype wasteful goods-based GDP growth in the global economy without also measuring toxic wastes, resource depletion, dirtier shrinking water supplies, polluted air, unsafe streets, drugs, money laundering, poverty and global epidemics.

In mature OECD countries, the limiting factor is now time rather than money. There are only 24 hours in each day and already, in the USA for example, the average citizen now spends 9.5 hours per day (up from 7.5 hours in the 1980s) watching TV, movies, etc., or online. If GDPs were recategorized and recalculated for the USA and similar OECD countries, we would find that these information/services sectors are already dominant. For example, mass media and entertainment are a growing percentage of global trade, while tourism is the world's largest industry at ten percent of global GDP. In response, 28 percent of US citizens are down-shifting—a form of tuning out this dominant culture of information overload and costly mass consumption oriented value system, as reported by the Merck Foundation in 1995. They are choosing more free time and less monetary income and moving to quieter, less expensive, rural towns where life is slower and communities are still intact. Consumers are seeking their own (not advertisers') definitions of quality of life.

These Attention Economy characteristics include concern for more caring, attention-based health services geared to self-knowledge, prevention and wellness, as well as cleaner, greener products, eco-labeling (e.g., Germany's Blue Angel and US Green Seal) and the newer social seals of approval (e.g., CEP SA8000 labor standards) as well as the rise of socially responsible investing. In addition, there are increasing demands for global corporations to reduce emissions and employ fair labor standards and promulgate Codes of Conduct (e.g., the CAUX and CERES and McBride principles). The clash is escalating between individual value changes, concern with community and quality of life *vis-à-vis* market driven globalization of finance and trade. This leads to further domestic political turmoil in OECD countries, as their information-overloaded citizens try to sort out all the issues of globalization. Meanwhile, their politicians' mixed messages do not help in that they support more free trade and globalization and then cite the resulting global competitiveness as excuses for their own refusal to cooperate in global and regional standards on domestic issues: unemployment, social safety nets, social and environmental regulation, taxes and budget deficits. All this will require facing down global corporations' demands for tax holidays and more deregulation in their location decisions. National governments must soon face up to the new Era of Corporate Mega-mergers, which will further erode national sovereignty.

Global Standards

The UN has reached a crucial phase in its 52-year history, as it wrestles with reform and reinvention for the onrushing 21st century. The funding crisis at the UN, due to the $1.3 billion US arrears, has spurred the new interest of many UN agencies in forging partnerships with businesses and newly powerful civic society organizations (CSOs or more familiarly NGOs). Such partnerships with business, especially green businesses, should be encouraged. Many of today's issues involve the global commons: air, oceans, biodiversity, the electromagnetic spectrum, low earth satellite orbits, climate and outer space, including the newly perceived commons of global cyberspace. Such issues can only be addressed with new cooperative initiatives between all three sectors: governments at all levels, businesses (from global to local) and CSOs. Governments oversee the rules and standards regimes; businesses can operate the market-based domains; and CSOs can provide innovations, input and feedback from users. I have been working with others recently to assure that UN agencies promulgate their own global standards for partnerships and contracting with private corporations based on its 50 years of treaties and protocols on human rights, labor and workplace standards and environmental treaties, from Agenda 21, the Montreal and London Protocols to the Kyoto Agreements on climate change in December 1997.

UN standards will also do much to dispel the growing suspicions among NGOs and smaller companies that the UN seems to favor the World Business Council on Sustainable Development (WBCSD) and other global corporate giants of the Industrial Era. Even as the giants strive for eco-efficiency, their power over governments still allows them to keep their huge, perverse subsidies, which still hamper the shift to sustainability. Meanwhile, the smaller, cleaner, greener businesses that have been pioneering uphill in the face of such subsidies feel shut out of the very game of sustainable development that they with NGOs have worked so hard for decades to create. It took decades of NGO pressure to get the World Bank to discover micro-enterprises and micro-credit. The WTO is already in a firestorm of criticism for its high-handed and ignorant rulemaking. The UN can do much better. By proactively embracing ethical and socially responsible small and medium-sized businesses (which are now recognized as the real engines of global job creation), the UN can demonstrate its commitment. Millions of businesses worldwide can benefit from UN partnerships for sustainable development. The UN can, where necessary, assist those which need help in meeting its standards.

The UN convened a series of these summits on the real agenda of We the Peoples of the Earth (in spite of much opposition from their national governments): food, shelter, population, health, children, human rights, science and technology, poverty and unemployment, cities, environment, women and development. Because mass media covered these UN summits they became hot topics in many countries, whose reluctant politicians were pressured to deal with them. No wonder the UN is in such a crossfire, as its nation members alternatively use the world forum (the UN has no power beyond its members) either as a fig leaf for their policies, as George Bush did in the 1991 Gulf War, or as a scapegoat, as both Bill Clinton and Bob Dole did as presidential candidates in 1994. Both erroneously and shamefully portrayed US command failures in Somalia and Bosnia as the fault of the UN. Such policy disinformation, as well as deceptive advertising and media campaigns, are now a major block to a sustainable future.

Dealing with today's accelerating destruction of our global commons requires the UN, as the only international body with the mandate of We the Peoples and the broadest membership of all the nations. If it were not there, truly we would have to invent it. This is not to deny that the UN, like most bureaucracies and large corporations, needs restructuring for the future. A problem for the UN is that powerful global corporations have captured the World Bank, the IMF and the WTO originally within the UN's mandate, while succeeding in shutting down agencies they opposed, including The UN Center on Transnational Corporations, and crippling UNESCO, UNCTAD, UNIDO (seen as controlled by developing countries) and marginalizing the International Labor Organization and the UN Environment Program. The UN Development Program devoted to poverty eradication and sustainable, human development is seeking partnerships with corporations, provided they meet its high standards. Any contracts with polluting, employee-exploiting or otherwise irresponsible companies would also harm UN credibility.

- Corporations have historically captured local, national markets by capturing standards, rule-making (e.g. Windows/Intel, Telecom policy).
- Now standards going global (private, WTO, etc.), e.g. banking, finance, accounting, etc.
- Some companies try to lower, others to raise standards.
- Past and future-oriented management

Amortise	Investment emerging
Investment	Future markets, innovate
'*Risk budget*'	'*Risk budget*' redeployed:
Insurance	process retooling, new products,
Public relations	'market creation,' global scanning
(Short-term)	(Long-term)

Figure 10. Global Standard-Setting: increasing activity, voluntary partnerships between companies, government agencies and civic groups (e.g. ISO 14000, Codes of Conduct, Best Practices, etc.)

One of the most interesting features of today's globalization phenomena is this new world game of capturing global standards (see Figure 10). The G7's 30 October proposals for stabilizing world markets join civic groups in advocating standards of transparency and accountability on the IMF, banks, corporations in private sectors worldwide. We see this trend clearly in technology and network markets, where market dominance depends on rapid capture of technological standards, even if the product or service must initially be underpriced or given away. Economist W. Brian Arthur has termed this 'technological lock-in,' while system theorists refer to the phenomena as classic effects of positive feedback in non-linear systems (See Figure 11 below). Whether it is Microsoft and Intel's Wintel standard or earlier battles over 19th century railroad gauges and 20th century electrical system specifications, we are all familiar with such phenomena in network markets as, for example, today's internet. Most markets evolve by capturing government standards and regulations—first at local levels—over zoning, property, public transport, infrastructure and land use regulations (Henderson 1996). As markets thus become structured, companies grow and form trade associations to capture national regulatory and investment standards. Today the game is that of capturing a host of newer regional standards (e.g., European Union, NAFTA, MERCOSUR, ASEAN, etc.), as well as global standards via the WTO and GATT rule-making, ISO, and those of the United Nations on Human

STABLE, EQUILIBRIATING SYSTEM (morphostatic) (structurally stable), e.g., thermostat-controlled mechanical system, early agrarian or small-scale production economies (as conceived .in market equilibrium supply-demand theories), reversible components and decisions

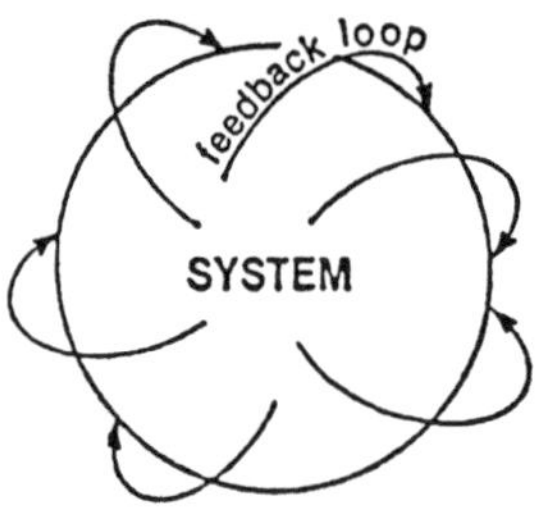

System internally dynamic, but stable structure maintained and governed by *negative* feedback loops.

UNSTABLE, DIS-EQUILIBRIUM SYSTEM (morphogenetic) (evolving new structure), e.g., living, biological systems, human societies, large-scale sociotechnical economic systems, rapid innovation and structural evolution, many irreversible components and decisions

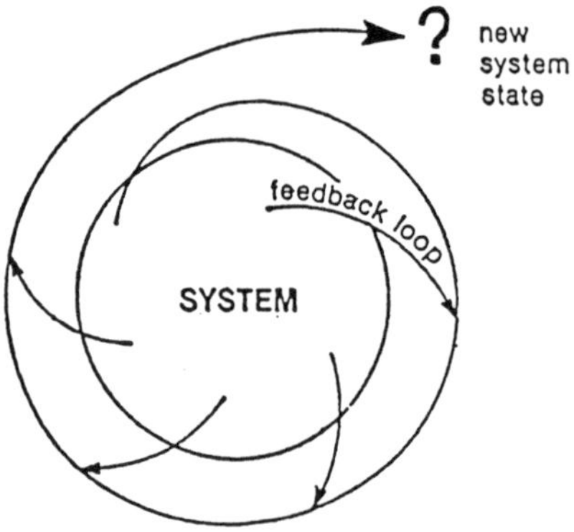

System internally dynamic *and* structurally dynamic, governed by *positive* feedback loops, which can amplify small initial deviations, which sometimes break through thresholds and push the system to a new structural state.

Figure 11. Simple Diagrams of Two Major Types of Cybernetic Systems

Rights, Labor, and Environment (e.g., the Action Plans of UN Summits, ILO, WHO protocols), as well as others mentioned earlier.

Institutional investors and corporations continue and broaden their standard-setting activities in partnership with relevant government agencies, civic and consumer groups. They build on the ISO 14000, 14001 and Environmental Management Systems (EMS), eco-labeling and the prior 100 years of such voluntary standard-setting across a range of products from electrical goods to pharmaceuticals. Corporations continue to publish codes of conduct and foster such global standards and best practices (See *Business Week* Special Report, October 1995 and October 1996). The International Organization of Securities Commissions (IOSCO) has taken the leadership in bringing a greater transparency and order to global securities, currency and futures markets. The Big Four accounting firms and hundreds of new companies are increasing environmental and social auditing of corporate performance. Many institutional investors and portfolio managers have joined with these business leaders and those which have signed on to the CERES (Coalition for Environmentally Responsible Economies) Principles, the Sullivan and McBride Principles, CAUX Principles, and those of the Minnesota Center for Corporate Responsibility. Much of this activity in assessing corporate performance owes its impetus to the pioneering work of New York's Council on Economic Priorities and its much-honored founder, Alice Tepper Marlin, and that of other innovators such as Amy Domini (See Domini and Kinder 1984) and the Domini 400 Social Index, which regularly outperforms the Standard and Poor's 500.

Some 90 percent of global industrial companies lobby to keep and capture standards at current levels while often succeeding in reducing their regulatory requirements. The other ten percent are the contrarians: i.e., the mostly smaller, younger, innovative enterprises, investment funds, venture capitalists, and investors already positioned in the cleaner greener social markets of the 21st century. These firms are also organized, but in less powerful trade associations. They lobby to raise global standards to higher levels of social and environmental accountability. Such trade associations include the US-based Business for Social Responsibility, the Future 500, the Minnesota Center for Corporate Responsibility, which has urged full US payment of UN dues and arrears, the Social Venture Network (USA and Europe), the US and UK-based Social Investment Forum, the Prince of Wales' Business Leaders Forum, the Copenhagen Centre for Social Responsibility, the Business Council for the Social Summit, the Caux Roundtable and others. Newer efforts include The Task Force on Socially Responsible Business of the World Business Council For Sustainable Development. Many such groups promulgate their own more stringent codes of conduct and are willing to be audited by the legions of accounting firms now offering social, environmental and ethical audits. By thus raising the ethical floor under the global playing-field these contrarian companies can win. Their analyses of their markets are systemic and future oriented, rather than focused on traditional short-term economics and market returns. For example, SafeScience, Inc., of Boston is building this global brand by linking and licensing many small firms which complement its own line of biodegradable pesticides, fungicides, and other natural products. I am an investor in SafeScience, Inc.

Today, most companies and countries are still steered by the dominant short-termism and capturing markets for goods and commodities for export-led growth. These strategies succeed at first, but not every country can win in such a win–lose global game. For example Korea's *chaebol* did bring jobs and prosperity for many years, providing half the country's jobs and most of its exports. But growing their global market share becomes very costly—as Boeing and other US companies have found. Only changing the global economy from a win–lose toward a win–win, cooperative structure can constrain the rules of the competition and prevent cut-throat, beggar-thy-neighbor policies and allow more poor people still in need to participate in a fairer world economy. A new network of global institutions is needed, not only to contain and channel market activities, but to implement the new human and environmental security proposals which have emerged in the Action Plans of major UN summits, from Rio in 1992 to Istanbul in 1996. As the lessons of unsustainable global GNP growth sink in, we must surely move faster to correct traditional economic textbooks and statistics with longer-term and broader indicators of social capital, quality of life, environmental sustainability, and human development as I have outlined. I have been spearheading the new Virtuous Circle Global Bond Fund^{sm}, which will invest in the bonds of the most responsibly managed countries with superior performance on social and environmental, human rights, labor and democracy criteria. Such funds can not only reward good governments, but also provide investors with enhanced political risk assessment.

Money Isn't Scarce

Perhaps the biggest paradigm shift involves the new information-based electronic markets—from local to global. The implications for both central banks and private banks are vast. If money creation and management as well as money-based transactions and credit availability are not overhauled drastically to serve the new needs of 21st century consumers, businesses, employees and investors, they will simply go around banks and money-based transacting to pure information-based transactions (i.e., high-tech barter, local scrip currencies, LETS systems payments unions, counter trade, etc.). Banks are busy buying computer and information technology to reimpose scarcity and money-based transactions, particularly on electronic commerce via e-cash, credit and debit cards, virtual banking, etc. The new competition from money-free, information-based, high-tech exchange will not go away. Banks and money-based exchange systems are very useful, but they now have competition for their basic functions of intermediation, for which the internet is ideally suited. For example, floor-based open outcry stock exchanges are being replaced daily, and seats on the New York stock exchange have lost half their value since 1998.

I have argued (1991) that the newest global commons is the internet and the world wide web as well as financial cyberspace—all largely unregulated and with a host of issues concerning their use piling up. For example, the internet's protocol and language codes are still informal and controlled by a handful of early technological innovators and programmers serving as volunteers on *ad hoc* standards committees. Worse, while the internet expands access to information, there is no agreement on information quality (i.e., relevant to human and ecosystem health and survival) let alone facing the problems of disinformation or moving toward knowledge or greater wisdom (see Figure 12 below). Little legal underpinning exists for the internet, a common resource funded by tax dollars and currently overwhelmed by free riders. For example, the internet's enormously profitable franchise to assign website domain names and addresses was given to one private company, Network Solutions Inc. (NSI) by the US National Science Foundation without a open bidding process. NSI promptly went public, providing a windfall for its founders. I expect to see in the next few years some kind of International Internet Standards and Oversight

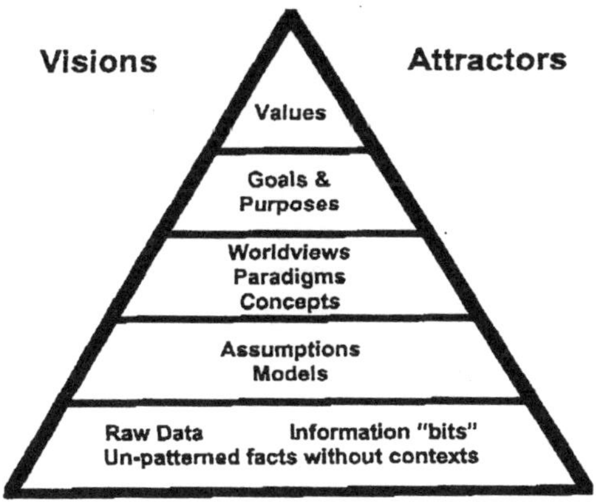

Figure 12. Information Quality Scale: (i.e. meaning of information as relevant to human purposes)

Agency to deal with all of these free rider and commons issues while interfacing with established agencies such as the World Intellectual Property Organization (WIPO) and the International Teleommunication Union (ITU).

As more citizens and businesses move their transactions into cyberspace, what are some key and broader implications? Let's start with electronic commerce. Most companies assume that money-based transactions will monopolize cyberspace through better security, encryption systems, credit card handling and e-cash systems. However, electronic commerce does not require money-based transactions, but could lead to pure information-based transactions, i.e., high-tech barter. The implications of this are clear: money and information are now equivalent—we are already off the money and gold standard and on the information standard worldwide. Banks thrive on money-based scarcity and, understandably, are trying to control cyberspace transactions. Yet today, billions of dollars of services and goods are bartered each year in the USA by corporations and individuals on PC-based electronic trading networks. The implications for the world's central bankers are clear: if they don't improve their currency issuance and monetary management and control operations, through overhauling the Bretton Woods institutions and making credit widely available—not just to their cronies in governments and corporations, they will be bypassed by pure info-based transactions. Today's state-of-the-art computer-based markets in cyberspace can make such info-based, high-tech bartering efficient with minimal transaction costs. Developing countries will no longer need to earn foreign exchange but can trade all their commodities among themselves—doing three, four, five and six-way trades with the computers keeping the audit trails as to settlement agreements (which is what money is and does while also serving as a store of value). I have spelled out the implications of all this, including the need for three different kinds of currency: a) a global reserve currency, b) national currencies and monetary unions of them, where appropriate, and c) local currencies to clear purely local markets (Henderson 1996a, Chapter 9).

Nations will need to regain some of their lost sovereignty in order to maintain their political legitimacy and manage their domestic economies democratically for the benefit of the majority of their citizens. All this will now require international agreements to tax electronic commerce and global mechanisms to protect human citizens, employees, and investors as opposed to paper financial institutions. I expect a shift to safe haven, high-tech barter transactions both locally and globally in order to create full employment and clear local markets. Local currencies and PC-based trading systems are flourishing in the USA, Canada, Europe, Australia and New Zealand. Today they are needed in Russia. Indeed, I have used them as leading indicators of the incompetence of central banks and macroeconomic management authorities in many countries. Let us now look at the taxation issue more closely. At the global level, tax evaders are catered to by increasing numbers of small, island countries and regimes deliberately offering anonymity, dummy corporations, money laundering and tax havens. Internet-based commerce and intranet-based trading make all of this easier (*The Economist* 1997b). Conservative financial advisors are telling investors how to move offshore, obtain duplicate passports and dual citizenship, buy small islands, and other manoeuvres to evade taxation. Nation states, now with chronic budget deficits due to tax losses from deregulation, are breaking up and some predict that there will be about 1,300 countries in a few years.

Local governments can resist pressures from global retailers, services chains, and mall developers to displace local merchants. These global TNCs still operate as free riders on infrastructures at below-cost energy prices and at the exclusion of many social and environmental costs. This allows them to penetrate local markets with below-true-cost prices. Then, after locals have been put out of business, they can raise prices without their competition. Development banks, local credit unions and micro-credit groups should be favored over branches of large national and global banks free riding on the unregulated infostructures of financial cyberspace. These banks, tied into the global casino, accept local deposits and paychecks but these funds tend to be vacuumed out of the local branch bank each day onto the global electronic funds transfer systems (EFTS) to be lent out worldwide. At average global interest rates, local communities and businesses can no longer afford these interest rates to borrow back their own deposits for local development purposes. It is also important for local communities to engage in as much barter as necessary, including high-tech exchanges using personal computers, such as local exchange trading systems (LETS) and the many kinds of local scrip currencies now circulating in towns in the USA, Europe and other OECD countries. These tools can complement scarce national currencies where monetary policy is ill-conceived or too restrictive so as to help clear local markets, employ local people and provide them with alternative local purchasing power. Indeed, such local currencies in every state and most cities in the USA during the Great Depression helped local communities survive (Mitchell and Shafer 1984).

The continued growth of electronic commerce into today's autonomous global casino will continue to erode the power of governments while also denying them the tax revenues they formerly received from domestic bricks-and-mortar commerce. On the national and micro level, the tax issue will involve a fight for equitable tax treatment between these traditional bricks-and-mortar businesses and those in cyberspace (Barnett 1998). There are already two kinds of web-based businesses: those which link and empower existing bricks-and-mortar retailers (such as those in the jewelry business linked on the Colorado-based, worldwide Polygon Network)—and those which bypass bricks-and-mortar local, retail businesses (such as bookseller Amazon.com). When the Clinton administration, prematurely pandering to the 'digerati sector', announced that it would not tax transactions on the internet, it heard an instant chorus of complaints from local governments and bricks-and-mortar businesses across the USA, which might thus be condemned to penury. Yet, the internet itself is very fragile, with a few voluntary standard-setters and little legal underpinning to protect the growing global activity it carries, as I outlined to a resistant audience of technological enthusiasts at the Comdex Computer Convention in Chicago.

New Partnerships for Social Innovation

Lastly, new partnerships for social innovation are essential. (See Figure 13 below). New global systems of political risk management are now possible, to deal with small domestic conflicts and terrorism, centered around strengthening the International Criminal Court. Although the US government foolishly weakened it, a large majority of US citizens (80 percent) approve of a strong Criminal Court.

- United Nations Security Insurance Agency
- Global public facility for currency trading
- 'Virtuous circle' global bond fund
- International bank for environmental settlements
- WETV—The global public access network (already in 31 countries)
- TV series 'The Ethical Marketplace'

Figure 13. Partnerships for Social Innovation

Hopefully, its cases can be televised also before the ultimate court of world opinion. We can safely reduce the world's military budgets, by employing insurance instead of weapons. For example, the Global Commission to Fund the United Nations has proposed the United Nations Security Insurance Agency (UNSIA), a public–private–civic partnership between the UN Security Council, the insurance industry and the hundreds of civic, humanitarian organizations worldwide which engage in conflict resolution and peacebuilding (Henderson and Kay 1995). Any nation wanting to cut its military budget and redeploy its investments into its civilian sectors could apply to UNSIA for a peacekeeping insurance policy. The insurance industry would supply the political risk assessors and write the policies. The premiums would be pooled to fund both properly trained peacekeepers and a rapid deployment, online network of existing civic, humanitarian organizations on the ground to build trust and confidence. The UNSIA proposal is now backed by several Nobel Prize winners, including Dr. Oscar Arias and other leaders, and is taught at the London School of Economics and other major institutions. UNSIA was debated in the UN Security Council in April 1996, the first time that body had considered the need to bring civic humanitarian organizations into peacekeeping operations. In May 1996, the Security Council called on the Secretary-General to investigate the feasibility of 'a rapid-deployment humanitarian force' and, in October 1996, the Norwegian government pledged $1 million to this project.

Finally, it is imperative that at least one global TV network be devoted to exchanging information on the many paths to sustainable development. I am delighted that global, multicultural public access TV is now a reality. Here again, Canada has provided global leadership in launching WETV (the WE stands for We the Peoples and the Whole Earth). Citizens in mediocracies and Attention Economies are already sick of much of the content of online, cable and broadcast media. They demand more useful content and coverage of community problem-solving, higher quality entertainment, education, and children's programming. WETV, headquartered in Ottawa, is a public–private–civic network with a state-of-the-art multimedia backbone now in 31 countries with programming for human development—allowing selfexpression from NGOs and the grassroots on global and local issues. We are learning that cultural diversity is as important as biodiversity, and both are the bedrock wealth of nations. WETV is growing through program bartering and partnering with similar media. Funded by the humanitarian aid programs of seven countries, led by Canada's IDRC and CIDA, WETV has obtained rights to all UN television programming and that of many other public service producers. WETV is now opening some ownership to private investors and I am proud to be one of its first. As a member of its Business Advisory Council, I am now working to bring in other socially responsible investors and businesses who will accept WETV's stringent code of conduct and standards for all private sector partners. Even more innovative is WETV's proposal for equity participation by civic groups and NGOs which provide programming for WETV distribution. This kind of entitlement to shares in WETV can both incentivize their audience-building outreach and earn dividends when WETV is profitable. WETV is launching a TV series, *The Ethical Marketplace*, which will cover socially responsible businesses and investing, green technologies, social auditing, corporate codes of conduct and global ethical standards-setting. Such creative hybrids as WETV (accessible at *www.wetv.com*) are typical of Information Age based companies and can open up new grassroots, multicultural communications far beyond the reach of the internet alone and still unavailable to most people in the world.

As the G7 30 October communiqué showed, old balance-f-power politics is transforming into strategies of global cooperation. Companies and countries are shifting slowly from competitive strategies toward partnerships and international agreements. A key criterion for human societies and their relationship with ecosystems is sustainability over the long term—as proposed by the Brundtland Commission in *Our Common Future* (World Commission on Environment and Development 1987). This implies equity, not only within and between societies of the present but intergenerational equity as well—as complex a set of tradeoffs as our species has faced, as least consciously. Expanding to a multidisciplinary focus for both domestic and globalization policies can reveal all the positive sum, win–win games, the new public–private–civic partnerships and new strategies that can help all actors imagine, develop, and build toward a win–win world in the next century (see Figure 14 below). Humans must now acknowledge their responsibility for their active roles in the evolution of societies. Today, in a world we have made increasingly interdependent, we are learning the differences between money and wealth and that poverty can and must be eradicated. In a planetary context, we are finding that all our self interests are identical: morality has simply become pragmatic.

New markets	New commons
• Telecom services • Desert greening • Pollution control • Renewable energy • Recycling, eco-resource management • 'Caring' sector (day care, counseling, rehab, nursing) • Infrastructure (extending transport, telecommunications, etc.) • Eco-restoration, bio-remediation	• Space, Earth systems science • Electromagnetic spectrum • Oceans, water resources • Atmosphere, ozone layer • Security, peacekeeping • Forests • Health • Global economy

Figure 14. Exploring the Evolving Global Playing Field

Notes

1. The United Nations University pioneered such work. See the report of its 1984 symposium on *The Science and Praxis of Complexity* (1984).
2. The Alliance for a Caring Economy (801 Crocker Rd. Sacramento, CA 95864; Fax 916 486 5990 was founded by Riane Eisler, JD, author of *The Chalice and the Blade*, and will research these issues.
3. See, for example, *Economic Reform*, published monthly by the Committee on Monetary and Economic Reform, 3284 Yonge Street, Suite 500, Toronto, Ontario M4N 3M7 Canada. e-mail: *wkrehm@ibm.net.*

Part Two

CHAPTER 5

What is Globalization?

Wayne Hudson

Although there are countless references to globalization in the press and in diverse scholarly literatures, no single coherent account of what globalization means has emerged. Moreover, even if such an account appears, it is important to appreciate the plurality of different concerns passing under the term, not only in order to understand what particular authors are really talking about, but in order to grasp how different topics and concerns may or may not be related. We can then appreciate that the fact that the attempt by some authors to show a relationship between all the different topics discussed under the portmanteau of globalization is itself a part of the problem. For the unity and homogeneity the term is used to invoke may well be what is often lacking.

Initially it is useful to distinguish at least seven different patterns, each of which is often (singly or in concert) called globalization:

1. Emergence of global currency markets since the deregulations of the 1980s;
2. Transnationalization of technology and the rapidity of redundancy;
3. Competitive pressure of corporations to become global;
4. Globalization of political activity and transnational economic diplomacy;
5. Intensification of global cultural flows, communications and migration;
6. Breakdown of geographical boundaries and the emergence of new connections between cities, regions and governance structures;
7. Loss of faith in the capacity of government to manage domestic problems.

Similarly, it is useful to distinguish at least nine very common claims:

1. The globe is now a single unit for the purposes of decision-making;
2. Capital, goods and services move more freely throughout the world;
3. National economies have been opened up to global markets and are declining;
4. The role of the nation-state in shaping national policies has reduced;
5. The rate of economic interaction between nation-states and national economies has accelerated;
6. Organization of production has changed from Fordism to post-Fordism or has become flexible or been internationalized;
7. Social relations are acquiring relatively distanceless and borderless qualities;
8. The nation-state has been internationalized;
9. Migration patterns have shifted from South to North.

All of these claims are contestable and debated in the most learned literature. One minimal working definition of globalization provided by Holm and Sorensen (1995, p. 1) takes globalization to be 'the intensification of economic, political social and cultural relations across borders.' This definition invites historical exploration of the dynamics of social change, by which the permeability of the political borders of the nation-state has become intensified. This definition is also useful in stressing that globalization is not simply an economic problem (Holton 1998, p. 11). In pursuing a more adequate working definition of globalization, however, it is helpful to try to add a sense of greater complexity and an awareness of the existence of different worlds. One of the difficulties here is how simultaneously to draw attention to the development of the world as a single society, while doing justice to evidence of differentiation in the conditions of existence and forms of identity that the world's inhabitants express. Is globalization simply to do with the former, or is it intrinsically bound up with both processes?

Albrow (1990) takes up the former opinion, defining globalization as all those processes by which the peoples of the world are incorporated into a single society, a society in which 'humanity' becomes for the first time a 'collective actor'. This latter role is closely connected with 'globalism', defined as 'those values that take the real world of five billion people as the object of concern, the whole earth as the physical environment, everyone living as world citizens, consumers, and producers, with a common interest in collective action to solve global problems' (1990, p. 8).

Globalization, Albrow maintains, is directly the result of the interaction of 'nationalism' and 'internationalism'. Sociologists are inclined to adopt a novelistic interpretation of globalization as a 'process at a new level of social reality'. This 'new reality' is sometimes described by the term 'global society' (Albrow 1990, p. 9). But here poetics drive the rhetoric, and the existence of a global society is never proven.

Another approach to globalization is advanced by R.F.M. Lubbers, former Dutch Prime Minister and Professor of Globalization at the University of Tilburg, who characterizes globalization as:

> ... an abstract concept. It does not refer to a concrete object, but to [an interpretation of] a societal process. Therefore the concept can not be defined easily. To make clear what one means with 'globalization' it is necessary to explain the whole theory in which one's use of the concept is embedded. For some, globalization refers to Americanization, for others it is about the growing importance of the world market, yet others use it to describe a cultural or an ideological reality: globalization as the victory of 'market plus democracy'. For most authors, globalization is a complex concept that involves both political, economic and social–cultural changes. Usually, globalization is also meant to refer to the consequences it has. Thus, globalization is often seen not just as a 'one-way process', but as a dialectal dynamic (Lubbers 1998).

According to Lubbers:

> Globalization is a process in which geographic distance becomes less a factor in the establishment and sustenance of bordercrossing, long distance economic, political and sociocultural relations. People become aware of this fact. Networks of relations and dependencies therefore become potentially bordercrossing and worldwide. This potential internationalization of relations and dependencies causes fear, resistance, actions and reactions (Lubbers 1998).

Globalization is also about two types of consequences: consequences in terms of four deficits (the democratic, social, environmental and security deficits), and consequences as rebound effects in terms of attitudes and new institutions rebelling against globalization (Lubbers 1998). This account makes it possible to emphasize the importance of perceptions and subjective reactions. Whatever the 'objective' changes, there are real subjective changes which themselves then constitute objective changes, and globalization is understood as 'dialectical' i.e., as a subjective–objective reality. Globalization on this view may not imply homogenization, and if there is an emerging global umbrella civilization, there may be major cultural conflicts as well as very different subcivilizations beneath it.

Nonetheless, many writers seem to have objective changes in mind. Malcolm Walters, for example, defines globalization as:

> A social process in which the constraints of geography on social and cultural arrangements recede and in which people become increasingly aware that they are receding (Walters 1996, p. 3).

and further:

> The theorem that guides the argument about globalization is that: material exchanges localize, political exchanges internationalize; and symbolic exchanges globalize. As a given sector of social life moves from predominance of material through power through symbolic relationships, the tendency will be towards globalization (Walters 1996, pp. 9 and 93).

In related spirit, Brenner writes:

> Globalization is a process in which interdependencies among geographically dispersed social actors are radically intensified and through which social relations in geographically distant places and territories are intertwined (Brenner 1997).

Anthony Giddens, on the other hand, stresses the intensification of worldwide social relations:

> Globalization can thus be defined as the intensification of worldwide social relations which link distant localities in such a way that local happenings are shaped by events occurring many miles away and vice versa. This is a dialectical process because such local happenings may move in an obverse direction from the very distanciated relations that shape them. Local transformation is as much part of globalization as the lateral extension of social connections across time and space (Giddens 1990, p. 64).

Another entire literature equates globalization with the triumph of economic liberalism, or the application of economic rationalism to 'nation societies,' i.e., an approach which assumes: (a) that markets offer, at least in principle, the most reliable means of setting values on all goods; and (b) that economies and markets can, in principle, deliver better outcomes than states, governments and the law. On this view, globalization is a consequence of 'ideology,' and 'a bad thing'. This approach tends to obscure the distinction between technical changes and policy options in response to them. It often condemns a wide range of changes *in toto* because it opposes specific policy responses.

Obviously it is crucial to decide whether:

- globalization is a process of global integration occurring since the dawn of history, which has recently and suddenly accelerated;
- globalization is contemporal with modernization;
- globalization is a specific phase of capitalism;
- globalization is bound up with post-industrialization and/or post-modernization and/or the disorganization of capitalism.

These are hard decisions because the existing literature is saturated with conceptual inflation and logical slippage. For example, how can one establish that globalization is a process? Ian Clark denies that globalization is a process with its own logic. Instead, he argues that it has often been an effect of state policies; hence it is not irreversible. (1997, p. 195) Similarly, granted that (a) economic transformations; (b) technological changes; and (c) cultural changes are different things, with different logics and timeframes, it may be a mistake to fuse them into a single term. Is it helpful to posit and then relate economic globalization, technological globalization, and cultural globalization? Might it not be better to define globalization more narrowly, and then to distinguish how these three areas of change relate to it? Certainly the dubious learned literature on modernization supports the view that disaggregating the types of change and their concerns is preferable to bringing diverse changes under an inflationary portmanteau term.

Clearly one solution is to deny that globalization exists in one or more determinate senses. Hirst and Thompson, for example, summarize the vernacular understanding as follows:

> It is widely asserted that we live in an era in which the greater part of social life is determined by global processes, in which national cultures, national economies and national borders are dissolving. Central to this perception is the notion of a rapid and recent process of economic globalization. A truly global economy is claimed to have emerged or to be in the process of emerging, in which distinct national economies and, therefore, domestic strategies of national economic management are increasingly irrelevant. The world economy has internationalized in its basic dynamics, it is dominated by uncontrollable market forces, and it has as its principal economic actors and major agents of change truly transnational corporations, that owe allegiance to no nation-state and locate wherever in the globe market advantage dictates (Hirst and Thompson, 1996, p. 1).

They then argue that globalization in this sense is a myth. But this does not address the perception that the world has become 'a single place' (Robertson 1990, 1992) and the sense shared by many

Western elites that we are in the midst of an historical organizational shift. There is also a danger in focusing on specific trade figures rather than on changes of capacity for individuals, corporations and states to act transnationally. This, of course, implies that it may be a mistake to equate globalization with the weakening of the nation-state. Considered in these terms, globalization cannot be construed as merely negative. On the contrary, it is alleged to give rise to new systems of global governance and to global civil society. Once again, the evidence is less plentiful than the rhetoric might lead one to suspect.

At this stage in the discussion the crucial thing, I submit, is to demand a greater standard of logical clarity from writers on globalization about what types of theoretical entities they are deploying and what specific empirical data would or would not support determinate hypotheses or theses which they wish to advance. Without this, we will be subject to another worldwide explosion of ill-defined writing in which disciplinary specialists fail to address the matters which fall outside their immediate disciplinary concerns, while generalists will make inordinate claims in terms too rhetorical to ever be strictly true or false in principle. Likewise, the political and ethical biases which run through the existing literature need to be disentangled so that those who oppose liberal capitalism do not write up their judgments as economic and political analyses, and those who seek to promote global governance and global citizenship do not describe their lofty ideals as current facts, except insofar as they are so. Without such clarifications, we will not get past the residues of Marxism as a political religion or escape secular eschatology dressed up as ethical globalism. Nor will we articulate policies that actually empower people in developing countries, especially women. Nor will we effectively protect working people all over the world whose living conditions are under threat. No doubt my scholarly scruples may strike some as conservative. They are not. On the contrary, they support a radical cosmopolitan republican politic which seeks to change the existing state system fundamentally. However, they do imply that talk of globalization currently covers different problematics, and that we would do well, both in theory and in practice, to distinguish them.

CHAPTER 6

The Challenges and Tensions of Globalized Space

James N. Rosenau

Having long proceeded from a broad social science perspective that is global in scope (rather than regional or country-specific) and that focuses on enormous changes I perceived to be transforming world affairs, I argue here that the dynamics of economic globalization, new technologies and evolving global norms are clashing with equally powerful localizing dynamics. The resulting encounters between diverse interests and actors are seen as rendering the boundaries between domestic and foreign affairs ever more porous and as creating a new political space that I variously call the Frontier or Globalized Space (Rosenau 1998, pp. 145–69). It is in this Space where the quest for control in world politics is joined. Indeed, I contend that it is along the Frontier, and not in the international arena, that issues are contested and the course of events configured (Rosenau 1997a).

Within this broad context, here I am specifically interested in the main agents and processes that sustain world affairs. More specifically, this inquiry focuses on the roles played by leaders and ever more skillful citizenries in shaping both the day-to-day events and long-term trends that mark our time and are likely to evolve in the coming decades (Rosenau 1990, Chapter 13; see also Rosenau and Fagen 1997). Equally of interest are the interactions between the forces promoting globalization and those fostering localization. These causal links lie at the core of present-day world affairs, but to date they have not been thoroughly probed. What follows is a brief elaboration of these concerns.

An Emergent Epoch

It may seem arrogant (as if I know all the answers), but I start with the presumption that the world is undergoing a profound transformation that is far deeper and far more pervasive than any of us appreciate, so much so that it amounts to the onset of a new epoch. And let me further presume that while people have difficulty articulating the transformation, there is a widespread awareness of it, a sense of underlying change that is spreading everywhere—in every country through every walk of life and across all the layers of class and community that comprise global affairs. Among elites the emergent epoch is intuitively understood in some detail; among masses it is grasped in bare outline; but whatever the level of comprehension, the central direction of the change is intersubjectively shared across cultures and all the other boundaries that differentiate communities and peoples.

And what are some of the main dimensions of the epochal transformation? At its root lies the premise that the order which sustains families, communities, countries, and the world through time rests on contradictions, ambiguities and uncertainties. Where earlier epochs had their central tendencies and orderly patterns, the present epoch derives its order from contrary trends and episodic patterns. People now understand, emotionally as well as intellectually, that unexpected events are commonplace, that anomalies are normal occurrences, that minor incidents can mushroom into major outcomes, and that fundamental processes trigger opposing forces even as they expand their scope.

This is not to say that people have adjusted comfortably to these new circumstances. On the contrary, a high level of disquiet and uncertainty persists and will doubtless continue until such time as a new, presently unforeseeable epoch replaces the one now emerging. Rather, it is only to assert that what once seemed transitional is now accepted as enduring and that the complexities of modern life are so deeply rooted as to infuse ordinariness into the surprising development and the ambiguities and anxieties that attach to it.

Being complex, the new conditions that have evolved in recent decades cannot be explained by a single source.[1] Technological dynamics are major stimulants, but so is the breakdown of trust, the shrinking of distances, the globalization of economies, the explosive proliferation of organizations, the information revolution, the fragmentation of groups and the integration of regions, the surge of democratic practices and the spread of fundamentalism, the cessation of intense enmities and the revival of historic animosities—all of which in turn provoke further reactions that add to the complexity.

Cast in terms of contradictions that have become customary, the emergent epoch is marked by a pervasive multiplicity of opposites. The international system is less commanding, but it is still powerful. States are changing, but they are not disappearing. State sovereignty has eroded, but it is still vigorously asserted. Governments are weaker, but they still possess considerable resources and they can still throw their weight around. Company profits are soaring and wages are stagnant. Scenes of unspeakable horror and genocide flicker on our TV screens even as humanitarian organizations mobilize and undertake heroic remedial actions. The United Nations is asked to take on more assignments and not supplied with the funds to carry them out. Defense establishments acknowledge that their roles have drastically altered and continue to adhere to traditional strategies. At times the public are more demanding, but at other times they are more pliable. Citizens are both more active and more cynical. Borders still keep out intruders, but they are also more porous. In sum, we have come to know that we live in a world that is deteriorating in some areas, remaining fixed in others, and thriving in still others.

The Need for a New Lexicon

Attaching a label to the new epoch is no simple matter. In good part the huge gap between our sense of profound transformation and our ability to grasp it stems from a huge shortage of the tools needed to narrow the gap. A new lexicon is needed for this purpose. Notwithstanding the widespread recognition that vast changes are unfolding, our vocabulary and conceptual equipment for understanding this emergent world lag well behind the changes themselves. We still do not have ways of talking about the diminished role of states without at the same time privileging them as superior to all the other actors in the global arena.[2] We lack a means for treating the various contradictions as part and parcel of a more coherent order.[3] We are experiencing considerable difficulty in expanding the concept of security beyond the military realm.[4] Aside from vague uses of the concept of interdependence, we are deficient in our capacity to work around and through the overlap between domestic and foreign affairs.[5] We are short on incisive understandings of the nature of transformative dynamics and ways of differentiating between transitory changes and those that are profound and enduring. We are bereft of analytic equipment that allows us to treat the US as both the world's most powerful country and one that shut down its government twice in 1995. We sense that the concept of territoriality is being shorn of meaning, but we still find it easier to think in terms of landscapes rather than ethnoscapes, technoscapes, financescapes, mediascapes and ideoscapes.[6] We do not have techniques for analyzing the nonlinearity and simultaneity of events such that the full array of their interconnections are identified.

In short, the need for a new vocabulary derived from new conceptual equipment is not trivial. Labels matter. They signify more elaborate content and, as such, they can serve as conceptual jails in which we become very comfortable and from which we are disinclined to escape. Without the rudiments of a new vocabulary, our descriptors reinforce our long-standing ways of thinking. They confirm our understanding of who the key actors are, what motivates them, and the processes that sustain their interactions. They impel us to privilege states by clustering all other collective entities in a residual category called 'nonstate actors,' to insist that the international system is anarchic or that it is marked by an underlying order, to affirm the importance of sovereignty by presuming that it still reigns supreme or that it has eroded somewhat, and so on across a number of long-standing presumptions that reinforce our conceptual jails. It is difficult to accord status to new actors, motives and processes unless one has a way of capturing their essential qualities through words that differentiate them from the prevailing conceptions.

There are a few indicators that this need for new conceptual equipment has begun to be felt on the part of those who analyze the course of world affairs. Or at least a vocabulary is evolving that departs from past practice as people seek new terms to account for phenomena that are no longer readily accommodated by the existing lexicon. Three terms are particularly noteworthy in this regard. They all involve the need to analyze collective actions across national boundaries that are organized but not formalized, amorphous but not ineffectual, imaginary but not inconsequential. As powerful forces shrink the world, erode boundaries, and shift loci of authority, observers now refer as much to 'the international community' as to the United Nations, as much to 'global governance' as to the leadership of great powers, and as much to 'coalitions of the willing' as to formal alliances, when discussing actions that governmental and nongovernmental organizations take or contemplate in concert with each other. These terms seem destined to become established ways of designating the considerable normative convergence and cooperative actions that now mark the global scene for which the lexicon of legal and political precedents makes no room.

On the other hand, none of these efforts to make up for the lag between changing practices and our descriptors for them hints at the mushrooming tensions between the fragmenting consequences of conflict and the integrative effects of cooperation. Accordingly, emboldened by these signs of terminological adaptation, let me dare to carry the practice a step further by offering a label that may seem awkward at first, but that has the virtue of calling attention to the transformative dynamics that have given rise to a new common sense of a new epoch. The label *is fragmegration*, a term that juxtaposes the processes of fragmentation and integration occurring within and among organizations, communities, countries and transnational systems such that it is virtually impossible not to treat them as interactive and causally linked.[7] From a fragmegrative perspective, the world is seen as short on clear-cut distinctions between domestic and foreign affairs, with the result that local problems can become transnational in scope even as global challenges can have repercussions for small communities. Viewed in this way, in other words, the global system is so disaggregated that it lacks overall patterns and, instead, is marked by various structures of systemic cooperation and subsystemic conflict in different regions, countries and issue areas.[8] Indeed, fragmegrative processes are so pervasive and generic that the emergent epoch seems likely to acquire a label reflective of them, although the term itself is probably too grating ever to catch on as the prime descriptor of the epoch. To speak of the Westphalian system as having been replaced by the fragmegrative system runs counter to the need for historic landmarks as a basis for thinking about global structures.

The Dynamics of Fragmegration

Sensitivity to the inextricably close links between the integrative and disintegrative forces at work in communities at all levels of aggregation is a major consequence of the diverse technologies that have collapsed time and space as well as expanded the visibility of underlying socioeconomic and political processes. In earlier times—i.e., during that long stretch of history when the boundaries between national and international systems were less permeable and when it took weeks and months for ideas, people and goods to move around the world—the occurrence of integrative developments such as the formation of states, the industrialization of societies, the evolution of empires or the opening of new trade routes were not readily apparent as sources of fragmenting consequences. Nor did the onset of fragmenting processes such as civil wars or class conflicts lend themselves easily to tracing their integrative consequences. Doubtless both sets of causal links did exist and could be discerned in retrospect if a decadal context was used. But only as technologies of communication fostered extensive overlaps among local, national and international systems did the simultaneity and interaction of fragmegrative dynamics became so readily evident, so widely pervasive and so fully operative as immediate stimuli to tensions that career back and forth through systems at all levels of economic, social and political organization.[9]

Indeed, so interwoven are these contradictory processes that is not far-fetched to conclude that most increments of fragmentation give rise to comparable increments of integration; that localizing and globalizing forces are products of each other.[10] Viewed in this way, it is hardly surprising that fragmegration constitutes the core of the emergent epoch. However they may articulate their understanding, people have come to expect, to take for granted, that the advance of globalization poses threats to the long-standing ties of local and national communities; that some groups will contest, even violently fight, the intrusion of global norms even as others will seek to obtain goods or increased market shares beyond their communities.

It follows that the forces of fragmentation are rooted in the psychic comfort people derive from the familiar and close-at-hand values and practices of their neighborhoods and nations. Contrariwise, the forces of integration stem from the aspiration to share in the distant products of the global economy, to benefit from the efficiencies of regional unity, to avoid the dangers of environmental challenges such as global warming, and/or to yield to the implications of the pictures taken from outer space that depict the earth as a solitary entity in a huge universe. The tensions inherent in these conflicting impulses dominate the agendas of political systems at every level of community. In so doing, they raise a number of crucial questions: How are both individuals and societies going to adapt to the transformations? How well, that is, will societies, groups and individuals be able to keep their essential structures intact and move toward their goals in the face of dynamic changes that are giving birth to a new epoch? In a decentralizing global system undergoing continual processes wherein authority is undermined and relocated, how can the public be mobilized and problems addressed? If the capabilities of states are eroding, are new political structures likely to evolve, or is the world headed for ever greater disarray?

New Social Contracts?

The answers to these questions are complex and elusive. While fragmegrative processes may be patterned, they are also inherently unstable and marked by recurrent imbalances. They unfold differently in different organizations, communities, countries, regions and issue areas. In some instances the tendencies toward fragmentation, localization or decentralization are predominant; in others, the opposite tendencies are more pervasive. In some cases the resulting tensions are intense and enduring, while in others they are episodic and cyclical. Uneven as the dynamics of fragmegration may be, however, they highlight the large degree to which the glue that holds communities and nations together is undergoing transformations—changes so profound as to necessitate the framing of new social contracts that can generate more effective forms of systemic coherence.[11] In the absence of progress toward the forming of new contracts founded on values that enable collectivities to remain intact and move toward their goals, it is reasonable to anticipate that the world is indeed headed for ever greater disarray.

But what might be the bases of new social contracts? Leaving aside the fact that they cannot be imposed from the top, or at least that they must resonate broadly with the affected publics, on what values should the new contracts rest such that localizing and globalizing forces can be reconciled and the tensions between them ameliorated?

In speculating along these lines, there is an ever-present danger of falling back on trite and simplistic, if not unrealistic, formulations. One important way to guard against this danger is to stress the complexity of the emergent epoch, to view it as sustained by a multiplicity of interactive dynamics, no one of which steers the processes of fragmegration. Such a perspective can be readily maintained if it is presumed, as elaborated elsewhere, that the major dynamics of the emergent epoch include an acceleration of their technological foundations; a decrease in the salience of territoriality, such that landscapes are being superseded by mediascapes, financescapes, ethnoscapes, ideoscapes and technoscapes; an increase in the analytic, emotional and imaginative skills of people everywhere; an enormous proliferation of organizations at all levels of community; an endless movement of people, goods and ideas that have vastly increased the variety and number of boundary-spanning activities and further confounded the meaning of territoriality; and a decrease in the competence and sovereignty of states corresponding to the enhanced vitality of the skill revolution, the organizational proliferation, the diverse boundary-spanning activities, and the new 'scapes' that crowd the horizon.[12]

Put differently, for all these reasons and others too numerous to elaborate here, the global stage has become highly dense and complex, marked by innumerable actors in a multi-centric world that sometimes cooperates with, sometimes competes with, but at all times interacts with the 190 nations recognized as members of the state-centric world. This bifurcation of the underlying structures of world politics has to be acknowledged in any effort to lay out the bases for new social contracts.[13]

Perhaps the most important implication of the foregoing dynamics is the question of who shall be the parties to the new social contracts? In the last two centuries the parties have been the national state on the one hand and its individuals and public on the other. But such contracts have lost some of their viability as the territorial state has weakened and the public have become more skillful, their organizations more numerous, their boundary-spanning activities more extensive, and their coalescence in cyberspace more secure. Clearly, then, the new social contracts must be among more than two parties; the state can no longer be the only collective agent who strikes a bargain with individuals, and the many collective agents cannot be exclusively founded on territoriality.

While these criteria for the new collective agents who will fashion and sustain the new social contracts are seemingly so unfamiliar as to make the task exceedingly difficult, a basis for developing them does appear feasible. As developed at length elsewhere, the collective agents with whom individuals may strike new social contracts are to be found wherever authority has been and continues to be relocated in the emergent epoch. That is, instead of viewing the world as organized in terms of sovereign states, the new epoch calls for viewing it as consisting of spheres of authority (SOAs).[14] Some of these may be partially founded on territoriality, but none are fully grounded in the same kind of geographic space that has marked the nation-state era. Rather, the boundaries of the bargaining agents, the SOAs, are defined by those entities to whom people accord legitimacy and thereby attach their loyalties. Thus an SOA can be an issue regime, a professional organization, a neighborhood, a network of the like-minded, a social movement, a local or provincial government, a diaspora, a regional association, and so on across all the diverse collectivities that have become major sources of decisional authority in the ever more complex multi-centric world. To be sure, the array of SOAs may include some states that manage to cling to sufficient authority to be the focus of the legitimacy sentiments of their citizens, but the advent of SOAs in the multi-centric world capable of drawing up meaningful social contracts with their adherents has reduced the number of states with the kind of unqualified authority that marked their counterparts in the past.

Put differently, if the nation-state is viewed as having always been an imagined community, a political entity that exists by virtue of the fact that its citizens believe it to exist and thus abide by its institutions, regulations and policies (Anderson 1991), the emergent epoch is one in which communities are being re-imagined (see Rosenau 1997a; and various essays in Archibugi *et al.*, 1998). The multiple dynamics of our fragmegrative epoch combine to allow people to envision themselves as tied to others whose connective tissues constitute an authority structure to which they are responsive. Such structures may be short-lived, as when a social movement achieves its goals and its SOA ceases to exist, but effective authority is embedded in their activities for whatever period of time they endure. The population of collectivities that comprise the multi-centric world, in other words, undergoes continual shifts in its composition.

Given a skill revolution that is enabling people to become increasingly adept at managing multiple identities and loyalties, in the early stages of the evolution of SOAs there is likely to be considerable overlap among them, with the result that their boundaries may initially be obscure and the scope of their authority ambiguous. Nor is there any certainty that eventually the boundaries of SOAs will evolve such that the overlaps are eliminated and SOAs become the focus of ultimate loyalties, much as the nation-state has long been the terminal community insofar as loyalties are concerned. Indeed, it is exactly the nature of the complexities underlying the emergent epoch that the notion of terminal loyalties has to be treated as highly problematic. Just because states have enjoyed such a status, it would be erroneous to view them as evidence that their successors will become terminal entities. On the contrary, given the large extent to which SOAs are founded on nonterritorial sources of legitimacy, the greater likelihood is that some overlaps will endure, that people will be responsive to one of their SOAs under certain conditions and to others of them under different circumstances, so that what evolves through time is clarity as to where the legitimacy of one SOA ends and where that of another begins.

This is another way of saying that the fragmegrative epoch will not be marked by neomedieval structures. Many observers have noted that if the interstate system breaks down, global structures will return to the arrangements that prevailed prior to the onset of the modern era of the nation-state. To be sure, the fragmegrative epoch will be distinguished by decentralized structures of authority and a vast array of political entities, but these will not resemble the medieval era in that people will have multiple loyalties toward and affiliations with numerous SOAs. In the medieval period individuals did have ultimate loyalties—to a king or fiefdom—whereas few SOAs in the fragmegrative era will be terminal collectivities. Rather, as stressed in the next paragraph, people will learn to balance diverse and even conflicting commitments in the absence of a terminal state.

Assuming a multiplicity of new social contracts between diverse SOAs and the individuals responsive to them, is there a core set of values on which all the contracts can be founded? While each SOA will doubtless have clauses in its contract that are unique to its circumstances, there are at least two clusters of values that come to mind as plausible core values. One involves an appreciation that no SOA has exclusive authority with respect to those within its purview. In a fragmegrated world, people have too many identities and affiliations to accord any SOA the sole legitimacy to make decisions about every aspect of their lives. Rather, recognizing that they cannot be responsive to the directives of all the SOAs to which they owe allegiance, their contracts are likely to require them to accept that their various SOAs might issue contradictory directives and that they are obliged to frame a set of priorities for responding to them. Second, faced with contradictory directions, people will be obliged by their contracts to be open to dialog across—as well as within—the various SOAs relevant to their circumstances. The agenda for such dialogs is likely to consist precisely of those contradictory issues which span their SOAs—issues such as when it is appropriate to accept or resist compromises on such matters, or under what conditions it is acceptable to move out of the purview of one SOA in favor of another.

The obvious question arises as to whether people will be amenable to adopting and living by these new contracts. Conceivably, it could be argued, the long-standing impulse to have a highest loyalty will prevent most people from abiding by a contract in which no SOA is accorded exclusive claims on those within its purview. And if this is the case, the argument would stress, surely there will be no basis for accepting an obligation to engage in dialogs that continuously redefine where the boundaries of SOAs are drawn. If the need for a terminal entity to which to attach the highest loyalty is strong, how can it be expected that the new contracts will attract sufficient signatories to be meaningful?

While this pessimistic line of reasoning can hardly be discounted, it may be exaggerated. It fails to allow for the power and urgency of the underlying currents sustaining the emergent epoch. The disarray that is likely to attend the dispersion of authority under pervasive fragmegrative conditions may well serve to encourage an appreciation of the need for a new social contract based on the foregoing criteria. To be sure, compliance with authority is rooted in habit-driven behaviour and people are thus likely to be slow in acknowledging the need for a new social contract and then agreeing to it; but at the same time most people are capable of learning and adapting when conditions change, so that in the long run it is possible to conceive of a readiness to negotiate new social contracts that are not founded on an exclusive acquiescence to the authority of states. Already a dialog and literature on the idea of a global civil society have evolved that are deep and broad enough to suggest movement in the direction of some kind of new contractual foundations. Moreover, if it is recalled that the age of fragmegration is pervaded with uncertainties, ambiguities and anomalies, there are ample incentives to seek, or at least accept, a new social contract which will do better in channeling, stabilizing or even reducing the instabilities of life than does its state-bound predecessor.

Conclusions

What does this analysis portend for the immediate and long-term future? My own estimate is that the dynamics of fragmegration may continue to unfold. There is no basis for anticipating that globalizing processes will decelerate, so that the trends toward integration in the worlds of business and government are likely to continue and they may even move more swiftly as regions begin to see virtues in special forms of cooperation, as businesses find that alliances enhance their bottom lines, and as states are pressed to share responsibility for common problems by forming regimes or otherwise integrating their policies. At the same time the negative, localizing consequences of globalization are likely to be ever more widely felt and to spawn increasing numbers of politicians like Patrick Buchanan of the USA,

Jean-Marie Le Pen of France, and Pauline Hansen of Australia, who appeal to local and racial identities as bases for exclusionary economic, immigration, and political policies.

It would be satisfying to conclude that the ultimate outcome of the clashes between these contradictory forces will amount to a continuing, if slow and halting, trend in which states and actors in the multi-centric world enter into new social contracts that manage to bring the fragmegrative dynamics under control and enable the world to move beyond its many contradictions toward less conflictual and more progressive values. Such an outcome, however, will depend on whether the dynamics of fragmegration are cyclical or dialectical. If they are the latter, as they may well be, then the new contracts may serve as the syntheses that emerge out of the globalizing theses that generate localizing antitheses.

Put differently, if the organization explosion continues at the grassroots and the multi-centric world thus becomes ever more populated and marked by an ever greater dispersion of authority, the contradictions of fragmegrative conditions are likely to beome increasingly intolerable and provide added weight to those who call for syntheses through new social contracts. Stated in still another way, since the powerful tensions that sustain fragmegration—the forces of fragmentation that are rooted in the psychic comfort people derive from the familiar and close-at-hand values and practices of their neighborhoods and nations, and the forces of integration that derive from the aspiration to share in the distant products of the global economy, to benefit from the efficiencies of regional unity, to avoid the dangers of environmental challenges such as global warming, and/or to yield to the implications of the pictures taken from outer space that depict the earth as a solitary entity in a huge universe—dominate the agendas of political systems at every level of community, they are as likely to highlight the virtues of achieving syntheses through new social contracts as they are to promote cyclical movement back and forth among the globalizing and localizing dynamics.

Notes

1. Since repercussions of the end of the Cold War were clearly evident at all levels of organization, it is tempting to treat this development as an epochal turning point. Such an interpretation, however, is misleading; it exaggerates the impact of a single historical moment and does not allow for the possibility that the end of the Cold War was the culmination of

underlying and long-standing processes of change which, as stressed here, ushered in a common sense of dynamics and structures that amounted to a new epoch.

For an analysis in which the Cold War is seen as having 'left so light an impact on the living memory of states and societies that it is already en route to oblivion' see Gambles 1995.

2. For a rare effort to come to terms with this problem, see Ferguson and Mansbach 1996.
3. Partial exceptions in this regard can be found in Holm and Sorenson 1995.
4. Attempts to confront these difficulties are undertaken in Lipschutz 1995.
5. For an elaboration of this overlap, see Rosenau 1997a.
6. For a discussion of these various 'scapes', see Appadurai 1996.
7. This concept was first developed in Rosenau 1983. See also Rosenau 1997a, ch.6.
8. For a cogent example of the vast array of circumstances in which fragmegrative dynamics are relevant, see Barber 1995.
9. For inquiries which, in one way or another, explore the tensions and posit them as central to the course of events, see Camilleri and Falk 1992; Zum 1995; Kuklinski 1990; Mlinar 1992.
10. Some analysts use the term *glocalization* to capture these causal links, but fragmegration is preferred here because it does not imply a territorial scale and broadens the focus to include tensions at work in organizations as well as those that pervade communities.
11. Although the conception of new social contracts developed here is not to be found elsewhere, pieces of it can be found in the following formulations: Hill 1995; Fleiner 1994; Tamas 1994; Turner 1993; Frankenfeld 1992; Henningsen 1989.
12. For elaboration of these various presumptions, see Rosenau 1997a; Rosenau and Fagen 1997; and Appadurai 1996.
13. The notion of bifurcated global structures is most elaborately developed in Rosenau 1990, Chapter 10.
14. The concept of spheres of authority is spelled out in Rosenau 1997a.

CHAPTER 7

Learning from Globalization: Issues and Obstacles

Stuart Rees

In simple terms, globalization means the use of financial capital to turn the world into one very competitive market (Martin and Schumann 1997, p. 5) In complex terms it refers to the various and often concealed means by which corporations promote their own interests, and to the social, political and environmental costs of such practices (Brecher and Costello 1994, p. 5)

Globalization can be viewed as a threat or it could be turned into a promise. In daily life its consequences could be perceived as overwhelming, or as one of several forces to be reckoned with. Which of these alternatives materializes could depend on what can be learned from current experiences of globalization. With that idea in mind, this chapter challenges prospective students about values as well as facts, and would examine them on their ability to develop socially just politics. The students could be any group—not necessarily enrolled in formal education—who want to discover the meaning of globalization and its impact on their own and other people's lives. The idea of building a curriculum is to take account not only of specific topics but also to ponder how students learn. Reflection on personal issues which affect understanding of an ambitious topic becomes part of the curriculum.

The diagram, *Learning from Globalization: A Curriculum*, shown in Figure 1 begins with prospective students' fatalism. It continues from the safety of old ideas to an emphasis on new concepts. Students' sense of direction will depend on whose voices are heeded and whether their agendas can be embraced. The study ends with reflection on the obstacles which hinder learning. A goal of this curriculum is that teachers, students and onlookers should be more politically and economically literate than when they started.

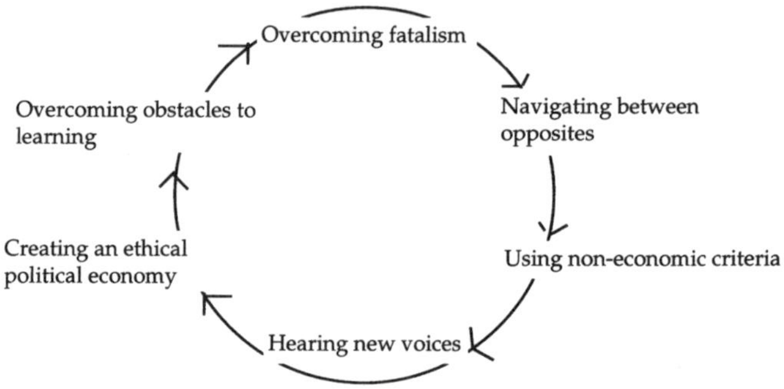

Figure 1. Learning from Globalization: A Curriculum

Overcoming Fatalism

It is not a new phenomenon for globally-wide force to affect the quality of life of all peoples. What is new lies in the irony that people's awareness of globalization makes them feel less equipped to cope with its consequences. This does not mean that previous ignorance about changes in international order was a blessing. It does present the challenge of conscientization (Freire 1972): raising awareness so that political and economic forces seem neither incomprehensible nor beyond our control.

Part of the fatalism rests on a view of corporate greed and social inequality as part of the process and outcome of economic globalization. It has been conceived as a race-to-the-bottom, hastened by policies which deregulate the labor market, abolish occupational health and safety measures and move companies to parts of the world where labor is cheap and very low wages can be paid (Brecher and Costello 1994; Mander and Goldsmith 1997; Hellyer 1999). Encouraged by benefits of deregulation, large corporations compound the powerlessness of poor countries and of poor regions within rich countries by minimizing their tax obligations and simultaneously demanding public subsidies for their activities (Martin and Schumann 1997).

International agencies with responsibility to set the rules of a new world economic order—the WTO and the IMF—collude with the interests of international capital. A condition of loans is that countries cut back on basic services for their people, lower the taxes which could have paid for those services and disempower the trade union movement. Under these circumstances vulnerable people have been deprived of forms of protection at a time when they most need them.

The fatalism of the poor and disempowered is based on the wretchedness of daily experience. The fatalism of critics of globalization is based on forecasts that the future looks no better. These forecasts revolve around two equations. One says that the world's economic policies already operate on a 40–30–30 basis; 40 percent of thc people are fully employed, 30 percent neither fully employed nor fully unemployed and 30 percent are virtually surplus to requirements (Hutton 1995). The other equation displays an 80–20 scenario; in the next century 20 percent of the population will suffice to keep the world economy going (Martin and Schumann 1997, p. 3) while the other 80 percent will have a struggle to survive. The world's rulers are moving their people toward a different civilization, if a society with 80 percent unemployed can be called a civilization.

A first step in overcoming fatalism has been achieved. Causes which may be beyond people's control have been identified and they need no longer blame themselves. Adding the burden of guilt to disempowerment is tantamount to drowning. A step beyond this understanding is to identify the familiar concepts which affect our assumptions. These concepts are useful but have been presented as either/or choices. In the next stage of the curriculum, the task is to navigate between them.

Navigating Between Opposites

Polarized ideas such as left or right, socialism versus capitalism, government intervention or market forces and regulation versus deregulation have influenced the way we look and what we see. They have determined political loyalties and policy priorities. Students have also been taught that these terms show how economic policics might be managed.

At first sight the polarization of opposing terms looks like a two-way choice. In fact economic think tanks (Wheelwright 1995) and international credit rating agencies have been telling politicians and civil servants that there is no choice. Only the market offers a solution. Apart from the intellectual poverty of this message it is also totalitarian in its content and style.

Students are asked to find a way between these opposite points but not simply by veering to one side or another. These points represent extremes of economic and social policies and the ideological basis of political allegiances. There is nothing in them which conveys human experiences, either the poverty of Africa or—in

Australia—the people struggling to live on a meager income and caricatured as Aussie battlers.

A goal in navigating between opposites is to depict people's hopes, constraints and aspirations, to find measures which reflect a common humanity.

Using Non-economic Criteria

If students and teachers are to escape from the constraints of these polarized ideas, they must use criteria which resonate with people's experiences. Hazel Henderson says that the recipes which politicians adopt as a result of their reliance on measures such as the gross national product (GNP) give a false picture of the quality of lives by, among other things, omitting the costs of environmental degradation (Henderson 1978; 1996). GNP criteria may reassure economists intent on measuring growth but they also omit reference to the caring work done by women. New Zealand economist Marilyn Waring has argued that activities which lie outside the production boundary—that is in every nation the great bulk of labor performed by women in an unpaid capacity—are left out of GDP as they are left out of the GNP (Waring 1988, p. 72).

In a study of 1,000 researchers from over 20 different disciplines Robert Lane assessed the effects of economic activity on learning and personal development. He found that what contributes most to satisfaction, happiness and human development are full employment, family life, friendship, intellectual growth, self reliance and self esteem (Lane 1993). Although economic criteria can measure some of these qualities, there are social costs of economic activity which seldom appear in official returns on the costs of growth. Personal costs of the alleged success associated with economic growth include insecurity, anxiety, competitiveness, dependence and subjection. In a plea for measures of economic globalization which reflect the humanness of existence, the Australian economist Ted Wheelwright argues that societies should be measured more on what they contribute to people's personal development and happiness and less on how efficiently they contribute to goods and services (Wheelwright 1995).

The criteria of economic growth and the presentation of opposites—either government regulation or market freedoms—are based on assumptions that rational choices will be made as when people act selfishly to foster their own interests. But they may wish to act on humanitarian grounds even if this looks irrational to public choice theorists. For example, there is evidence consistent with Lane's findings about the significance of personal happiness that large numbers of people choose to act altruistically and when faced with recession they insist that fairness should prevail, that cutting wages is never a solution to unemployment, that increasing taxes is a fair way to meet social costs (Hutton 1993).

The factors which enhance personal relationships have to be factored into economics. Even market transactions depend on bonds of trust and cooperation, qualities often referred to as social capital (Cox 1995; Putnam 1993). But globally, wide-ranging measures—cutting back on budget deficits, scaling back welfare provisions and lowering taxation—which have spread the benefits of growth so unequally and have led to social instability have ignored social capital.

The State has not reached the limits of what it can afford to do (Hutton 1994) but whether a new politics can be encouraged depends in part on whose voices will be heard and whether they will be taken seriously. This point is made because the goal of developing an ethical political economy—nationally and internationally—will be facilitated by weighing perspectives from different peoples and cultures. The forces of globalization are common but the impact has not been uniform.

Hearing New Voices

Unless the losers from financial globalization develop political clout, they will not be heard. Specific losers have been the poor in developing countries. The politician Bharati Ray from India emphasizes (1998) that in every culture the disempowerment of women has been hastened by the speed of economic globalization. In India the high rates of women's illiteracy make it almost impossible to comprehend new sources of disempowerment. In many developing countries, current struggles to survive have been compounded by skyrocketing food prices. In the labor market in developed countries, women are joining an informal sector or casual labor force. They also have to find solutions for the financial losses and other stresses associated with unemployment. They are paying the social costs of men's increased insecurity.

In Africa, Lawrence Schlemmer (1998) identified a cruel contradiction between the expectation of lifestyle improvements and the policy frameworks which have been imposed by global demands and are crushing people's hopes. In South Africa, the official unemployment rate may be 28 percent, but for dispirited people and those who are too poor to travel it is 38 percent, says Schlemmer. Without a basic government and non-government infrastructure, including well trained and well resourced staff, even influential leaders within poor countries can at best be only defensive in their responses to globalization.

The link between globalization, employment and quality of life is intriguing but it is important not to attribute every experience of disempowerment to one cause. Other global processes have affected people's wretchedness. For example, in five southern African countries—South Africa, Botswana, Namibia, Swaziland and Lesotho—the Aids epidemic has infected as many as one in four people and cut life expectancy by one quarter.

Indigenous voices have joined a chorus demanding that human rights be given due recognition. Yet the chances of indigenous peoples' voices being heard, or their claims acknowledged, are lessened by the ideology that insists that unless corporations maintain control of land and mineral resources they cannot compete. So, the story goes, it would not be in corporations' global interests to advocate indigenous peoples' rights. On the other hand, globalization of communication has facilitated the achievement of worldwide alliances between indigenous peoples. Aware of the United Nations 1986 convention on the right to development, indigenous peoples are insisting that governments' major responsibility is not to hinder development. The issue then arises whether indigenous peoples' pleas for reconciliation, for investment and for control of local economies can be a feature of a new and ethical global politics.

There is always a chance that attention paid to hearing new voices may achieve little. Like the optimism created by community development in the 1970s, action may occur at the periphery but real power remain at the center. On the other hand, in the 1990s two important victories have been achieved by activists within government and non-government sectors. The first occurred in relation to the postponing of the Multilateral Agreement on Investment (MAI). The second looks as though it is going to be achieved regarding debt relief for the Third World.

Regarding the proposed MAI Treaty, an international network of concerned citizens insisted that their voices be heard. For the time being the project has been shelved. A senior economist with the World Bank, Herman Daly, was one of the dissenting voices. In an article for *Scientific American* he wrote that 'when convenient, balanced international trade should be used but it should not be allowed to govern a country's affairs at risk of environmental and social disaster' (Daly 1993; see also Daly 1997). In an analysis of the proposed MAI Treaty called 'Globalization Gone Mad,' Paul Hellyer quotes John Maynard Keynes: 'I sympathize therefore with those who would minimize rather than those who would maximize economic entanglement between nations. Ideas, knowledge, art, hospitality, travel, these are things which of their nature should be international. But let goods be homespun whenever it is reasonably and conveniently possible; and above all, let finance be primarily national' (Hellyer 1999, p. 65).

The second globalization issue about which dissenting voices have been effective concerns the relief of Third World Debt. In a campaign known as Jubilee 2000, the proposal was made to offer relief to the world's 45 poorest nations by the year 2000. Jubilee is based on a story of biblical precedent in Leviticus in which every 50 years was designated as the year of the jubilee, a year of rest, renewal and fresh start. (Paul Hellyer goes further than advocacy of debt relief. He argues for a write-off of all the money owed to the IMF, the World Bank, Regional Development Banks, individual country loans and private bank loans to debtor governments.) The campaign is about the difficulties of improving the lot of people who are poor. It is not merely about debt relief. The campaigners argue for reform of structural adjustment programmes of the IMF. They want measures to ensure that debt relief goes to those who need it, not into Swiss bank accounts or to arms dealers. The campaign has included some who argue that debts should be suspended, the suspension renewable on an annual basis under certain conditions. The Jubilee 2000 campaign is a reassuring example of a globalization initiative from the bottom up. It has been identified as a 'triumph for morality, a triumph for conscience and a triumph for good'. It is a deeply significant moment for grassroots activism and democracy (Elliot 1999, p. 12).

Principles concerning the prevention of the MAI Treaty and the implementing of Jubilee 2000 imply an ethical political economy, nationally and globally. That's the curriculum topic to which we now turn.

Creating an Ethical Political Economy

Before diving into a subject as apparently abstract as 'an ethical political economy', we might pause to review what has been learned so far. The assumption that everything is beyond our control has been criticized and we've been critical of the simplified view of the world provided by polarized points of view. We have become aware of the significance of non-economic criteria to portray wellbeing. The need to hear what the poor and powerless say has been emphasized in unison with the voices of some successful protesters. We are now in a position to sketch a political economy capable of satisfying human needs and freedoms.

To make the globalization curriculum manageable, I'll finish with brief reference to three principles. Others could also be developed, but the three chosen provide a basis for building an ethical political economy: a commitment to achieving human rights, the goal of work for all who want it and attention to an economy of time.

People from every walk of life can be conversant with the principles of human rights and with the small print of the covenants which oblige governments to implement those rights. An objective of human rights covenants concerns the ability of individual citizens to participate fully in public life but the powerlessness engendered by economic globalization has shown the rights of citizenship to be nebulous unless a country invests in social capital (Falk, 1993). In this respect, international financier George Soros contrasts the powerful mechanisms of a global economy with the limited means of preserving peace and preventing the excesses of financial markets (Soros 1998).

However, the Declaration of Human Rights does at least present a vision of a more equitable world. Mary Robinson, the UN Commissioner for Human Rights, says that the Declaration 'has become an elevating force on the events of our world because it can be seen to embody the legal, moral and philosophical beliefs held true by all peoples and because it applies to all' (Robinson 1998, p. 11).

Teaching about human rights is one way to combat fatalism about economic globalization. In that teaching it is important to maintain students' hope that an ethical way of conducting government can be attained. Nelson Mandela says of the Universal Declaration of Human Rights that in the darkest days of apartheid 'the simple and noble words of the Universal Declaration were a sudden ray of hope. It was proof that (we) were not alone, but rather part of a great global movement against racism and colonialism, for human rights, peace and justice' (Robinson 1998, p. 9).

The right to work challenges those equations which say that the world's economies can be run efficiently with only a small percentage of the population in secure work. In addition to job creation programs the politics of job sharing also need to be addressed. Such sharing addresses issues about quality of life and commitment to a common good. A happy medium has to be found between the competitive rush nurtured by globalization and the waste of human energy inherent in being unemployed and living in poverty.

Time and attention have become as valuable as money. People are profoundly disturbed about both the waste of time and the lack of time. The leaders of countries and companies claim that if they are to stay internationally competitive, time has to be rationed even though the rush implied by rationing time has adverse effects on health, friendships and education. For example, in Australia, tertiary education is faced with the paradox that everyone is a full time student but virtually no one is a full time student. Faced with increased fees and the prohibitive costs of finding somewhere to live, few students can afford to be 'full time'. But they are expected to engage in a curriculum designed for full time students.

This globalization curriculum finishes with a story. Its lesson is that politics and economics have to be reformed with a view to time being regained. The story refers to the significance of an economy of self sufficiency providing not only sustenance but also benefits in physical and mental health. Benefiting from group solidarity and enjoyment of the environment is contrasted with the consequences of involvement in individual competition whatever the costs.

The King of Thailand is a devout Buddhist. In cities and in the countryside he is regarded as being in touch with his people. He is highly respected. In response to the Thai economic crisis from 1997, the king's advice to his people has been to value and foster a system of economic and social sufficiency. Adapted to farming, this means the abandonment of mono-cropping favored by those who have advocated the highest return for highest yield of a crop that was marketed once or perhaps twice a year. Instead of mono cropping, Thai farmers have been encouraged to return to diverse farming to take account of the benefits of year-round work. As an alternative to mono-cropping, Thai farmers are encouraged to grow vegetables as well as rice, to produce fruits and different forms of animal husbandry. Academic and community development activist Dr Jitti Mongkolchaiarunya from Thammasat University says that farmers who have heeded the king's advice, and returned to a self sufficient economy, report improved mental and physical health. After a day working in his newly created fishpond one farmer is reported to have said: 'After working in our fishpond, we have a cool mind. Our food problem is secure.'

The essence of Buddhism is living in harmony with natural

resources and with one's fellow human beings. Thai commentators acknowledge that when ideas about the supremacy of international markets operated, the king's advice was not heeded. Now the worst consequences of globalization have provided an opportunity.

Overcoming Obstacles to Learning

In following this curriculum, an objective has been to promote an ethical politics in which measures which reflect the quality of people's lives would become well known. Thus informed, the public would be better prepared to advocate democracy in many forms and never again be overawed by corporate agendas.

That sounds noble but the exercise would only be realistic if the obstacles to learning are identified: (a) the problem of unreflectiveness; (b) the disproportionate influence of American corporate culture; (c) the promotion of alleged rational thinking.

(a) Developing a capacity to reflect contributes to self-confidence and self-reliance. It also enhances a capacity to solve problems and encourages qualities of humanness. Yet the forces of financial globalization have discouraged this capacity for reflection. Australian sociologist Michael Pusey has observed that it is remarkable how unreflective economic policymakers have been, in particular when they tell politicians that the rules of international competition demand that there be no alternative to deregulation and letting the market decide. In education circles it is often felt that there is little time to reflect. Cost effectiveness in the use of time demands that a priority task in communication is to master computer technology. Means have become ends.

(b) In examining globalization with a view to producing an alternative politics, it is risky to finish with a point which sounds like an exercise in xenophobia. Yet globalization often looks to be synonymous with the promotion of North American corporate interests. In that respect an element in the demise of the MAI Treaty was said to be the determination of some powerful nations to protect their cultures against encroachment by the United States.

Any all-embracing culture hinders the exploration of other ways of thinking and acting. It can never be just let alone liberating to claim that one culture has found a utopian existence, hence the emphasis on challenging monolithic corporate influence. This challenge depends on revitalizing democracy, as in promoting awareness of human rights and the means of attaining them.

(c) A capacity for reflection should enable students to ponder diverse points of view and discourage that linear thinking which implies 'this is the rational way to look at the world, we have found the answer.' Such rationalism has produced economic dogma even though it has been paraded as choice. Under the influence of only one form of rationalism it is difficult to ponder the content of an ethical political economy. In addition, students perceive the invitation to appear rational in support of the growth and prosperity generated by globalization to be very appealing. The forces of the media, of many governments and most corporations foster such a view, yet being limited to one orthodoxy shows a fatalism not dissimilar to people's feeling that globalization was beyond their control. That is the challenge with which this curriculum ends and with which it began.

CHAPTER 8

Globalization and the Impacts of Economic Rationalism on Quality of Life in 'Advanced' Societies

Michael Pusey

Together with other contributors to this volume I am faced with a daunting question ... Is life getting better or worse: and how should the judgments be made? I ask this already too large question in relation only to 'First World,' or so-called developed, capitalist nations with comparatively very high standards of living (Eckersley 1998). What are the impacts of globalization on wellbeing and quality of life in these societies? And how should we begin to evaluate the transformations that globalization has brought upon us?

In what follows I will try to give an in-a-nutshell *prècis* of the impacts of globalization. It goes almost without saying that evaluations of wellbeing and progress do not easily command consensus and that they must, of necessity, issue from an intellectual framework that is contestable and which needs, for just this reason, to be declared. How then should we approach these daunting questions? It seems to me that one has to clear the ground by addressing at least three paradigmatic questions.

Perspective and Framework

Are modernization and modernity still acceptable beacons for progress and for judgments as to whether life is improving? For the most part the answers may be more settled than we think. In these 'First World' nations basic legal, political and human rights are taken for granted and affirmed (however imperfectly) as basic conditions for a personal autonomy that is deemed by most people to be a *sine qua non* for happiness and wellbeing. As we speak at the start of the third millennium one is surprised by the eagerness with which people seem to seize what they see as an expanding freedom of choice, lifestyle, and belief in what looks like a celebration of limitless individuality. Apologists and advocates for First World standards want to claim that modernization and modernity are now coterminous with turn-of-the-millennium post-industrial capitalism. Modernity is held to go hand-in-hand with a liberal democracy and a liberal pluralism that gives primacy to a 'self that is prior to the ends that can be affirmed by it' ... in a world where ... 'even a dominant end must be chosen from among numerous possibilities' (Rawls 1984, p. 5). We have no single 'moral consensus' and no trump cards for settling questions of morality, need, or entitlement; no commanding traditions and, in short, no templates for the good life that can be taken 'off the shelf'. These are the certainties of an age in which we speak now of a 'reflexive modernity', in a 'risk society', in which even these fruits of modernity seem to be 'saturated with contingency'. And yet doubts about the achievements and burdens of modernity quickly re-enter assessments of the wellbeing of national populations at several points. It could be, first, that much of this celebration of freedom and choice boils down to nothing much more than the meretricious self-consciousness of an upper middle class of 'self-actualizers' who are busy enjoying their own success (perhaps even at the expense of others?). And yet it is true that globalization has enhanced cultural freedoms and even shown that there is no 'zero-sum' relationship between individual freedom and 'collective' morality. On the contrary, a well-ordered society should be based on binding rights and obligations that allow individuals to flourish in spontaneous diversity. But since these rights are inherently procedural and abstract we are led to ask whether they can secure the 'hearts and minds' of whole populations in a way that can command popular legitimacy. Will they be adequate to sustain whatever minimum levels of 'mutual recognition' and social cohesion may be necessary to secure social peace? Other doubts hang over the viability of an ever growing disaggregation and compartmentalization of value spheres—private/public, family/work, religious/secular, etc—each with its own 'autonomy'. In short, we do not know whether modernity will on balance undermine or renew the foundations of our institutions.

In what respects do standard economic indicators reflect the real wellbeing of national populations? This is a paradigmatic question—with a vengeance—because, as Hazel Henderson and others have shown, the GNP as a measure of 'development' does not even measure natural assets of a material kind, such as resources, climate, land, etc. Nor does it measure the depletion of non-renewable resources and environment costs. And still more fundamentally we see that GNP devalues, or completely ignores, precisely those non-material resources that count most both for production and well-being in First World countries. These include social peace, stable time horizons, generalized confidence in 'the System', human capital, intellectual creativity, cultural diversity and political stability. Most of these deficiencies stem, paradigmatically, from several systematically distorting assumptions (Bell 1981, p. 56) that are set into the architecture of both modern economic theories and the standard economic indicators. These assume, first, that wellbeing must be measured in terms of economic wants that are idiosyncratic and psychological and not in terms of social needs that are common to all (these are paradigmatically excluded). A second assumption is that social welfare is defined only in terms of the welfare of individuals; a third assumption prescribes that the individual is the only judge of his or her own welfare; and a fourth decrees that the social welfare of individuals cannot be compared. Moreover, despite incontrovertible evidence—even in First World nations (Veenhoven 1996)—of a strong correlation between inequality and wellbeing the economic indicators will not allow any reckoning of 'who gets what' to tarnish the blind artificiality of the metric. Distribution is allowed to enter the paradigm only in terms of its impact on economic efficiency. The effect is to reduce wellbeing to 'utilities' that are then measured only by prices through the market. On the positive side it must be accepted that the 'consumer society' is here to stay; that the market economy does indeed 'reduce complexity'; and even that it provides people with a structure of incentives that they largely accept. However, the greater problem is that the standard indicators assume a 'commodification of everything' that attacks those fundamental constituents of quality of life that people in First World nations routinely value much more highly than commodities, consumption and material wellbeing. A typical list in rough hierarchical order puts personal autonomy and good health at the top followed by friendships, social peace, domestic felicity and tension-free leisure: with material wellbeing near the bottom of the list and never accounting for much more than ten percent of the variance (Lane 1991).

Should wellbeing be measured subjectively or objectively? It is no accident that the English speaking nations with the strongest commitments to economic liberalism are those most wedded to subjective indices of wellbeing and quality of life. Typically these indices are based on self-reported life satisfactions given in answers to such standard questions as: 'how do you feel about "your life as a whole"; about "your income and financial situation"; about "your marriage"; about "your job"'; etc? The plausible defence for this approach is that 'the individual knows best' about his/her own life and that no one else, least of all experts of any description, should presume to judge how another person should evaluate his or her own life. This would violate individual rights and invite 'social engineering'. However, as with the economic indicators, the problem with this disingenuous prescription is a blindness to distribution that puts those with fewer resources in double jeopardy. More specifically, it ignores the regularly reported finding that something approaching one half of the most deprived people in any First World national population (typically those in the bottom decile of the income range with no assets and no jobs), will routinely say they are 'satisfied', or 'very satisfied', with their lives. It puts them in double jeopardy because their 'virtue' in having adapted to unfavorable circumstances is then met with the policy prescription that they are coping and no further call on resources is justified unless it is asked for. To avoid these distortions the European 'level of living' indicators have always concentrated on objective measures of wellbeing. These indices are based on questions that ask people, for example, not how they 'feel' about their housing but rather how many rooms they have to live in—and likewise with other items such as health, nutrition, spending money per person, holiday time, etc. The underlying assumption is that public policy, and where necessary welfare state provisions, should ensure that everyone has objectively adequate resources for a decent 'level of living'. The disadvantages are obvious: the costs are considerable and imply higher taxes and, on balance, a larger welfare state. But is it 'social engineering'? Surely not. Part of this answer is given in the fact that the Nordic societies which use this paradigm not only have the most equal distribution of income but also very high, or the highest, levels of subjective wellbeing as well. Moreover, these Nordic (and other western European) societies seem on most conventional economic criteria to have fared better than those more aggressively liberal economic nations that have chosen more anti-state, pro-market approaches to reform.

Globalization and Structural Change

Majid Tehranian succinctly explains globalization as a reconfiguration of the international political economy that is attempting to integrate pancapitalism around the interests of some 40,000 transnational corporations currently operating in over 100 countries. To define globalization in these terms correctly identifies the structural aspects of a process that is everywhere 'de-traditionalizing' settled ways of life, undermining established authority (whether benign or otherwise), and producing a hitherto undreamed of interaction of ethnicities, religions, world views and local and national cultures. All this is unleashing a breathtaking diversity of new human possibilities, both negative and positive.

What matters is that we understand the structural engines and impacts of a process that is brought on primarily through a program of economic restructuring and liberalization coordinated through such international economic organizations as the World Bank, the International Monetary Fund, the World Trade Organization, and the OECD. At the national level the structural adjustments have involved a change in the way nation-societies are organized that is perhaps best understood as a shift in the balance of coordination from states, governments and law on the one side to economies, markets and money on the other. The effect is to weaken the social protection afforded by governments to groups and individuals, and to increase their dependence on economies, markets, money and corporations. Indeed we may define globalization as a process that is driven by a neoliberal economic rationalism which assumes: (a) that markets offer, at least in principle, the most reliable means of setting values on all goods; and (b) that economies and markets can always, in principle, deliver better outcomes than states, governments and the law (Pusey 1998).

In the Anglophone neoliberal economies this process has been gathering pace for nearly a quarter of a century since economic restructuring was first packaged as a political program with the appearance in 1975 of the Report to the Trilateral Commission on the '*Crisis of Democracy*' (Crozier *et al.* 1975). I am dating the emergence of neoliberal economic rationalism as a dominant policy prescription from the publication of this report because, in my view, it turned economic rationalism cum neoliberalism from an economic doctrine into the political program that was first deployed by Australian Prime Minister, Malcolm Fraser, (in a soft form) and thereafter (the harder form) by the governments of Margaret Thatcher,

Ronald Reagan, the New Zealand Labor Party, and thereafter again in Australia by Prime Ministers Bob Hawke and Paul Keating. In most First World nations, but most especially in these Anglophone countries, this program of economic rationalization, structural adjustment, economic liberalization, *laissez faire* (the terms all mean the same thing) has produced several clearly marked structural changes (I will occasionally use Australian examples as illustrations) as follows:

(a) *A major redistribution of power, incomes, resources and opportunity* along the following lines:

from ... the public sector	to ... the private sector
from ... the bottom 70 percent of wage and salary earners	to ... the top ten percent
from ... wage and salary earners	to ... corporations
from ... small business	to ... big business
from ... the 'bush'	to ... the city
from ... consumers	to ... producers
from ... households	to ... the market

(b) *A selective running down of those civic associations and public sector institutions* that have traditionally served to moderate the distribution of income, to secure the mutual recognition of social needs, rights, entitlements, and of collective identity and common citizenship. We see a program of funding cuts and of sponsored challenges to the legitimacy of community and social advocacy organizations (e.g., with respect to tenants' rights, social services, environmental protection, minority rights, consumer protection, media regulation and community health); and, similarly, attacks on public provision, and on basic 'public infrastructure' institutions such as the High Court, Parliamentary committees of review, houses of review, the Industrial Commission, the publicly owned media and local governments.

(c) *A transformation of the broad middle class* as job re-engineering, downsizing, unemployment, underemployment and the casualization of work have variously fractured, unsettled, 'hollowed out' and weakened the broad middle class.

(d) *An experience of enormous change without rewards* as forced structural economic adjustment has coincided with stagnating or falling real standards of living for most of the population and produced the first strong economic recoveries in living memory in which few, or none, of the rewards have been shared with the broad majority of the population.

Impacts on Quality of Life

Impacts on regions and communities

Increasing unemployment and falling incomes are concentrated in urban and rural areas with populations that become increasingly dependent on falling welfare provisions, poor schools and poor access to new jobs. House prices fall and the middle class exits as the affected areas retain or attract disproportionate concentrations of young people and new immigrants with low skills, and poorer aged persons without the resources to support households. The result is that several forms of deprivation interact to produce 'ghetto' and underclass conditions. Pre-existing forms of class, status and gender stratification are overlaid with spatial, inter-generational and ethnic/racial inequalities in complex and self-reinforcing patterns that together attack both subjective wellbeing and the objective foundations for quality of life (especially social peace, personal security, stable households, and paid work) (OECD 1997).

Impacts on households and families

Stagnating or falling living standards, falling real single incomes, unemployment, under-employment, insecure job tenure and casual work all combine with rising real housing costs and educational expenses to increase the real financial and social burdens of household/family formation. Consequently family formation is abandoned or postponed by an average of several years (or takes place in a context of unwanted dependencies, as with single parents who are forced to move back 'home' with parents.) Family units with dependent children run out of coping strategies: they take on more work, give up shared leisure time (weekends, evenings), relocate in search of better employment, and incur unserviceable housing and consumer debt with mortgages on the deceitful promises of improvement to their living standards in the future.

Impacts on the person

Objectively precarious market incomes, insecure work tenure, and increasing separation and divorce rates impact on personal expectations and combine to shorten time horizons in both the private and work spheres at the same time. Persons are forced to reinvent themselves as time managers, risk takers and strategic actors in an environment offering less generalized confidence in 'the System' and fewer resources for the temporal projection of the self forward into realistic and fulfilling futures. As the public and moral environment of the self becomes more unsupportive, disenchanted and 'saturated with contingency', a greater number of people are affected by chronic insecurities that overburden their personal relationships and their sense of wellbeing. The chances of living well, or even flourishing in the face of these new uncertainties, are unequally distributed and stratified along lines that are increasingly visible. Those with the material and intellectual resources to 'make the world their oyster' (typically those in the top ten percent of the income distribution) will experience this dimension of globalization as full of stimulation, challenge, opportunity, choice; and perhaps as an emancipation from 'traditional' constraints. In this increasingly abstract environment others, with fewer cognitive problem-solving skills and with less capacity for critical self-reflection, will increasingly take risks and make 'mistakes' with their material assets and resources, and with their personal relationships. They will succumb to excessive demands for continuous self-transformation and 'individual adjustment' with which they cannot adequately cope.

Impacts on sociability and association

The volatility of the labor market and the pressure on persons and families to relocate in search of employment endangers or reduces the social support available from friends, from other family members (grandparents, parents, and siblings) and from neighbours. Individuals lose social skills and variety in their contacts with significant others as well as a broader understanding of how others live. They retreat into a private sphere that is defined passively, and with reference mainly to mood states, as 'rest and relaxation'. These factors together diminish the energies and commitments necessary to participate, actively and creatively, in civic, community, and political arenas beyond the workplace. This leads to a running down of 'social capital'.

Addressing the Issues for Reform

Restoring collective intelligence to public policy

There is need to restore and enhance the capacity of peak public policy institutions to generate impartial and broadly informed policy advice for ministers and parliaments. Over the last 20 years, narrowly trained technicians, most of them economists and business professionals, have taken over the top echelons of the policy apparatus and reduced public policy to economic policy, narrowly conceived in asocial or anti-social terms, as whatever structural, distributional and institutional changes best serve the interests of corporations. These policy 'elites' are ill-equipped to address the basic long run failures to their own free market economic policy paradigm. There is need for a new corps of more broadly educated and responsive public policy professionals with both a 'hands on' experience of real living conditions *and* the intellectual strengths to transcend the limits of what has become a deaf and self-referential economic paradigm.

Restoring institutions and social capital

In Anglophone nations public policy has tended to follow the mistaken assumption that political participation and deliberation are inherently frustrating, and hence that markets offer the only reliable means of resolving conflicts and reducing complexity. This has gone hand-in-hand with the assumption that 'the economy' must have functional primacy in every sphere and with a perverse redefinition of public, civic and welfare institutions as 'vested interests' that must then be cast as the targets of 'reform'. Instead they should be included in a larger circle of partners in social reconstruction and development.

Internalizing the 'externalities'

Aggressive and wide-ranging programs of economic 'reform' have followed a perverse economic logic that has set economic growth, and even increases in standard of living, in contradiction both to subjective wellbeing and to objective quality of life. These pathologies are accurately captured in some of the more sophisticated alternative economic indicators such as the Bennet Index of leading Cultural Indicators, the Fordham Index of Social Health and, most notably, the Genuine Progress Indicator. With these and other instruments there is a need to more accurately measure the social costs of production and distribution; to 'reinternalize the externalities' (pollution, unemployment, stress, defensive expenditures, community breakdown etc.); and to civilize and re-regulate the behaviour of corporations in the light of more comprehensive indices of real and sustainable development.

Moderating the redistribution of incomes and resources

Most Anglophone nations have experienced a marked upward redistribution of incomes that generally reduces subjective wellbeing, creates damaging social conflicts, endangers social cohesion and effective governance, and negatively impacts on the health of populations. Job sharing and active labor market programs must be combined with social security provisions to gradually raise the living standards of households in the bottom quintile of the income range (without creating reactive resentments in the middle class). The sharing and active labor market programs must bc combined with social security provisions to gradually raise the living standards of households in the bottom quintile of the income range (without creating reactive resentments in the middle class). The effectiveness and accountability of governments should be measured on performance in reconciling investment policies with a more equitable redistribution of resources and incomes.

A restoration of the public sphere

Nations suffer long-term damage from 'elite politics' that promote a 'government of corporations, by corporations, for corporations, that is busy fooling all of the people all of the time.' There is need for new 'constitutional' guarantees for active citizenship that are better suited to contemporary circumstances in which the privately owned media have accrued enormous power at the expense of other voices in the public sphere. In these new conditions where communication is increasingly impossible without material resources, public support must be available, at arm's length, to any *bona fide* group with a message, program, grievance or claim to public attention. Legally enforceable ethical codes must be developed to prohibit cynical abuses of the media for private ends where these are damaging to social cohesion and respect for others. The strategic (willful) subversion of communications and of institutional solidarity and connection among those who are perceived to be opponents must be proscribed as an evil.

Prospect and Discussion

In pondering what ought to be done we return to evaluative judgments that were made at the beginning; and to a few general, and I hope cautious, observations that have been implicit in what we have said so far.

In making judgments about the consequences of high modernity for quality of life in these First World nations we would seem to be looking at cultural impacts that are mainly positive and structural impacts that are mainly negative. Multiculturalism, cultural diversity and the universalistic moral values generated by the green, feminist, and peace movements must all be counted among the fruits of modernity—most of them well on the way to being institutionally secured in First World countries. But structurally, we see instead a caving in of most of the economic 'guarantees' that an earlier post-war generation took for granted. For the vast majority of individuals who must still earn their livelihood from wages and salaries, economic restructuring delivers a future that looks bleaker by the day. In these nations young people are increasingly excluded from full time work until they reach their mid or late twenties and, on present trends, they can expect to be pushed out of the labor market by the age of 55. With increasing life expectancy and decreasing public provision for retirement support, no one knows where they will find the resources to sustain them for some further 25 years or more. Equally, at the front end of the equation, no knows what will happen to household formation and to families that are fast running out of resources and coping strategies. Since we have already passed the point where small incremental adjustments to the distribution of income could fill in the structural 'black holes', we must assume that the social repercussions will be enormous.

This observation delivers its own judgments on the limitations of the conventional economic indicators and, more broadly, on the market as the single best means, or even the only means, of coordinating nation societies. We know that cultures and civil societies are dynamic, resilient, creative, and adaptive. But do we know their limits? We know that we cannot plausibly recreate the remembered past or use some *status quo ante* as a static point of reference to 'freeze' a process of structural change that always leads from a future that is largely unknown. Self-renewing and inherently innovative modern cultures have, for the most part, produced the needed intellectual and moral resources to deal with what sociologists have for a long time called the 'unanticipated consequences of purposive action'. Yet we seem to be entering a situation in which these capacities may be damaged or exhausted—if only because the changes outstrip our capacity to make sense of what is happening and to project ourselves forward into a 'normal' future. In these so-called advanced post-industrial societies it is well recognized that the fuels for economic development are no longer material resources like iron, coal or water but rather culture itself. The resurgence of religious fundamentalisms and of tribalisms of various kinds deliver their own unheeded warnings. The war on tradition, meaning, memory and coherence could be dangerous! Increasing rates of crime, suicide and stress-related breakdowns should be read as signs that cultures are thinning as they are put into the furnace to force new economic growth that is then wrongly measured with indices that are incapable of measuring the social and cultural costs to social solidarity and quality of life.

A third flaw in the self-understanding of the most ardent pacesetters of 'reform' in the First World has to do with attitudes towards government, or, more accurately, the prejudice against government. Neoliberal governments have become instruments for an economic re-engineering of society that is driven, with naked power, by multinational corporations and big business interests. As the momentum of economic restructuring increases, governments compete with each other to deliver privatization, corporate welfare, 'competition policy', lower corporate rents and taxes, the destruction of labor unions, labor market deregulation, and cuts to government programs. Gradually national populations are treated not as the originating subjects of good (representative) government but rather as the objects of politics, and as 'material' that has to be manipulated and re-moulded. Inasmuch as this is done in good faith it is driven by the belief that the market alone can 'reduce complexity', and hence relieve governments of burdens and obligations that they cannot ostensibly honor. Money and prices will settle all or nearly all the conflicts that arise from the clash of incommensurate value claims in the modern order. What is not seen is that the 'reforms' unleash, on an unprecedented scale, a huge surplus of new uncertainties, new complexities, and new social needs, that only governments can properly address. Indeed the reforms have committed most First World societies to enter the new millennium with less government—and with weakened institutions—at a time when they palpably need more (good) government—and stronger institutions—to deal with mounting problems presented by demographic change, the misallocation of resources, environmental dangers, an uncontrolled upward redistribution of incomes, mass unemployment, over-work, destroyed social time, broken communities and social and ethnic strife. In the face of such problems the underlying assumption of the new global policy apparatus is still that the consent of the governed, and legitimacy itself, can be replaced by the 'dull compulsion' of the market—without a system breakdown! Even rising popular cynicism towards elites in all these nations is frequently welcomed as another positive sign of success in 'reducing expectations' of government. And this is occurring in the completely new circumstance where already very high living standards are running into structural limits, and more seriously still, in the face of seething, and potentially reactionary, discontents among the broad middle classes on which stability most depends.

Most of the contributors to this volume believe that (economic) globalization has, in varying degrees, undercut the power of governments to control its negative impacts on wellbeing and quality of life in the third millennium. They also agree that global civil society, and global democracy, are, as Majid Teranain puts it, the *sine qua non* for the survival of the world. Yet no one seems very sure about what this would mean for the future of government and of the institutional architecture of First World societies. With a characteristically American leaning, Hazel Henderson seems to have given up on government altogether. These several uncertainties leave us wondering how a global commons would be organized. My answer is that the creative energies of NGOs and of other citizen, community and regional organizations will not be enough to restrain or control corporate power without strong and effective governments.

I also believe that appropriate models are already available from among an array of different combinations of capitalist market economy, government/state sector, and civil society. On closer view we see that in the contemporary world we have not a single all-or-nothing capitalism but more probably five models: 'crony' capitalism (in Indonesia and Korea, for example); the Anglophone radical free market model that is the rule in what Nettl once called the 'great stateless societies' of the US and Britain; the Nordic welfare state model; the western European corporatist model (Germany and Holland); and the Mediterranean model. Even among the three continental European groupings there are great differences in the roles that are assigned to markets, governments, and to families and civil societies. Comprehensive comparative empirical studies of the western European democracies point to the superior performance of the Nordic countries, and to some degree also, the corporatist nations (Holland, Germany) in delivering strong social *and* economic welfare without too much damage to civil society and social solidarity (Vogel 1998). Many of these most successful nations are, perhaps for this very reason, under enormous coercive pressures from the European Commission to fall in with a diluted version of the Anglophone model. Indeed the criteria for choosing among these contending First World capitalisms are clear. Individuals in democratic, plural, First World nations will have the best chance of flourishing in societies with strong markets, strong governments and strong civil societies. If any one sphere 'colonizes' another, human wellbeing is endangered as it is today by the economic imperialism of the new global order.

CHAPTER 9

Globalization, Quality of Life and Women in India

Bharati Ray

This chapter argues that the chief aim of governance is to improve the quality of life of people, and the instrument of governance, that is, the State or any other body entrusted with the power of governance, must aspire to achieve it. The question may easily be asked, quality of life for whom—for all people? For the rich? For the middle class? For the man on the street? For women? For a section of people, for the majority or the minority, and so on? Does the impact of globalization affect all in the same manner, or has it varying effects on different segments of society? There are obviously tensions within classes and communities, and therefore what ensures good quality for one group may not do the same for others. In a democracy, the greatest good of the greatest number is the accepted guiding principle. In this chapter, which focuses on the issue in the context of the Republic of India, we will look at the problem in an Indian setting and from the women's standpoint. Having said that, it is necessary to assert that it is the existence of peace, both internal and external, which is the prime necessity for safeguarding good governance. And therefore, any policy which foments internal factionalism or dissension or disturbs peaceful co-existence in the world will act against ensuring a good quality of life.

Quality of Life: The Indian Context

What is this concept of quality of life? Simply stated, it is grounded in the belief that it is not just the quantitative measurement of a nation's wealth, but the qualitative assessment that is equally important. The GNP *per capita* is not the sole indication of a nation's progress; a wealthy country does not necessarily connote that its citizens enjoy a high quality of life. If suicide, mental illness or violence afflict a people's existence, would we agree that their quality of life is commendable? In trying to evaluate the standard of life, no doubt we have to take note of the basic needs of people—security of food, of shelter, of drinking water, access to healthcare and education, and right to employment—and so on. However, we must remember another equally important aspect for ensuring good quality of life—psychological security—and which generates peace, happy family life, tolerance for others and togetherness. And we must explore whether human rights are respected, and investigate whether there is any disparity between races, classes or gender.

From earliest times, Indian culture has emphasised *atmajnan* (self-realization), *shanti* (peace) and *ananda* (physical and mental happiness or bliss) as the ultimate objectives in human life. D.P. Chattopadhyaya (1988 and 1997) has competently dwelt on the subject, after the Indian savant of the 20th century, Sri Aurobindo (Aurobindo 1972), and has stressed that the Indian ideal encompasses both the physical and the mental states of existence and requires the fulfilment of some basic physical, sexual as well as spiritual needs as for example, education, freedom from strife, employment, security, sexual fulfilment, religious duties. India has, moreover, from time immemorial advocated universal love, universal tolerance, and what is described in modern terms as universal co-existence. In the *Upanishads*, in Buddha's teachings, and even in the *anushashans* (edicts) of a king—King Ashoka—the same principles have been emphasized. If this be the age-old goal sanctioned by Indian culture, this chapter would argue that an Indian person's quality of life would be determined by his or her 'capability' of achieving the goal.

In other words, a person's wellbeing may be understood in terms of his or her 'ability to do valuable acts or reach valuable states of being'. The expression capability, says Sen, is meant to represent 'the alternative combinations of things a person is able to do or be—the various 'functionings' he or she can achieve' (Sen 1993). The capability approach to a person's wellbeing would, therefore, entail assessing that person's ability to achieve various valuable functionings and the ability to choose from a combination of alternatives in leading a life.

What are those functionings—for doing as well as for being? To be free from hunger and diseases? To acquire economic self-reliance? To be employed according to one's choice and potential? To satisfy basic sexual desires? To be guaranteed human rights and dignity? To enjoy some means of freedom—religious, social and mental? To be psychologically secure and be happy and peaceful? I would argue that it is a person's ability to have some amount of all these functionings as well as the availability of opportunity of choice from different combinations of these that would ensure for him or her a good life. Given this definition of quality of life, it is our purpose to examine the impact of globalization on Indian women's life-situations and to explore the possible ways of improving the situation, if necessary.

Globalization: The Indian Scene

Globalization is based on the concept that the globe is a single unit for decision-making. It means free movement of goods, services and capital throughout the world. It connotes the opening up of national economies to global markets and a reduction in the role of the State to shape national policies. However, the interaction between developed and developing countries poses some critical questions. To what extent should globalization be allowed to undermine the State's capacity to formulate policies, especially for the benefit of the poor? Should not globalization also connote free movement of labor? When there is no discrimination between national and international capital, should there be differentiation between national and international labor? Could globalization be a political construct, promoting but limited globalization? Further, globalization has brought in more knowledge-intensive and capital-intensive industries. The question is: at whose initiative, and on whose terms? What will be the mechanism to check the adverse effects on a developing country's economy and society, if free inflow of capital is followed by free outflow as well? And finally, has the policy been conducive to globalization of love, of compassion, of co-operation, and the formation of a global human society based on equity and equality?

As is well known, structural change, an integral part of globalization, is a process of transformation of agricultural economies to industrially developed ones and the process is largely shaped by exposure to international markets both in terms of production and of consumption. Obviously, the crucial factor in garnering the benefits of the process depends on a country's ability to compete internationally. But the world order is unequal, so competition is also unequal. The question naturally emerges: how far can a developing country like India meet the challenges of unequal competition, and how far can it absorb the shocks of inequality in its socio-economic system? Since globalization is meant to work through domestic structural adjustment policies (SAP), by shifting emphasis from the State to the market, the impact of SAP depends largely on a particular country's pre-existing circumstances, infrastructure and policy framework. How would it affect the teeming indigent masses, who form the majority of Indian people? And, in a developing country like India, does the SAP as a policy package serve the interests of women, especially poor women, both at home and in the workplace? Should not there be a number of 'safety nets' provided by the State and international agencies to counteract adverse effects, if any, of SAP?

The Gender Dimension

In most countries of the world—if not all—women form a disadvantaged section *vis-à-vis* men. India is no exception. If the country's economy has to fight an unequal battle with the developed countries in the international market, its society is doubly burdened by the inequities suffered by women, enhanced by the effects of this unfavorable competition. It is true that a section of Indian women—the elite and the upper middle class—has gained by the exposure to the global network. More women are engaged in business enterprises, in international platforms like the Inter-Parliamentary Union, and have greater career opportunities as a result of international networking. Freer movement of goods and capital is helpful to this section. In India, statistics show that the unemployment rate for educated women (and for that matter for educated men as well) has declined considerably throughout the late 1970s to early 1990s, though it is still very high. It was 22.36 percent of the total female population in 1993–94, *vis-à-vis* 41.89 percent in 1977–78 (Hirway 1996). The work participation rate for women with graduation or higher level educational qualification in rural India was 22.0 percent in 1983 and 29.3 percent in 1993–94, and in urban India 27.9 percent and 28.2 percent respectively (Deshpande and Deshpande 1998). There has been some increase in highly educated women attaining coveted positions in Government services, and indeed the increase of women in such jobs has often been at the cost to men, as Table 1 indicates. It has to be borne in mind that these jobs were opened to women in the late 1950s and some restrictions on women (e.g., regarding marriage of women in the Indian Administrative Service) were only gradually removed.

But what about the majority? To identify only a few areas of concern regarding them:

Table 1 Personnel by Sex in Some Important All India and Central Services

	1993		1994		1995		1996	
	M	F	M	F	M	F	M	F
Indian Administrative Service	4427	455	4427	483	4473	492	4546	501
Indian Customs/Excise Service	1502	107	1519	112	1520	117	1531	130
Indian Foreign Service	507	57	489	59	481	66	NA	NA
Indian Revenue Service	2032	224	2022	246	1980	276	NA	NA

Source: Government of India 1997. Women in India: A Statistical Profile, 158–159

First, since globalization is introducing technological inputs, women are being marginalized in economic activities, men traditionally being offered new scopes of learning and training. Scholars of women's studies have pointed out that women have gained very little from technological changes taking place in India (Bannerjee 1996). It has bypassed them and has caused the economy to undergo a transformation biased in favour of the males, and degeneration of occupations specific to women. Inventions and innovations do not normally occur in the sectors/occupations where women predominate (Ghosh and Mukhopadhyay 1984; Ghosh 1990). As a consequence, female workers are joining the informal sector or casual labor force more than ever before. In agriculture, for instance, technological change has adversely affected female employment. While new rice technology has given rise to higher use of female labor, the increased workload for women is in operations that are unrecorded, and often unpaid, since these fall within the category of home production activities. Again, for female casual labor (wage employed) in agriculture, technology has been found to exert strong negative effects on their employment. For example, application of commercial chemical inputs (fertilizers and other plant treatment), essential for new (HYV) rice technology, is done exclusively by men—displacing women in the process. Women normally perform similar activities for traditional varieties of rice (Ghosh and Mukhopadhyay 1988). Furthermore, women continue to work in areas/operations where there has been little technical progress. In most activities, especially agriculture, household industries and informal sectors, there is a sex-specific allocation of different operations involved. Women typically work in the fields or in unhealthy work environments, spending most of their time in unpleasant, tedious and laborious jobs which have seen no innovation over the years (Ghosh 1995).

Although agriculture is the main occupation of Indians, other sectors of the economy have been adversely affected by aggressive market competition, more so where women are especially involved. Obviously, for industry the process of marginalization of women has been more marked. Without any professional skill and technological know-how, women were edged out of high productivity manufacturing sectors and left to the tertiary and service sectors.

Again, fishing, a lifetime occupation in coastal India, changed its character first with the rising demand for prawn (the 'pinkgold') in the international market and then the advent of the fishing trawlers from European countries and the use of 'inappropriate technology.' The country fisherman, with their small fishing boats and meager capital, are no match for the huge capital and technology invested in the foreign apparatus. Many of them were thrown out of employment, and many became impoverished. Women, who play a crucial role in indigenous fishing practices, looking after the nets, the catch, the preservation process and the sale, were deprived of their work and the opportunity to add to the family income. Although in traditional fishing communities, women were not paid for their labor, nonetheless, they are the beneficiaries of the family earnings. What is worrisome is that fishing trawlers are mercilessly exploiting coastal water for many a mile—a distance not reached by local crafts—and this is reducing the fish population in the sea. This problem is specially acute in Kerala, the leading maritime state of India, where the policy of 'the judicious exploitation of maritime resources, giving primacy to the accumulated skills of the fishermen' had been traditionally followed (Kurien and Thankappan Acharia 1994). It may be mentioned here that in the Budget session of the Parliament of India 1998, in the Rajya Sabha (Upper House), a vociferous debate took place, the members demanding a total ban on trawlers. While a partial ban has already been imposed for a period of time, the Government has promised to look into the problem.

Examples may be multiplied by referring to the weavers, the food processing industries, the dairy business, in all of which women have a crucial part to play—not always paid but as part of family participation in self-employed occupation. In these spheres, the globalized market economy has hurt women by reducing subsidies, importing drinks like *Coca-cola* and foreign processed food, and in fact through the media creating a new food-and-drink taste instead of the traditional one. There is a craze for the so-called global brands. *McDonalds* have opened their food shops, designer shoes, tee-shirts and jeans are being made popular through aggressive advertising, and the indigenous style of cooking or dressing is yielding place to the cosmopolitan. The common people's—specially women's—homespun and homemade clothes or recipes are increasingly being spurned and hence adversely affected.

In an overall assessment, as Hirway has shown, there has been an increase in female employment since 1987–88, but the growth rate has been fairly low—1.27 percent per annum during 1987–88 to 1993–94—and much lower than the earlier growth rates of female employment—2.06 percent during 1977–78 to 1983 and 1.71 percent during 1983 to 1987–88—and the gap between the growth rates of male and female employment has gradually increased over the years. Moreover, the growth rate of female employment has been higher in urban areas and lower in rural areas—only 0.87 percent. Hirway argues that this is due to the growth of production in industries (5.10 percent per annum), and a growth in female employment in the tertiary sector—specially the service sector—and that the low employment in the rural sector is due to the relatively low rate of growth of agricultural production (3.85 percent per annum), or/and low growth of the non-formal sector in the economy (Hirway 1996). An analysis of the statistics of the past five NSS Rounds, including the 50th Round (1993–94) shows the percentage increasing from 38.6 in 1987–88 to 42.9 in 1993–94 (Table 2).

What is more alarming is that the increase in female employment has been at the cost of self-employed women. Their percentage has declined from 53.1 to 48.8 during this period. Their share of regular employment has remained static overall. Importantly, however, in the rural area both self-employment of women and their regular employment have declined, and casual labor has increased from 40.2 to 45.3 percent. Deshpande and Deshpande, while analyzing the favorable and unfavorable impact of liberalization on the labor market in India, have also concluded that rural women, classified as workers by their usual status, formed a smaller share of their population after liberalization than before, and that regular wage and salaried women among them lost absolutely: 'Fewer of them were employed and mostly on wages that failed to buy for them the basket of goods they bought before liberalization.' Further, research based on the NSSO and Government of India's Economic Survey,

Table 2 Percentage Distribution of Workers (UPS) by Category of Employment

	Rural			Urban			Total		
	M	F	T	M	F	T	M	F	T
Self-Employment									
50	56.9	51.3	55.1	41.1	36.4	40.3	52.9	48.8	51.9
48	60.3	54.8	58.6	40.8	36.4	39.9	55.6	52.2	54.7
47	59.2	52.3	57.1	42.5	41.9	42.4	55.3	51.0	54.1
46	55.2	54.5	55.0	40.4	43.9	41.1	48.0	51.0	48.8
45	59.1	56.6	58.4	41.3	43.5	41.7	55.3	54.9	55.2
43	57.5	55.1	56.7	41.0	38.6	40.5	53.8	53.1	53.6
Regular: Salaried Employment									
50	08.5	03.4	07.2	42.7	35.5	41.5	17.0	08.3	14.7
48	08.4	03.5	06.9	39.8	33.9	38.8	15.9	07.7	13.6
47	09.3	03.8	07.7	40.3	30.7	38.6	16.6	07.3	14.1
46	13.1	04.5	10.6	44.5	30.1	41.7	28.3	13.1	24.4
45	10.0	03.4	08.0	42.0	33.0	40.0	16.9	07.1	14.2
43	10.4	04.7	08.6	44.4	34.7	42.7	18.0	08.3	15.2
Casual Wage Employment									
50	34.6	45.3	37.7	16.2	28.1	18.2	31.0	42.9	33.5
48	31.3	41.7	34.5	19.4	29.7	21.3	28.5	40.1	31.7
47	31.5	43.9	35.2	17.2	27.4	19.0	28.1	41.7	31.8
46	31.7	41.0	34.4	15.1	26.0	17.2	23.7	25.9	26.8
45	30.9	40.0	33.6	16.7	23.5	17.9	27.8	38.0	30.6
43	32.1	40.2	34.7	14.6	26.7	16.8	28.2	38.6	31.2

Source: NNS Rounds (cited Hirway 1996).

1996–97 indicates that 'gender-based wage differentials widened among regular wage/salaried rural and urban workers' (Deshpande and Deshpande 1998). Women were always paid less than men, but more so after liberalization than before. What quality of life does globalization offer to this colossal segment of women comprising a third of India's working population without any job security, or appropriate wages or prospect of improving their life situation? What forms of security, *shanti* and *ananda*? What can be their impetus for developing concepts of international citizenship or co-existence?

One important point must not escape our attention while discussing globalization. Consumerism, fanned by captivating advertisements (enormously exaggerating the usefulness or attraction of the articles), has come to shape the market in India, and the pattern of demand in India. Consequently, not just the Indian market, or the Indian women workers, but Indian culture itself is under assault from outside. At the recently concluded All-India Sociological Conference held at Aligarh, in an interesting paper entitled 'Pepsitisation of Society in India,' C.A. Somnasekharappa, of Karnatka University, India, observed that 'Globalization of the Indian market has led to the over-riding effect of Western culture and civilization on our society so much so that in every walk of life in India, there is a conspicuous presence of Westerness' (Somnasekharappa 1998). Today's Indian youth are not thinking of quality of life in the Indian cultural connotation; they are perceiving it from the Western angle. And there is competition to outshine neighbors and friends in trying to adopt the latest fashions in imitation of the rich and the West as mirrored in advertisements, Western movies (and imitating Hindi movies) and cable TV. The whole concept of Indian social life is facing an unprecedented crisis. And as a fall-out, women—who in almost all the countries around the world, and certainly in India, are regarded as the preservers and upholders of tradition—are worse off socially and losers of the traditional position in the family.

There is an unfortunate impact of the swift economic changes on Indian family life, especially on women. SAP has led to the unemployment of a large number of men, as global competition forced employers to mechanize and rationalize labour. This has increased men's (the main bread earners') frustration, tension and fear of job insecurity, and also affected those who are intermittent and casual workers, or those who fear laying off; women are being made to pay the social cost. Family violence has increased, rape has become an everyday event, and dowry deaths (a fall-out of consumerism) are escalating (Ray 1999). It is not possible to have a true picture of the home scenario, and hence any perfect statistics, since most cases are

Table 3 Incidence of Crime Against Women by Crime Head 1990, 1994

	Rape	Dowry Deaths	Torture	Molestation	Sexual Harrassment
1990	9,518	4,836	13,450	20,194	8,620
1994	12,351	4,935	25,946	24,117	10,496

Source: National Crimes Record Bureau (Cited in Government of India 1997, Women in India: A Statistical Profile)

not reported—tradition and social pressure operate against it—and far too many are not properly investigated. We can only cite government statistics, unsatisfactory though they be (See Table 3).

This is happening in a country where women were/are traditionally held in high regard socially and where incidence of torture of women and molestation of women were not so conspicuous as to attract newspaper reporting or demand police intervention, although some incidents must always have been there.

The economy, strained to the utmost under the challenges of globalization, is unable to bear the burden of necessary healthcare and educational expenses. The weaker sections, especially the women, are denied the physical care they deserve. Maternal mortality is extremely high (2.3 percent in 1994 according to the Annual Report of the Office of the Registrar General), anaemia is common, nutrition deficient, (Chatterjee 1996) and women die in large numbers from communicable diseases while increasing use of amniocentesis is killing yet-to-be-born women, (Mallick 1998), over 30 percent of women are illiterate, and the drop-out rate among girls in schools is excessive (37 percent after the primary stage). Skyrocketing food prices and an export-oriented cropping pattern in agriculture contributes to women's declining access to food and nutrition. The recent dearth of onions and potatoes in the Indian markets leading to a great outcry of the people is a pointer to the growing essential food crisis in the country, while imported luxury food articles are widely available in the market. The less than satisfactory public distribution system deteriorates under the SAP—there is a growing demand in Parliament for a better organized PDS—and brings extra sufferings to women, especially to women heading households (and women-headed households are on the increase in India mainly because of the increasing occurrence of divorce, separation and desertion).

There is, thus, hardly any ability for the majority of Indian women for valuable functioning; the capability to choose from alternatives is conspicuous by its absence. In terms of the age-old Indian concept of life, the SAP has not provided any physical or psychological base for *ananda*, the increase in violence on women makes a mockery of peace, and lack of education and nutrition is not the best means for attaining self-realization.

This is not to suggest that all this is the result of globalization, but to assert that globalization/SAP has not ensured a good quality of life for the majority of Indian women; on the other hand it has reinforced the existing gender inequalities. The key point in this discussion is that for a developing country like India, where infrastructure is inadequate, resources limited and society slow to change, free and unregulated competition with powerful developed countries cannot prove to be the best policy. Unequal competition, like all forms of inequality, is not beneficial to the disadvantaged.

Question of Accountability

It is one of the axioms of this chapter that good governance promoting the citizens' quality of life is a duty of the Government, which must be accountable to the people. The international organizations formed to advance national and international peace and prosperity also have a responsibility to the weaker sections of the population. If the poor countries of the world become poorer and face acute financial crises in order to undergo domestic structural adjustments under external market mandates, the international communities have the responsibility for playing an effective role to counteract the forces. The implications of SAP for poverty have been debated by economists, social scientists and policy framers, as well as the United Nations. This led the World Bank to prescribe certain mechanisms to provide some support to the indigent people at least for a temporary period during the transition to a market economy. The Bank advocated the creation of an 'enabling environment' for the private sector. It also urged the State to intervene to formulate effective policies to alleviate poverty. The poor people can certainly improve their situation, if they are given the required support. Roy ably argues that there is plenty of evidence to indicate that the poor can improve 'the quality of their life and create sustainable self-supporting status', provided their need for such critical inputs as land, credit, employment and basic infrastructures like education, healthcare, drinking water, housing etc. are met (Roy 1997).

The question is: whose responsibility is it to provide means to satisfy these needs? How do we do this? And what will be the implementing agencies? Obviously, the main responsibility lies on the State and, therefore, it must not shy away from intervention whenever necessary. It is for the State to provide basic education and healthcare, to guarantee employment to all (so that the poor do not remain poor), and adopt a number of poverty alleviation policies. The civil society has to be made an active partner of the State in this difficult task. The NGOs, which in a way represent community endeavor, should be enlisted for support. They enjoy a greater access to and communion with the poor, who have to be motivated to organize themselves for their own survival. In the ultimate analysis, they must be part of the strategy to generate the quality of their life-situations. Here one may mention the example of the NGOs in Bangladesh which are effectively networking among women and building up an aware women's movement.

With almost one-third of the world's absolute poor living in India, the government has to take special measures to give protection to them. The public distribution system has to be streamlined, employment schemes formulated and access to education and health provided at the expense of the Government. The Government must invest more in infrastructure, credit and technology that can be easily adapted to the local environment. In the specific context of India, traditionally an agricultural country, it is sound policy to promote agricultural growth and invest in the agricultural sector, since that will induce industrial growth as well. For that, it is essential to offer some subsidies to the poor agriculturists, because if left entirely to the market forces, with their low *per capita* income, they will not be able to survive ruthless competition from the external competitors and multinationals. Although this approach will be at odds with the basic tenor of SAP, it may be strongly argued that if our peasants—who form the bulk of our population—become prey of unequal competition and of starvation, for whose benefit is the economic transformation consequent on globalization meant? While it is true that the process of globalization cannot be reversed, it is equally true that in the Indian context the State has to be combined with the market in order to enhance the country's development. India's globalization policy has to be modified so as to direct foreign investment flow in a way that it can dovetail with the domestic infrastructure and domestic development priorities. For example, both domestic and export-oriented growth have to be stimulated in 'labor absorbing and skill enhancing' areas. Simultaneously, labor, when redundant on the closure of any sick industry, has to be retrained for absorption in the new industries that might come up.

As far as women are concerned, the problem is much more acute; they constitute the largest portion of the country's poor, and do not have the wherewithal—as explained earlier—to improve. And especially in India women have the sole responsibility to serve food to the family. The unemployed son comes home—as sons tend to live with parents until settled and employed—and asks his mother for a meal. 'Give me food, mother, I am hungry.' And the mother has to try her best to provide food for the hungry son. Special efforts, therefore, need to be made to empower women politically and economically. What can those be?

In the first place, the State has to provide support by adopting poverty alleviation policies, both short-term and long-term. The most important of these must be generating employment. Here the quality of State intervention is crucial. Mere employment is not enough, it has to be fruitful and conducive to national development and, therefore, carefully planned. The 'safety nets,' like the Social Funds (SFs), for poverty reduction have not been very effective. In fact while foreign finance is welcome, foreign designing and planning may not be best suited to local needs. Locally designed programs such as the Maharashtra Employment Guarantee Scheme, which served as a model for the Rural Landless Employment Guarantee Programme (later merged with the National Rural Employment Programme into the Jwahar Rozgar Yojana), are expected to be more useful (Roy 1997). To give women access to credit—so essential for self-employed women—the Government of India has set up Mahila Kosh Nidhi. Experience shows that women return credit much more honestly than men. The Bangladesh experiment of Grameen Bank has given an excellent paradigm. If followed and expanded, it can prove to be a boon to women and enable self-employed women to be economically self-reliant and even well-to-do.

Second, high quality basic education has to be provided free of cost to women. It is often claimed that an educated mother makes educated children. Be that as it may, the education of women is of critical importance for their own sake, and to enable them to lead a better life. Financial capital through foreign investment cannot answer India's special concerns. We need to have more human capital and, if a new term can be coined, more 'women-capital'. The State has to arrange for the access of women to greater healthcare and nutrition, and chart a widespread consciousness-raising agenda. In this area, the NGOs can be of active help. International organizations can also furnish models and short-term financial help.

Third, the State has to intervene to create opportunities for women to acquire skills and to get training in technology, initially low-tech, and then high-tech. The gender bias against women going in for science and technology can to a great extent be reduced by the State adopting a positive approach. And in the context of the fast-developing/changing world economy and mind-boggling technological innovations/inventions that are taking and going to take place, women's acquiring higher skills in the new processes is essential. Lawrence Schlemmer observes in the context of South Africa, 'I have reached the conclusion that intensive training for self-reliant small-scale production is essential' (Schlemmer 1998). So it is in the case of Indian women, especially for new technologies.

But then, it is equally essential to see that women are not driven away from their traditional skills in the lure of the 'new learning.' It is absolutely necessary to help women develop their traditional skills, and give support, both financial and technical, to their age-old expertise and arrange for the marketing. For example, women's skill in making *kanthas* (traditionally made out of old clothes for the use of the family in winter) is now being promoted, used in new garments and shawls, and commercialized. Huge prospects lie in women's traditional craft of making and dressing dolls from rags, of painting earthen clay pots with locally available colors and various other forms of stitching, knitting, embroidery and crafting. Most importantly, women's homemade medicine and knowledge of the medicinal properties of common herbs and plants have to be carefully cultivated and promoted, and precaution and protection be provided against bio-piracy. Unless active Government assistance is provided, these skills, not supported by either money or publicity, will die in the face of competition from stronger forces.

It is essential for the State to intervene in all matters where violence against women is involved, be that in the public or in the private sphere. Unless protection from sexual harassment and physical violation is pledged, how can a woman ever live with dignity and peace of mind? The task is not easy, since it is deeply connected with the general scenario of frustration and depression. State intervention to solve these complex problems is a prerequisite for the improvement of women's lives.

Women, especially poor women, must have a role in shaping their own destinies. Only political power can enable them to share with men the decision-making processes. And therefore, it devolves on the State to devise schemes for the political participation of women in local and national political and administrative institutions, such as the *panchayats* (local rural and urban bodies), Assemblies and Parliament. India has made a 33 percent reservation for women in rural and local bodies. But a reservation for women in State Assemblies and Parliament has also to be ensured. A Bill is pending in Parliament—already approved by the joint Parliamentary Committee—but it has not yet been put to the vote. One hopeful sign is that women's political participation shows an increase as the Table following indicates.

Table 4 Political Participation of Women: Number of Contestants and Those Elected to the Lok Sabha by Sex, 1952 to 1996 (roughly every 10 years)

	Contestants		Elected	
	M	F	M	F
1952	1,831	43	475	14
1962	1,951	70	459	35
1971	2,698	86	497	21
1980	4,478	142	514	28
1991	8,374	325	484	37
1996	13,353	599	503	40

Source: Government of India: Women in India: A Statistical Profile, 1997, 213

One notices that although the number of women contestants has increased over the years, the number of elected members has increased but slightly during the last 30 years, from 1962 to 1996. In the *panchayat* bodies the record is much better. To give but a few examples: in Karnataka the percentage of women in *panchayats* is 44 and in West Bengal it is 34, higher than the statutory 33 percent reservation of seats for women.

Finally, the most important step for women is to organize themselves. SEWA in Ahmedabad has set a model for such organizations (Bhatt 1998; Jhabvala 1995). These are women's own poverty reducing programmes and deserve unstinted support from the State. Organized women producers may withstand the challenge of competition from large multinationals. It is also important for women to form their own NGOs—fortunately a number of them are cropping up, some being really effective—and form alliances with other disadvantaged groups. They must function independently, if necessary collaborate with the State, or otherwise challenge the State to minimize social, political and economic marginalization (Bannerjee and Mitter 1998). The women's movement all over the world, and certainly in India, needs to work both on the economic and social fronts, aiming at greater economic power, political participation and decision-making authority at the familial level. It needs to ally with movements for environmental protection, children's rights, human rights and so on. The civil society has to be strengthened as a check to economic malaise.

Conclusions

To conclude, it is obvious that the process of globalization cannot be reversed. It has come to stay. As the Chief Minister of West Bengal succinctly put it, 'In an increasingly multi-polar world we have to ultimately adjust to the new world order of globalization and mutual inter-dependence' (Speech in Delhi, *The Telegraph*, 14 November 1998). India as a country cannot remain isolated—it is not possible to remain isolated—from the global economic forces. It is equally obvious that the SAP in India has not met the needs of the common people, especially women. Not only in India, as the East Asian crisis has proved beyond doubt, unregulated globalization and sudden exposure to a free economy can be an unmitigated disaster. Walden Bello has given an analytical account of the downside of globalization in the Philippines and Thailand, and the adverse impact of the 'exit race' of foreign capital from East Asia. In the whole process, common people had not been the actors, but were acted upon and, consequently, suffered (Bello 1998). In fact, world economic thought is veering towards an evaluation of the total free economic policy. The UNDP *Human Development Report* 1998 reflects this worldwide concern. It has commented that 'Globalization is integrating consumer markets around the world and opening opportunities. But it is also creating great inequalities' (UNDP 1998, p. 6). According to the *Report* market research has identified that globalization has broken down local and national boundaries in the area of consumption and that many options are now available to the rich and upper middle class consumers, while the poor are left out in the cold for their inability to afford the goods they are made familiar with through advertisements. The poor countries must have the capacity to shape their own future, and to follow their own courses to accelerate their consumption growth—the priority being the consumption of the basic necessities of life—and to adopt pro-poor policies, creating more employment, ensuring greater access to education, healthcare, housing, safe drinking water, etc., and develop or borrow technologies best suited to their own needs. In view of the tremendous importance of information technology, this tool needs to be fully utilized and socially conscious telecommunication be created to promote development and foster a link between the people and Government policies.

I would like to end on an optimistic note. Since in the depths of their hearts, ordinary citizens everywhere are truly cosmopolitan and desire peace and a healthy, happy life, alternative strategies are bound to be found for the advancement of the quality of life of the common people. New strategies will inevitably be formulated 'that can help actors imagine, develop and build towards a win–win world in the next century' (Henderson 1998).

In other words, in the Indian situation, development strategies have to be reoriented, and the State has to intervene to regulate to some extent the market forces. In the context of gender in particular, State support is needed, and an international–national public–private–civic partnership engineered for ensuring to women a good quality of life. Unless material needs are satisfied by guaranteeing some gainful employment, mental advancement is secured by education and training, and freedom from violence is assured, women in India cannot achieve their goal—*atmajnan, shanti* and *ananda.* Globalization is welcome in India, but with a human face, and indeed with a feminine face.

CHAPTER 10

Globalization and a Welfare State

Brian Easton

Globalization challenges us with a question: What choice (or what control), if any, does a society open to the globalized world have over its social and cultural policy? A common view is that international competitive pressures are so strong that they will drive every country down to the lowest common denominator of a pure market economy, with a minimum of government intervention.

For instance, suppose a society wanted to have a welfare state, providing a degree of public social security. That would involve taxing the incomes of factors and individuals. This would either raise the costs of production, so industries would move offshore to countries where they were not taxed, or it would depress the returns on factors of production such as capital and labor, which would migrate to countries where their return was not so depressed. The logic of this account is that all countries will be pressured towards minimizing taxation, forcing them to dismantle their welfare state and shift to the private provision. There may be some taxation and government spending, but only that which promotes the efficiency of economic production, such as the provision of law and order.

I want to play down the pious argument that all government spending promotes economic efficiency. While some public spending enhances productivity, the argument misses the central problem because it leads to the conclusion that only government spending which contributes to productive efficiency can be justified. This chapter's concern is to what extent spending justified on other grounds can be pursued.

To make this issue clear, consider public provision for the elderly, which is a feature in most rich nations to a lesser or major extent. Arguments that this adds to the productive efficiency of an economy are very tenuous, since the spending is on those who have left the workforce. The implication of the international competitiveness argument is that countries whose State machinery ignores their elderly will have lower taxation, attract more capital and labor, and so prosper. (If, as a result, the elderly die sooner, *per capita* income will be even higher, but the argument does not rely on this.) Moreover, competitive success will force other nations to pursue similar low-tax policies, and so the theory predicts the dismantling of public provision for the elderly as globalization intensifies. Some seize on such predictions, arguing that retirement provision should be privatized, and there are analogous arguments for other forms of welfare spending.

Suppose the nation collectively agrees to accept higher taxation, in order to supply services or transfers by the public sector, where the private sector fails to do so adequately—say supplying recreational, cultural and environmental services. It has two problems. First, public spending requires a public ethos which values such collective actions. But this is being systematically challenged by the anti-collectivists, sometimes with silly arguments, sometimes with shrewd ones. For instance, why should the young, interested in pop music, contribute to the cost of the nation's symphony orchestra? The collective-supply rebuttal is that the young do not directly contribute to the orchestra. Rather everyone contributes to a pool, which funds a lot of public services including the orchestra, sporting facilities used more by the young, and so on, and everyone benefits by getting more out of the pool than they put in, because of the efficacy of public supply in these instances over private supply (a gain which advocates of privatization would deny as possible.)

Second, however, some taxpayers may get little or no benefit from the spending, and can move to another jurisdiction. The group for whom this is most obvious is investors, who can shift their capital reasonably easily between countries. (Note that the investors will find it more difficult to shift their residence, and so local investors can be taxed on their income and spending, subject to the caveat in the next paragraph.) The import is that taxes to fund such collective services have to be on the beneficiaries as income recipients or spenders and not the factors of production.

The argument for the limitations from factor mobility applies to those individuals (workers or investors)—typically those on high incomes—who can easily move to another country. A taxation regime which does not give them a net benefit may result in their migration. (An interesting case was that after one Australian state abandoned estate duties, others felt compelled to follow in order to prevent the retired rich moving to that state.) Thus it appears that a limitation on the tax regime is that it cannot be too progressive on individuals because it will lead to their migration.

Thus far we have identified the following opportunities and limitations in a globalized inter-nationally competitive and mobile world.

Government spending remains viable which:

- promotes economic efficiency and growth;
- provides desired public goods and services which are poorly supplied by the private sector.

Taxation is limited upon:

- highly mobile factors (such as capital) which do not benefit from the spending;
- mobile individuals, who can migrate if the burden of taxation relative to any personal benefit from the spending is high.

Tax avoidance further complicates the story. For instance, there is a case for zero company taxation, but if the company tax rate is below the top personal tax rate, a private company can be created which reduces the liability for income tax. It may seem this can be overcome by shifting the tax balance to a higher proportion of revenue from indirect taxes, but this encourages overseas travel and global shopping via the internet.

Thus there appear to be severe limitations to a tax system being able to raise taxes on capital, or to have a progressive structure. Both suggest more limited government spending, and a restricted welfare state, compared to that of the recent past. The bleakness of this conclusion is moderated by at least two considerations.

First, factors and individuals are not perfectly mobile. Some may be willing to accept higher taxes because they are offset by a better (including more secure) economic, social and political environment. (Government spending may contribute to this superiority.) With more space one could argue that eliminating the welfare state can lead to a society in which life is Hobbesian: 'No arts, no letters, no society; and which is worst of all, continual fear and danger of violent death; and the life of man solitary, poor, brutish, and short,' offset by extraordinary private expenditures by those who can afford to maintain their person and property security. Thus mobile economic actors may be charged a fee—in the form of the taxes they pay—to be allowed to benefit from the superior social (and physical) environment. Even so, the rich will complain about any such levy, using the rhetoric of international competitiveness in a global environment to justify its being reduced for them.

Second, insofar as there are enforced international standards, they prevent the signatory countries undercutting one another—an example is the social chapter of the Maastricht Treaty of the European Union. Currently, however, comprehensive international standards are mainly developed for human rights, rather than economic rights (although there is some overlap). Where comprehensive international economic standards exist they tend to promote mobility of products (i.e., international trade,) and investment (the aborted MAI). Even so, in these economic agreements there may be some measures which give a nation control over some aspects of its destiny. One element in the demise of the MAI was that some powerful nations wanted to be able to protect their culture against encroachment by the all-pervading American culture.

Is there an option of closing the economy to the outside world at least to some degree? My view is that while there is no need to be completely open ('trading naked' as it is sometimes called), the opportunities for major gains from closure are limited in a small country, such as New Zealand, which has a high demand for foreign goods and services and numerous options to effect that demand via overseas travel (and the internet). A politically open society also has the threat of migration if conditions (including access to goods and services from other economies) become too unattractive. So while some measures or interventions to reduce the openness of the economy may have some positive effect, in total they are limited.

Thus the answer to whether a nation open to the globalized world has choice or control over its social and cultural policy seems to be 'some' but 'less than it had in the past'. However we should not get too romantic about the past: a country with a colonial history—such as New Zealand—never had much freedom then either. Nevertheless within these limitations there remain opportunities to design a better society rather than simply follow the lowest common denominator in the international market. Some of the initiatives (providing the tax burden or intervention is carefully designed) are evident from the above analysis:

- government spending which enhances productivity and reduces costs;
- government spending which adds to the social, cultural and physical environment, and to community security;
- industrial relation interventions which enhance productivity.

In addition, a considerable effort should be put into maximizing employment, and alleviating the burden of unemployment (especially as it will contribute to some of these objectives—productivity, a lower tax burden, community security, less poverty, a better society).

What at this stage I remain unsure about is the question of redistribution in the welfare state. Some may enhance productivity or provide cheaper supply than the private sector (e.g., sickness benefits and public healthcare), because collective supply is more efficient than private supply. Full employment reduces some of the social security burden. Insofar as they succeed, they will make the income distribution less unequal. But it may not be enough to reduce the inequality to past levels, while the pressures from international prices are likely to increase wage inequality, since unskilled workers are more reasonably competing with low income 'Third World' workers. Protection may raise the wages of the unskilled, but the higher costs of their produced goods will generally lower the real incomes of the more skilled and investors, so there is only a very limited opportunity from protection.

The welfare state has not necessarily been distributionally vertically progressive, transferring income from the rich to the poor. The New Zealand case suggests horizontal transfers have been more important, providing (limited, minimal) protection from unemployment, sickness and handicap. Most important has been its intergenerational transfers, from the working population to the young and old. Arguably, under the pressures of globalization the social insurance element can be maintained as a more efficient means of providing the protection than private provision. But the public intergenerational and vertically redistributional transfers are more problematic. A noble sentiment is that a society ought to provide for the young, old and needy—a central notion of the New Zealand welfare state from the 1930s. But what if capital and skilled labor migrate to societies with less noble aspirations?

In summary, globalization poses substantial challenges to the public-spirited and welfare state, in that capital and labor mobility (in addition to international trading relations) limit the autonomy a nation has over its economic policies. Yet providing there is an understanding of these limitations, there remains opportunities for it to fashion a society which is not the market—nature raw in tooth and claw—but one which provides a degree of protection for its weak, and collective goods and services for all. Even so, because of the intensification of globalization in recent decades, government involvement in the economy may be different from that of a quarter of a century ago, and it will have to take into consideration the globalization pressures.

CHAPTER 11

The Human Right to Food

Graham Riches

This chapter is adapted from G. Riches. 1999. 'Advancing the Human Right to Food in Canada: Social Policy and the Politics of Hunger, Welfare and Food Security', which appeared in *Agriculture and Human Values*. It argues that at the dawn of this new millennium, two significant obstacles stand in the way of advancing the quality of life of the world's most vulnerable people—the hungry, the poor and the socially excluded. These are (a) the increasing commodification of human life and nature, and (b) the power exerted by global markets over democratic life and decision-making.

I engage these questions by addressing the issue of 'First World' hunger in developed market economies and liberal welfare states in terms of the politics of welfare reform and food security in one such society, Canada. I specifically ask how the economic and social rights of citizenship (e.g., to employment, adequate incomes and a decent social wage) can be advanced on a global basis, when the world's wealthiest countries are themselves adopting food and welfare policies which neglect basic human needs and fail to respect, let alone advance, the human right to food.

It is correct that hunger in Canada has been one factor—along with unemployment, child poverty and homelessness—prompting a progressive policy analysis of the restructuring, if not the dismantling of the welfare state. This has, rightly, focused attention on the need for adequate incomes, full employment and more effective social programs. Yet this critique is limited.

On the one hand, full employment remains light years away and on the other, welfare reform policies following OECD 'active' as opposed to 'passive' labor market prescriptions have resulted in increasing numbers of Canadians falling through the social safety net of employment insurance and social assistance schemes. Canada, which tops the United Nations Human Development Index, is home to one in five children living below the poverty line and charitable food banks are used more than 3.3 million times a year (CAFB 1999) to feed hungry people.

On the other, food security and the human right to food have remained largely unconsidered as being essential both to the eradication of hunger and to the advancement of social and economic rights. For example, there has been little criticism of the federal and provincial governments for neglecting their domestic obligations ratified in international law to 'respect, protect and fulfill the right to food' (Robertson 1990, p. 185) and issues of food security as they relate to domestic hunger have largely been ignored.

The Right to Food and Food Security

According to Robertson, the right to food means 'a condition in which each person can eat food which, by prevailing medical standards, is judged adequate for the full realization of physical and mental health. A person's diet should also consist of food which satisfies cultural preferences. The food should be obtainable in a manner which is not an affront to the dignity or self-esteem of the person. The process by which the food is made available should be stable and sustainable, thus ensuring continuing access to food of acceptable standards' (1990, p. 188).

This definition reflects the prevailing international consensus that the right to food is a right for the individual while food security conditions are normally thought of as the conditions of a unit of society (state, community, household) under which the individual may have her/his human right to food realized. Definitions of food security suggest that a society or community enjoys food security when all people at all times have physical and economic access to sufficient, safe and nutritious foods to meet their dietary needs and food preferences for an active healthy life. Food security is a right and includes, at minimum: an available, adequate, dependable and sustainable food supply and an assured ability to acquire nutritious and culturally acceptable foods through normal food distribution channels (Houghton and Riches 1997, p. 2).

It is perhaps unwise to make the *reductio ad absurdum* argument and claim that all human rights depend on the right to food, though it is difficult to imagine life, and living, without food, water and air (Macrae, 1997). Yet it is difficult not to agree with Alston that the right to freedom from hunger is a fundamental human right (1984,

p. 162) and essential to economic and social wellbeing. That being the case, it is critically important to engage a range of interconnected/transdisciplinary agricultural, cultural, ecological, economic, health and social justice perspectives as they bear upon the growth of hunger in affluent societies, and indeed, within the global context.

Barriers standing in the way of achieving food security include the increasing commodification of welfare and the corporatization of food, and the depoliticization of hunger and the loss of food sovereignty. Not only are the forces of globalization reasserting the commodification of welfare whereby citizens' rights to adequate social security are being increasingly subjected to labor force participation, but at the same time, the increasing corporatization of food is both creating and exacerbating conditions of food poverty and unemployment in countries of the South and North. In the process, food sovereignty is being denied. These are important questions if we understand hunger and food security as political and structural issues and matters of distributional justice which directly engage the democratic rights of citizenship.

The Commodification of Welfare and the Limits of Welfare Liberalism

Australia, Canada, New Zealand, the UK and the USA have been described as constituting 'liberal' welfare state regimes (Esping-Andersen 1990, pp. 26–7 and 52). This cluster of Anglo-Saxon societies, Esping-Andersen suggests, comprise residual welfare states lacking any commitment to full employment and seeking to maintain a state/market dualism in which the state defers to the market. This is true not only of welfare policy but also of food policy. Their welfare arrangements are characterized by: 'means tested assistance, modest universal transfers or modest social insurance plans ... Benefits cater mainly to a clientele of low income, usually working class, state dependents. In this model the progress of social reform has been severely circumscribed by traditional, liberal work ethic norms: it is one where the limits of welfare equal the marginal propensity to opt for welfare instead of work. Entitlement rules are therefore strict and often associated with stigma; benefits are typically modest. In turn the state encourages the market, either passively—by guaranteeing only a minimum—or actively—by subsidizing private welfare schemes' (Esping-Andersen 1990, 26–7).

In this context people's entitlements to welfare assistance, and thereby to food security, are directly related to their capacity to sell their labor power as a commodity in the marketplace. This is particularly problematic in conditions of chronic unemployment. The point which Esping-Andersen makes is that the commodification of labor power means that 'people's right to survive outside the market are at stake' (1990, p. 35). The fact that the ideology of 'workfare' now permeates the welfare system, coupled with stringent cutbacks and punitive eligibility criteria (see the doctrine of less eligibility), means that increasing numbers of people are denied adequate assistance and any hope of achieving an enriched quality of life. For many, low wage, part-time employment is the only alternative to hunger and joblessness and dependence on charitable food banks. The driving force behind this is globalization (deregulated financial markets) and international competitiveness and the use of welfare policy to drive down wages and maintain large pools of reserve labor. No government pursuing such policies wishes to be reminded of its international commitments to fulfill the right to food.

A central concern therefore arises with the capacity of 'liberal' welfare states to promote the decommodification of social rights, that is 'the degree to which individuals, or families, can uphold a socially acceptable standard of living independently of market participation' (Esping-Andersen 1990, p. 37). If access to welfare is only to be determined by people's ability to participate fully in the marketplace, particularly when there is no political commitment to full employment policies, the future is indeed one of risk and increasing vulnerability.

The Commodification and Corporatization of Food

Inasmuch as welfare has been commodified, food, as Winson notes, has also 'become a commodity—one in a long line of goods and services produced and sold. This means that the production, transportation, distribution and consumption of food are subject to the same fundamental social forces and economic "laws" that work on and apply to other commodities' (1993, p. 1). Of course food has always been a commodity, yet Winson eloquently argues why we need to understand food as a different kind of commodity and appreciate it as a social and cultural good.

He suggests that within capitalist society many commodities (e.g., automobiles, houses, Nintendo games) serve to fragment our lives while food, in terms of the rituals of food preparation and communal consumption, acts as an integrating force and helps establish 'human existence as social existence' (1993, p. 2). He sees food as having a special role in the reproduction of our species in that its consumption 'often provides the context for the initiation and development of romantic and sexual relationships'. And he makes the telling point that if 'food and drink have become commodities, they are "intimate" commodities like perhaps no other. In the process of their consumption we take them inside our very bodies, a fact that gives them a special significance denied such "externally" consumed commodities as refrigerators, automobiles, house paint or television sets' (1993, 4). Food is, therefore, not only essential to human existence but to the quality of our lives, to cultural identity and freedom itself. To deny access to the means of life is also to deny community and democracy.

The evidence is all around us. As a result of the corporatization of the food industry too many farmers are no longer in control of their land nor the food they produce and too many people are no longer in control of what they eat—particularly those with insufficient income. Local control of the production and distribution of food has been taken over by the giants of transnational corporate agriculture and the food industry, in particular retail and trade (Kneen 1993; Lang 1997), where the bottom line is food for profit, not for nutritional value and the health of the community. Kneen refers to the development of this global food system as a process of 'distancing: separating people from the sources of their food and nutrition with as many interventions as possible' (1993, p. 7). The result is that individuals, families and communities have become disempowered and deskilled in terms of their capacity to produce their own food, make sound choices when they purchase food and feed themselves nutritional and well-balanced diets. The role of consumer, not citizen, is how we might best describe our relationship to the food we produce and eat (Lang 1997).

In terms of achieving food security, the decommodification of social rights implies recognizing people's need for food and nutrition because we are interdependent members of society with rights of citizenship, and because food is a social and cultural good essential to health and societal integration. It also implies acknowledging the need for democratization and community control. In other words people as citizens and as members of local communities (rural and urban) have the right to control their food systems locally and nationally. What are the prospects for such developments?

The Depoliticization of Hunger and the Loss of Food Sovereignty

Since the early 1980s there has been considerable international evidence from Australia, Canada, New Zealand, the UK and the USA regarding the depoliticization of hunger or the failure by governments to protect and fulfill the right to food. By deferring to the forces of the global marketplace, governments have denied the existence of food poverty, neglected their international human rights obligations and abandoned domestic food security, refused to acknowledge the inadequacy of welfare benefits, framed issues of social security costs in terms of fraud and abuse, consistently blamed the victim and implemented punitive systems of welfare reform (Riches 1997). Internationally these states have committed themselves to the human right to food and the eradication of poverty through the ratification of such conventions as the International Declaration on Human Rights (1948) and the UN Covenant on Economic, Social and Cultural Rights (1966). In Canada, these commitments have not been enacted in domestic legislation and governments have downloaded their responsibilities to the voluntary sector in the form of emergency relief programs such as food banks. And caught in this trap, food banks themselves have aided the depoliticization of hunger.

While food banks reflect a concern for individuals, a faith in humanity and community altruism—all significant liberal values—and can provide immediate and practical short-term relief, their existence nevertheless obscures the underlying causes of hunger. While they appear to be an effective response, they cannot guarantee an adequate supply of nutritious or culturally appropriate food, they are often short-staffed and complain of donor fatigue. Indeed the churches and voluntary agencies complain that the task is too large to contain, let alone arrest the growth of hunger. As a result of their work food banks, unless they have acted upon a progressive educational and political analysis, assist the state in undermining social and economic rights. They enable governments to look the other way and deny food security. Indeed governments will frequently refer welfare claimants to charitable food banks, clearly indicating that international commitments to the human right to food are not worth the paper they are written on.

The commodification and increasing corporatization of food has also resulted in the loss of food sovereignty (FAO/NGO-Rome 1996; Lang 1997). Trade liberalization has granted more powers to transnational corporations including the food giants (e.g., Cargill, Monsanto), thereby undermining not only the sovereignty of nation-states in relation to their agriculture and fisheries policies (food policy) but also to health and social policy. The global marketization of the food system (which results, among other things, in the loss of community-based agriculture through practices such as mono-cropping, genetic engineering, exploited labor and corporate ownership of agricultural production) is at the same time destroying biodiversity and eroding the capacity of nation-states and local communities to feed themselves. The result is increasing food poverty and unemployment both within and between countries of the South and North. Of course the scales are stacked against the South, and the North's food security—such as it is—is being achieved at the expense of food security in the South.

Conclusions

Asserting and fulfilling the human right to food is essential to human existence, to the quality of life and to the exercise of democratic freedoms. If hunger is now being tolerated in affluent 'First World' societies and accepted as part of the 'natural' order there is little prospect that the economic and social rights of citizenship (to full employment, adequate incomes, a reasonable social wage and quality of life) and to democratic participation will be advanced. Moreover if First World societies are convinced that the human right to food should not be applied to their own peoples, there is little prospect that they will seek to further this right in the global community where the issues are most severe. The key question perhaps is whether societies can accept and apply the principle of the decommodification of social rights.

CHAPTER 12

The Failures of Globalization—Ignored at What Cost

Edna Ross

For 25 years, proponents of globalization have sold the integration of the global economy as inevitable and beneficial for all. The integration of the global economy, particularly through the liberalization of trade and investment, was seen as the vehicle for rapid economic growth, the reduction of poverty and the spread of democracy.

In recent years, evidence has been accumulating that many aspects of the globalization process are not yielding the expected results. Critics of the deregulation of trade and investment in particular, and of the dominant economic development model more generally, have pointed to the downside of the policies flowing from it. The failure of governments and international organizations—which are driving these policies—to address the concerns and criticisms has resulted in a polarization of the debate.

Advocates of globalization hold the view that globalization can deliver unparalleled growth and perhaps even provide the salvation to all the world's problems. At the other end of the spectrum is the view that globalization is a process which will undermine human development and human rights.

While the impacts of globalization on ordinary people's lives are complex and diverse and its implications not yet clear, reactions to globalization are strong. The rapidity of change and its huge impacts on every facet of life are eliciting fear.

Undoubtedly, increasing global integration opens opportunities for economic and social progress not available before. However, its benefits and costs are not evenly distributed. To date, the governments of most industrialized countries, international institutions such as the WTO, World Bank, IMF and OECD, corporations, and economic commentators have focused almost exclusively on the benefits of opening markets and borders. They have not acknowledged—let alone explored ways to address—the social cost of these policies.

The failure of governments and international institutions to address the social cost of globalization has contributed to a growing backlash against it. The growing criticisms of deregulation and liberalization policies and of the institutions that drive them is evident in both industrialized and developing countries. The continuing failure to address the criticisms and concerns of ordinary citizens is providing succour to fundamentalist political parties with isolationist and xenophobic policies.

This chapter argues that continued failure to address the social and environmental costs of the deregulation of trade, investment and financial flows is likely to result in a backlash against global integration, international cooperation and international institutions. The potential benefits of globalization will be lost as will the potential for greater international cooperation, at precisely the time when such cooperation is essential. The backlash will also result in a rejection of international institutions, essential for developing and implementing collaborative strategies to address global problems.

Main Causes of Concern

In recent years, meetings of citizens' organizations have been held in parallel to meetings of the WTO, NAFTA, APEC, World Bank, IMF and other international organizations promoting the liberalization of trade and investment. These meetings of development, environment, labor and human rights groups have articulated their concerns and criticisms of aspects of the globalization process and of the institutions driving these processes. Increasingly, as evidence accumulates that many of the fears and concerns voiced by these citizen organizations are valid, similar critiques of globalization are being articulated by academics, writers, World Bank officials and even financiers. The areas of concern can be grouped as follows:

- Globalization, as it is currently proceeding, is exacerbating inequity, contributing to the widening gap between rich and poor both between and within countries.
- Globalization processes are contributing to social and economic insecurity and uncertainty and an erosion of human rights and consumer standards.
- Globalization is eroding democracy and reducing the capacity of national governments to make decisions in the national interest.

This, in turn, is contributing to a growing cynicism and loss of faith in government, leadership and political processes, among citizens around the world.

Growing Inequity Between and Within Countries

The theory that liberalizing trade and investment would lead to rapid economic growth to the benefit of all is not being supported by the reality. While there has been a substantial increase in world trade and investment (world exports increased from US$1.3 trillion in 1977 to US$4.8 trillion in 1995), and while the ensuing economic growth has benefited many countries and people, the real picture is more complicated, as the financial crises which have hit East Asia, Brazil and Russia clearly show. The evidence is that not all trade is good, not all investment is productive and not all economic growth is linked to improved human wellbeing.

Growing inequity between countries

The UN Conference on Trade and Development's (UNCTAD) 1997 *Trade and Development Report* warns of the threat to globalization posed by growing economic polarization and income inequality (UNCTAD 1997). It notes that evidence is mounting that slow growth and rising inequalities are becoming more permanent features of the world economy. The income gaps between North and South have continued to widen. In 1965, the average *per capita* income of the G7 countries was 20 times that of the world's poorest seven countries. By 1995 it was 39 times as much (UNCTAD 1997). Looked at another way, the gap in average *per capita* income between the industrial and developing worlds tripled from $5,700 in 1960 to $15,400 in 1993 (UNDP 1996).

The United Nations Development Program's (UNDP) 1996 *Human Development Report* found that, despite rapid integration of the global economy, growth has been failing over much of the past fifteen years in about 100 countries, with almost one third of the world's people. The *Report* concludes that over the past fifteen years the world has seen spectacular economic advance for some countries and unprecedented decline for others. While a surge in economic growth in some fifteen countries has brought rapidly rising incomes to many of their 1.5 billion people, the economic decline or stagnation affecting 100 countries has reduced the incomes of 1.6 billion people (UNDP 1996)[1].

Figures illustrating the growing gulf between rich and poor

countries are truly staggering. For example, of the $23 trillion global GDP in 1993, $18 trillion is in the industrial countries, leaving only $5 trillion in the developing countries, even though they have nearly 80 percent of the world's people. The poorest 20 percent of the world's people saw their share of global income decline from 2.3 percent to 1.4 percent in the past 30 years, while the share of the richest 20 percent rose from 70 percent to 85 percent (UNDP 1996). Yet policymakers have tended to ignore these figures and focus simply on the quantity of growth.

What the 1996 *Human Development Report* highlights so starkly is the need for policy-makers to be much more concerned with the structure and quality of growth. Greater equity, it found, led to much better sustained growth. As the *Report* points out, current patterns of growth are widening the disparities in economic performance, creating two ever more polarized worlds (UNDP 1996).

There are numerous ways in which trade liberalization could benefit many developing countries and contribute to reducing the inequity between North and South. For example, agricultural protectionism in the European Community (EC) and the US has pushed down prices of agricultural produce, making it impossible for vulnerable smallholder producers in developing countries to compete. A reduction of the European and US agricultural subsidies, consistent with trade liberalization philosophy, would benefit small producers in developing countries.

Similarly, tariffs imposed by industrialized countries on manufactured goods deny developing countries the opportunity to reduce their reliance on extractive industries such as tropical forest logging and mining and to move to earning foreign exchange by exporting manufactured goods.

Unfortunately for developing countries, liberalization has tended, so far, to proceed in a lopsided way. The rules of global free trade have been drawn in favour of the world's richest countries—the playing field is not level. In areas where trade liberalization would assist developing countries, progress is very slow. This was reinforced at the first meeting of the World Trade Organization (WTO) in December 1996 in Singapore. Developing countries repeated their concerns at the slow pace in the reduction of EU and US domestic support and export subsidies in agriculture and the absence of significant reductions in quotas on textile exports from developing countries.

UNCTAD makes the point that, contrary to much current economic thinking, increased global competition does not automatically bring faster growth and development. Nor do growth and development automatically bring about a reduction in inequality. The Report points out that the lopsided way in which liberalization of the world economy has proceeded 'tends to prejudice the growth prospects of developing countries by discrimination against areas in which they can achieve comparative advantage. Liberalization of trade in goods has proceeded more slowly in those sectors where developing countries are more competitive' (UNCTAD 1997, p. vii).

The huge increase in private investment flows to developing countries as a result of the liberalization of trade and investment is another area in which the reality does not match the potential to promote development. The bulk of private investment has been to a handful of developing countries (around a dozen, mostly in East Asia and Latin America). Much of it is to China. Since the crisis there has been a further narrowing of the countries to which capital is flowing. A 1999 OECD report shows total net private flows fell sharply in 1997, down by $30 billion, due largely to a drop in bank lending to Asia. Very little is flowing to the least developed countries. Further, private investment flows do not go into social sectors such as health and education, sectors which are essential to equitable development in which the benefits of growth are more widely spread.

In addition to the uneven distribution of private investment flows, lack of controls on private investment has resulted in large sums of non-productive, speculative investment—investment looking for quick returns. The resultant currency volatility and devastating instability have been starkly demonstrated in the Asian crisis.

Liberalization of financial markets is of major concern to developing countries, whose nascent financial institutions are not in a position to compete with the well established ones in industrialized countries. Recent events in Indonesia and Thailand illustrate the dangers of too rapid liberalization without adequate institutional preparation. Further liberalization will exacerbate the problem of speculative capital increasing the pressure on fragile financial systems.

The turnover in international currency markets is $1.5 trillion every day, of which 90 percent is speculative—i.e., unrelated to trade or the real economy. Rapid liberalization has delinked finance from trade and investment, siphoning off capital from productive investment.

The financial crisis has highlighted the serious economic and social dislocations which can be caused by unregulated financial markets. Markets are inherently unstable and cannot be left to correct their own mistakes. How to preserve stability in financial markets and channel capital into productive investment are two major challenges facing the international community.

Growing inequity within countries

Polarization between countries has been accompanied by increasing income inequality within countries. The UNCTAD *Report* notes that the income share of the richest 20 percent has risen almost everywhere since the early 1980s, with the richest 20 percent receiving over 50 percent of the national income in more than one half of the developing countries. Those at the bottom have failed to see real gains in living standards and in some cases endure real losses. Increases in the share of the richest 20 percent have also been associated with a fall in the share of the middle class—a 'hollowing out' of the middle class has become a prominent feature of income distribution in many countries (UNCTAD 1997).

While economic growth need not lead to increased disparities in wealth within countries if policies are adopted to ensure the benefits of growth are equitably distributed, rising inequity has been associated with liberalization in many countries. Income inequality was fairly low in Sri Lanka in 1970, with the Gini coefficient at 0.35.[2] When Sri Lanka began to liberalize its economy in the late 1970s, inequality rose. By 1990 the Gini coefficient had risen to 0.51. Similar increases in inequality of income have occurred in China when it began to open its economy to international trade and finance (Gini coefficient rising from 0.33 in 1979 to 0.38 in 1988); in Mexico, when it began to liberalize its economy in the mid 1980s (Gini coefficient rising from 0.43 in 1984 to 0.48 in 1992); and in Chile, where the Gini coefficient rose from 0.45 in 1970 to 0.57 by 1990 (UNDP 1996).

The link between growing inequality within countries and rapid liberalization is due to liberalization's favoring certain income groups over others. Growing wage inequality between skilled and unskilled workers is becoming a global problem. According to the UNCTAD *Report*, wage inequality has increased in almost all developing countries which have undertaken rapid trade liberalization, 'most often in the context of declining industrial employment of unskilled workers and large absolute falls in their real wages, of the order of 20–30 percent in some Latin American countries' (UNCTAD 1997).

Subsistence farmers are being hurt by the removal of import restrictions on agricultural goods. The UNCTAD *Report* notes that, contrary to expectations, agricultural price liberalization has not resulted in improvements in the domestic terms of trade for agriculture in many countries which implemented reforms. Liberalization tended to boost the incomes of traders rather than farmers.

An Oxfam UK study which looked at the impacts of liberalization on maize farmers in the Philippines found that the average household income of maize farmers will be reduced by as much as 30 percent over the next six years as cheap imports from the US drive down prices in local markets (Watkins 1997). This is in a context where one-quarter of maize-producing households already lack sufficient income for adequate nutrition, and where one-third of children in these households suffer from malnutrition. The social consequences will be devastating. Up to half a million livelihoods are under immediate threat.

Such problems arise because, as noted earlier, trade liberalization is not being played out on a level playing-field. As currently practised, liberalization has meant increased access to developing countries' markets with negligible reductions in subsidies to US farmers. The US supremacy in world markets derives from the access of farmers to subsidies. The OECD estimates that each US farmer receives a subsidy of about $29,000. This is roughly 120 times the average income of maize farmers in the Philippines. US grain surpluses can therefore be sold at prices equivalent to one-half of the cost of production, destroying local agriculture and creating a captive market in the process (Watkins 1997). While the US has the power to force developing countries to remove barriers to US imports, the US and EU have made little progress on reducing subsidies.

The perception that the rules of trade are not drawn up fairly and that inequality between and within countries is growing has a firm basis in fact. Thus, the UNCTAD 1997 *Trade and Development Report*'s warning—that failure to address growing divisions between and within countries poses a serious threat of a political backlash—should be heeded (UNCTAD 1997). Future trade negotiations must address the imbalances in liberalization of sectors of traditional interest to developing countries. They must also identify and address the negative impacts of liberalization on developing countries and on poverty and inequity.

UNCTAD's warnings of a backlash against the liberalization of trade and investment, arising out of the inequitable effects of these processes on industrialized and developing countries, have been echoed in other arenas. In a book resulting from a series of policy dialogs on APEC, Charles Morrison of the East–West APEC Study Center notes that, while there is little doubt about the overall positive benefits to both developed and developing countries in reducing economic barriers to flows of goods, services and capital,

> the least flexible and economically disadvantaged groups are likely to suffer . . . those who are disadvantaged cannot be dismissed, and they will make the trade and investment liberalization agenda inherently difficult and conflictual (Morrison 1997).

A major challenge posed by globalization is how to ensure that the benefits it offers are more evenly distributed.

Social and Economic Insecurity and Uncertainty

A second area of concern contributing to a widespread backlash against globalization relates to feelings of insecurity about employment, health and safety, environmental safeguards and threats to human rights, engendered by competition between countries for investment. Such competition is exerting pressure on working conditions and labor costs, driving these down to maximize profits on investment and creating a potential race to the bottom. Concern about reactions to job insecurity in industrial democracies has been expressed in a number of forums, extending beyond 'the usual suspects' of labor unions, NGOs and others who advocate on behalf of the poor.

Klaus Schwab and Claude Smadja, president and managing director respectively of the World Economic Forum (WEF), which produces the annual *Global Competitiveness Report*, put it thus:

> [t]he lightning speed at which capital moves across borders, the acceleration of technological changes, the rapid evolution of management and marketing requirements increase the pressure for structural and conceptual readjustments to a breaking point. This is multiplying the human and social costs of the globalization process to a level that tests the social fabric of the democracies in an unprecedented way (Schwab and Smadja 1996).

Similar warnings come from economist Lester Thurow and historian Ethan Kapstein. Thurow argues that the fall of communism has removed the factor which curbed the excesses of capitalism, especially the tendency for new technologies to lead to job losses and cause downward pressure on the wages of the unskilled. He warns that the very poor will retreat into religious fundamentalism and extremism (Thurow 1996).

Kapstein claims that the global economy is leaving millions of disaffected workers in its wake. He blames the coincidence of the fierce competition generated by the open global economy with pressure on governments to be fiscally conservative. Kapstein warns that:

> if the post-World War Two social contract with workers—of full employment and comprehensive social welfare—is to be broken, political support for the burgeoning global economy could easily collapse... [But] systemic pressures are curtailing every government's ability to respond with new spending. Just when working people most need the nation-state as a buffer from the world economy, it is abandoning them (Kapstein 1996).

Kapstein also echoes Thurow's warning about the rise in fundamentalism:

> Populists and demagogues of various stripes will find 'solutions' to contemporary economic problems in protectionism and xenophobia. Indeed, in every industrialized nation, such figures are on the campaign trail. Growing income inequality, job insecurity, and unemployment are widely seen as the flip side of globalization (Kapstein 1996).

In industrialized countries, pressure from competition of cheap labor and poor conditions is creating job insecurity and a growing wage gap between skilled and unskilled labor. The latter is becoming a global problem. As noted earlier, wage inequality has increased in almost all developing countries which have undertaken rapid trade liberalization (UNCTAD 1997).

Global competition for capital has also reduced the opportunities for workers in developing countries to negotiate improvements in their conditions. While liberalization and investment can create jobs, workers in developing countries are particularly vulnerable to exploitation and abuse. In a number of countries, workers who have sought to improve their conditions have been subjected to torture and arrest (Daniels 1996). The increased competition fanned by globalization, together with the impacts of structural adjustment programs imposed by the IMF, have also been linked to increases in child labor (UNICEF 1997).

Workers, particularly in developing countries, are also vulnerable to the volatility of financial markets and the global economy, economic downturns, sudden withdrawals of capital, and structural adjustment programs leading to massive job losses. In the aftermath of the Asian financial crisis, these factors have resulted in millions of job losses in Thailand, South Korea and Indonesia, which in turn have fueled social unrest and violence.

Evidence showing that there is no direct correlation between investment and jobs created has also contributed to growing disenchantment with the global economy. The 1997 UNCTAD *Trade and Development Report* found that capital has gained in comparison with labor: the share of income accruing to capital has gained over that assigned to labor (UNCTAD 1997).

The old assumption that economic growth would automatically expand employment and wages is increasingly questioned. The 1996 *Human Development Report*'s examination of the relationship between economic growth and employment opportunities concluded that, while growth in employment opportunities is strongly and positively correlated with GDP *per capita*, income growth will not invariably and automatically translate into expansion of employment opportunities. '[W]hether growth expands the opportunities for work—and contributes to human development—depends not just on the rate of growth but also on its pattern.' Factors such as what is produced, by whom and how, the organization of production and the distribution of productive assets such as land can and do affect the amount and type of employment generated. These are all responsive to policy (UNDP 1996, p. 91).

One aspect of global competition and integration that is contributing to jobless growth, unemployment and job insecurity is takeovers and mergers between companies. With intense global competition, the only way many companies can maintain high growth rates and survive being taken over by others is through mergers and acquisitions, which contribute nothing to creation, innovation or employment. While the sales of 200 companies represent 28.3 percent of the world's GNP, they employ just 0.75 percent of the workforce (Saul 1999). While the largest 500 TNCs have grown sevenfold in sales and productivity since the early 1970s, the number of workers they employ has remained flat at 26 million (Smillie 1998). The pressure to maximize profits in the interests of shareholders has led to reductions in the number of employees and increases in the output per employee (Soros 1998).

Unbridled competition for investment also exerts pressure on the environment and on health and safety standards. Threats to health and safety standards, in particular, provide further fuel for opposition to globalization. The outbreak of "Mad Cow" disease (BSE) in Britain in 1997 was a poignant example of the type of environmental disaster which could trigger widespread opposition to trade liberalization and support for protectionism and isolationism. There was universal agreement that the spread of the BSE virus could be explained by the unrestrained deregulation of the animal-feed industry in the mid 1980s by the government of one European state intent on promoting the global competitiveness of its food industry (O'Neill 1997).

How to prevent the natural conclusions of continued unbridled competition—a race to the bottom—and a concentration of power are two further challenges posed by globalization that the international community must address.

The social insecurity and uncertainty created by globalization processes and, in particular, by the deregulation of trade and investment, are exacerbated by the third major area of concern about globalization—the feelings of citizens that they have lost control over the processes; that globalization is being driven by forces beyond their control and influence and beyond the influence of their governments. The international institutions which drive the integration of the global economy are seen as lacking accountability, transparency and democracy. This perception is contributing to growing opposition to the authority of international institutions and support for isolationist and protectionist policies.

Globalization and the Loss of Democracy

Rapidly increasing integration of the global economy is eroding democracy in two ways: through the growing power of capital relative to the state, i.e., relative to the power of national governments, and through the growing power of international institutions such as the WTO, IMF and World Bank.

Numerous statistics point to the growing relative economic power of transnational corporations (TNCs). Fifteen of the world's largest TNCs have gross incomes larger than the GDP of 120 countries (Kothari 1994). A recently compiled list of the 100 largest economic entities contained just 29 countries—the other 71 were companies. Only ten countries in the world now have stock markets whose total worth is greater than the largest American conglomerates (Sheehan 1999).

The trend toward giant companies becoming bigger is likely to continue, further eroding competition and concentrating power in fewer hands. Already, there are only four major auditing firms left in the world; five companies control 50 percent of the global market in aerospace, electronic components, airlines, automobiles and steel; five companies control 70 percent of consumer durables; while *Microsoft* is on the verge of a worldwide monopoly (Soros 1998; Saul 1999).

Managers of publicly traded companies are as concerned with the market for their shares as with the market for their products—they seek to maximize profits rather than market share. This means that signals from the financial markets take precedence over those from product markets; managers will sell entire companies if this will enhance shareholder value (Soros 1998). Thus, decisions about how to use vast amounts of capital are made in the interests of a few (shareholders), rather than in the interests of the common good, which would entail, among other objectives, reducing unemployment.

As already noted, 90 percent of the $1.5 trillion traded daily in the global marketplace is speculative. This massive increase in financial flows means that international finance influences and constrains governments by affecting the exchange rate, giving finance quite a big lever to influence government policy (Crotty & Epstein 1996).

In addition to the influence of the large transnational corporations and the financial markets pressuring governments to support further liberalization, reduce corporate taxes, and reduce the protection of workers and the environment, the capacity of national governments has been eroded by the increase in power of international organizations such as the WTO, IMF and the World Bank. Increasingly, decisions which affect the lives of millions of ordinary people are made by these international institutions, which are unaccountable and undemocratic, and whose processes are not transparent.

Developing countries are particularly affected. As discussed earlier in the chapter, the international trade agreements promoted by the WTO usually reflect the interests of TNCs and the most powerful industrialized countries.

The IMF has substantial control over the economic policies of 75 developing nations (Sachs 1997). The measures associated with the imposition of the IMF's Structural Adjustment Loans and bailout packages continue to cause economic hardship to millions of people in the developing world. As noted by Harvard economist Jeffrey Sachs, 'It defies logic to believe that the small group of 1,000 economists on 19th St. in Washington should dictate the economic conditions of life to … 1.4 billion people' (Sachs 1997). It also defies democracy.

A further anomaly of the global rules is that, while international economic agreements are binding, agreements relating to protecting the environment, workers' rights, codes of conduct for TNCs, protection of human rights and promotion of development for developing countries—that is, treaties and agreements relating to the common good—are not binding. These are left to individual countries to implement, with the only international pressure being applied being that of moral suasion. The call by labor unions and some NGOs to incorporate these social issues into international economic agreements has, to date, been rejected by the WTO and APEC. Ironically, but understandably, the governments and some NGOs of developing countries object to such an incorporation of social and environmental issues, fearing it will disadvantage them further in the competitive global marketplace.

As John Ralston Saul (1999) pointed out in a recent lecture on Globalization and Democracy, removing power from the nation and putting it in the global arena without also transferring power of *citizens* to the global arena is not just weakening the nation-state, but weakening democracy. Given the huge impact of the economic policies being promoted on the lives of millions of ordinary people, the growing backlash against both the policies and the institutions implementing them is not surprising. Evidence of how the growing resentment can be harnessed was provided in the highly effective campaign against the MAI being negotiated in the OECD.

Redefining the role of the nation-state and developing governance mechanisms for international institutions which render these institutions credible are essential to addressing this third major area of concern regarding globalization.

Conclusions

After years of dismissing concerns about globalization processes expressed primarily by civil society—NGOs, environmentalists, labor unions, consumer and human rights organizations—there are the beginnings of recognition, even among its staunchest advocates, that globalization entails costs. This recognition is essential in order to shift the debate beyond the polarized positions that globalization is all good or entirely evil. It is essential in order to allow a fruitful exploration of possible strategies for addressing the failures of current theory and practice.

The costs of globalization, discussed in this chapter, were grouped into three areas of concern:

- The impact of globalization, and particularly of liberalizing trade and investment, on the growing gap between North and South and between rich and poor within countries;

- The pressures exerted by global competition for capital, on employment conditions, health and safety, environmental protection and human rights; and
- The erosion of democracy, due to the increase in power of private capital and international institutions relative to the nation-state.

These concerns pose a number of challenges to the international community:

- How to ensure the benefits of globalization are evenly distributed.
- How to preserve stability in financial markets.
- How to prevent the natural conclusions of unbridled competition—a race to the bottom in working conditions and the protection of health, safety and the environment, and a concentration of power through the unbridled natural tendency for monopolies and oligopolies to form.
- How to redefine the role of the state.
- How to establish credible, effective international institutions.

Failure to address these challenges will fuel the growing backlash against globalization evident in both industrialized and developing countries. It is the danger inherent in this backlash, together with the shock of the Asian financial crisis, which have served as the catalyst for broader acknowledgment that the downside of globalization must be addressed.

George Soros, regarded as the world's most successful market trader, warns of the possibility of the global economic system breaking down:

> We live in a global economy, but the political organization of our global society is woefully inadequate. We are bereft of the capacity to preserve peace and to counteract the excess of the financial markets. Without these controls, the global economy is liable to break down (Soros 1998).

Warnings were also sounded at the 1999 Annual Meeting of the World Economic Forum (WEF), at which over 2,000 leaders of world business, governments, and media gathered to discuss Responsible Globality: Managing the Impact of Globalization. The WEF has been a major proponent of market force economics and globalization for over 20 years. But as the title of the meeting indicates, the forum recently had a change in tune. While there had been some recognition, in earlier years, that all was not well in the deregulated global marketplace (Schwab and Smadja 1996), the firm belief in the virtues of unimpeded liberalization of global financial markets were replaced, at the above meeting, with apprehension. There was repeated recognition of the failures of globalization, with speaker after speaker expressing the need for 'responsible globality', 'putting a human face on globalization', 'taking into account the social dimensions of the global market', and 'sharing the benefits of globalization more equally'.

Claude Smadja, Managing Director of the WEF, suggested that the turmoil of the previous 18 months reflected the first systemic crisis of the global economy. 'It shows how much we are lagging behind in managing the implications of the globalization process and illustrates the urgency to put in place the structures and the process that will allow us to manage this new global reality in a responsible way' (WEF 1999).

Unfortunately, there was little evidence that the global leaders attending the Forum had a clear vision of what needs to be done. An Australian journalist reporting on the Forum noted that:

> On display in Davos was not just fear about an international economic crisis beyond the control of elected governments, but also deep alarm at spreading disillusionment among ordinary people with the economic policies which have led to this crisis ... what came through most clearly was that the capacity of experts to analyse the problems behind the crisis was being outstripped by the pace of change in the global economy (Kitney 1999).

It is to be hoped that this recognition of the social cost of globalization, and of the dangers posed by the political backlash against prevailing economic policies and the governments and international institutions driving them, will lead to some new initiatives.

Two recent speeches by the President of the World Bank, Mr Jim Wolfensohn, suggest that such initiatives are beginning to be developed by the Bank. In his address to the Board of Governors in October 1998, titled 'The Other Crisis,' Wolfensohn made the point that, in addressing the financial crisis, 'we must address this human pain. We must go beyond financial stabilization. We must address the issues of long-term equitable growth, on which prosperity and human progress depend. We must focus on the institutional and structural changes needed for recovery and sustainable development. We must focus on the social issues.' Failure to do so, noted Wolfensohn, will make political stability impossible, and without political stability, financial stability is impossible (Wolfensohn 1998).

Wolfensohn foreshadows the need for a new development framework, 'one that deals with the progress in structural reforms necessary for long-term growth, one that includes the human and social accounting, that deals with the environment, that deals with the status of women, rural development, indigenous people, progress in infrastructure, and so on . . .' (Wolfensohn 1998).

In a second speech, delivered at the Symposium on Global Finance and Development in Tokyo on 1 March, 1999, Wolfensohn elaborated on the Bank's vision of a comprehensive development framework, a Discussion Draft of which was circulated to the development community and posted on the Bank's external website in February 1999.

Wolfensohn's speeches and the Bank's Draft Comprehensive Development Framework are promising. They recognize the need to redefine development goals and indicators; to develop guidelines and benchmarks on social protection, service provision, employment and labor standards; to be inclusive in reaching international agreements on development goals and principles and to consult widely. 'I think you need to address a whole set of issues which are not typically addressed in the financial analysis alone. A stable financial architecture cannot be achieved without the proper structural institutional, social and human foundations needed to make a modern market economy work. Without these underpinnings, our building will collapse. It will also collapse if we are not joined in our labors by hands and voices from every corner of the globe' (Wolfensohn 1999).

While there is no consensus yet about how the global economy should be managed and by what type of institutions, a vast number of suggestions and possible strategies have been canvassed in various forums, including in this book. There is increasing agreement that the global economy and globalization processes need to be managed and regulated; that this needs to be done by pan-national institutions; that the institutions and processes for formulating policies need to be opened up to participation by civil society—they need to be democratic, accountable and transparent.

As a first step, governments and organizations such as the WTO, World Bank and IMF need to take the initiative and call a Globalization Summit for heads of state or government to address the challenges posed by globalization, as has been suggested by the Overseas Development Council (Sewell and McDowell 1998). What is required, however, goes beyond identifying strategies for regulating financial flows and other aspects of the global economy. There is a need to review the objectives of economic policies and how we measure success. The trend of the last 20 or so years, of having economic rather than social objectives determine policies, has led to ordinary people's growing disenchantment with politics, cynicism about and alienation from the political process. There is a longing for values, ethics and democratic processes to be reinstated in the formulation of public policy. The third millennium offers a timely opportunity for taking stock and restating what sort of society we want to live in and what sort of world we want to leave to our children.

Notes

1. These figures applied before the Asian crisis, which is estimated to have reversed many of the gains made in the previous decade in Thailand, Korea and particularly Indonesia.
2. The Gini coefficient ranges from 0 to 1, with 0 being perfect equality and 1 complete inequality.

CHAPTER 13

Prospect for Globalization, Employment and Quality of Life in the 21st Century

Akira Onishi

Introduction

The latest FUGI (Futures of Global Interdependence) global model 9.0 M200/M80 classifies the world into 200/80 countries and regional groupings, where each national/regional model is globally interdependent through international trade, financial flows and information flows.

The 200 or 80 national/regional models are incorporated into eight major sub-systems:

(a) Population
(b) Foods
(c) Energy
(d) Environment (ecosystem)
(e) Development
(f) Peace and security
(g) Human rights and
(h) Human healthcare.

The total number of equations is about 40,000 for the M80 model, or more than 150,000 for the M200 model. In order to make the computations for such an enormous global economic model, we require a very high capacity computer and a specially designed software package for use in modeling. The newest FGMS (FUGI Global Modeling System) software packages were developed at the Soka University Institute for Systems Science on the basis of the author's expert knowledge of global modeling in cooperation with systems engineers.

The FGMS software system allows large-scale integrated global modeling. It is designed in such a way that the following operations are consistently carried out:

- preparing the database for FUGI global model simulation;
- automatic estimation of the model's structural parameters using OLS and MLBM;
- dynamic model simulation testing; and
- pre-projection and projection using an automatic error correction system.

By applying this expert system on global modeling, the necessary manpower needs for global modeling and forecast simulation are kept to a minimum, and the work of computation is accomplished quickly and efficiently. In the absence of such progress in software, large-scale integrated global modeling and reliable policy simulations would probably be impossible to achieve. The FGMS software for the FUGI global model 9.0 M80 and M200 is available on the IBM RS/6000. (For further details on the FUGI global model, see *fugimodel.t.soka.ac.jp*.)

Globalization of Technology and Culture for Sustainable Development in the 21st Century

In the age of global interdependence, the population explosion should expand the needs for development. The destruction of the ecosystem, induced by global development coupled with military conflicts in various parts of the world; the destruction of the ozone layer, induced by harmful chemicals together with nuclear explosions and global warming gas, induced by the use of fossil energy have all caused serious issues for the global environment. On the other side, the 21st century might be an age of mass unemployment, as well as one incurring a vast increase in refugees, or displaced persons, derived from the destruction of environment, failures in development, lack of peace and violation of human rights. In order to cope with such global issues, progress is needed in both science and technology but also in human minds.

The new frontiers of science and technology in the 21st century will appear in the fields of space, of global environment protection including recycling and biotechnology, of new energy, new materials and information technology. Since these areas are closely interrelated, it is expected that these technologies will progress through the fusion of science and technology in the Space Age. The universe

Table 1 Outline of the Fugi Global Model 9.0 M80

Developed Market Economics		**Developing Economics**
Asia-Pacific		**Asia-Pacific**
1 Japan	WORLD TRADE	23 China, Mainland
2 Australia	MATRIX 80x80	24 China, Hong Kong & Macao
3 New Zealand		25 Taiwan, Province of China
		26 Korea, Republic of
		27 North Korea
		28 Indonesia
		29 Malaysia
		30 Philippines
North America	EXPORT	31 Singapore
4 Canada	IMPORT	32 Thailand
5 United States	PRICES	33 Myanmar
		34 SEAO
		35 Bangladesh
		36 India
Western Europe	OIL &	37 Pakistan
6 Belgium–Luxembourg	COMMODITIES	38 Sri Lanka
7 Denmark	PRICES	39 SWAO
8 France		40 Pacific Islands
9 Germany		
10 Greece		**Middle East**
11 Ireland	FOREIGN	41 Iran
12 Italy	EXCHANGE	42 Iraq
13 Netherlands	RATE	43 Israel
14 United Kingdom	ODA	44 Kuwait
15 Portugal	MATRIX	45 Saudi Arabia
16 Spain		46 MIDO
17 Austria		
18 Finland		**Africa**
19 Iceland	EXTERNAL	47 Algeria
20 Norway	DEBT	48 Egypt
21 Sweden		49 Libya
22 Switzerland		50 Morocco
		51 Tunisia
	LIBOR &	52 Ethiopia
	EURO	53 Gabon
Economies in Transition	RATE	54 Ghana
75 Bulgaria		55 Kenya
76 Czech-Slovakia		56 Liberia
77 Hungary		57 Nigeria
78 Poland	PRIVATE	58 Sudan
79 Romania	FOREIGN	59 South Africa
80 Former USSR	DIRECT	60 SOSO
	INVESTMENT	
		Latin America
		61 Argentina
		62 Bolivia
	FISCAL	63 Brazil
	MONETARY	64 Chile
	POLICIES	65 Colombia
		66 Mexico
	ENERGY	67 Ecuador
	POLICIES	68 Paraguay
		69 Peru
Mediterranean	ENVIRONMENT	70 Uruguay
73 Turkey	POLICIES	71 Venezuela
74 MEURO		72 LACO

is infinitely large. There are 500–700 million solar systems within only a single galaxy. In order to move by spaceship into outer space at ultra high speeds, we need high-tech engines utilizing cosmic free energy together with the use of flows of magnetic fields in the universe. The use of anti-gravity by magnetic coils, superconductors at normal temperatures and nuclear fusion producing clean energy will be necessary for developing the future technologies in the Space Age. These technological innovations will be able to bring about clean and inexhaustible energy in place of risky nuclear reactor powerplants and the harmful fossil energy currently inducing the destruction of global environments. The new materials include, for example, super alloy for superconductivity at normal temperatures, and artificial internal organs in place of transplantation of human internal organs. The next generation of high-tech information systems will be an innovation of multimedia not only for receiving but also for simultaneously transmitting information in forms of voices and moving color images over ultra-distances on the earth and into outer space.

It is worth noting that the cosmic minds or consciousness, through providing information on space technologies and cultural shocks coming from outer space, will awaken the peoples living in the global society. The progress of human society might be evaluated not only by the indicators of progress of science and technology but also those of spiritual minds through education and culture. Human spiritual progress will not be achieved by mere development of genetic information in many generations. It is expected that human spiritual progress would be very slow if we relid solely on sudden genetic changes such as mutation and self-organization. Human beings will be unable to construct a peaceful global welfare society if their mental progress fails keep pace with the speed of scientific and technological progress in the Space Age. Human spiritual progress may be achieved not by manipulation of genetic information but by the use of non-genetic information, which will be cultivated by the advancement of learning process and creativity though education and culture. One of the most important roles of the universities might be the human education for younger generations through self-awareness and practice of human behavior in accordance with the cosmic life systems, which will bring about a strong and merciful impetus for infinite creativeness and progress. As a result, a new global human culture harmonized with diversified local cultures will appear in global society in the 21st century.

Globalization of Economy; Prospect for the World Economy, 1996–2015

For the purpose of baseline projections of the global economy for the period 1996–2015 we have used the FUGI Global Model 9.0 M80. We have introduced the following future scenarios:

(a) Opening the market of the Japanese economy to the rest of the world through removing tariff and non-tariff barriers and imposing various regulations as well;
(b) Intensifying private foreign direct investment induced by globalization; and
(c) Increasing R&D for new technological progress and infrastructure investment for the purpose of opening the 21st century multimedia information society.

According to the FUGI model projections, the average annual growth rate of the global economy is expected to be 2.9 percent, 2.9 percent and 3.0 percent during the periods 1996–2000, 2001–10 and 2011–15 following an average growth of 2.9 percent in the 1980s and 1.9 percent during the first half of the 1990s. For the developed market economies taken as a whole, the average annual real economic growth rate was 1.7 percent during 1991–95 and is expected to recover to an average 2.4 percent, 2.3 percent and 2.4 percent in the periods 1996–2000, 2001–10 and 2011–15. It is worth noting that the Japanese economic growth rate decreased from 4.1 percent in the 1980s to 1.3 percent in the first half of the 1990s. For the period from 1996 to 2000, the annual percentage growth rate of the Japanese economy was estimated as 1.3 percent and it was expected to attain 2.5 percent and 2.6 percent for the periods 2001–10 and 2011–2015 because of new technological innovations as mentioned earlier.

In the developing economies, the average growth rate of 3.2 percent in the 1980s was accelerated to an average 4.7 percent in the first half of the 1990s. Due to the Asian financial crisis, the slowing down of real economic growth in the developing countries as a group may be anticipated, with the average annual growth rate of 4.2 percent for the period 1996–2000 sustaining 4.5 percent and 4.4 percent for the periods 2001–10 and 2011–15.

As for the Eastern European economies in transition, the average annual real economic growth rate fell from 1.1 percent for the 1980s to −1.1 percent in the first half of the 1990s. It was expected to recover to 5.6 percent, 4.9 percent and 4.5 percent for the periods

1996–2000, 2001–10 and 2011–15. In the former USSR, the average annual real economic growth rate was 2.7 percent in the 1980s and fell to –5.7 percent in the first half of the 1990s and was expected to recover to 2.8 percent, 3.1 percent and 3.0 percent for the periods 1996–2000, 2001–10 and 2011–15.

It is worth noting that the average annual growth rate of the developing economies in the Asia-Pacific region is expected to fall from 7.4 percent in 1991–95 to 4.8 percent because of the Asian financial crisis but to recover to 5.3 percent and 5.2 percent in the periods 2001–10 and 2011–15.

The Chinese economy recorded a high average annual economic growth of 10.3 percent during the period 1991–95, but also slowed down its high growth toward the end of the decade. The FUGI global model projected the Chinese GDP growth rate of an average 7.4 percent for the period 1996–2000. It was expected to further slow down to rates of 6.3 percent and 5.7 percent for the periods 2001–10 and 2011–15. As for the Southeast Asian group as a whole, several indications suggested a drastic fall of the growth rate from. 7.2 percent in the first half of 1990s to 0.9 percent during the latter half of the 1990s because of the sudden financial disturbances. It was however expected that the economic growth rate would recover to 4.2 percent and 5.0 percent for the periods 2001–10 and 2011–15.

If the developing countries in the Asia-Pacific region could succeed in overcoming the financial disturbances by self-supporting efforts together with international cooperation, this would contribute to open the Asia-Pacific age in the 21st century. For this region to stimulate positive global economic activities, technological innovations generated in large part by Japan, the EU and USA will no doubt be needed. Many indications point to the desirability of Japan, the EU and USA becoming a major research and development center helping to activate the world economy and to contribute to the solution of global environmental issues.

Globalization of Environment: Global CO_2 Emissions

According to the baseline projections by the FUGI global model 9.0 M80, the average annual increase in the rate of global CO_2 emissions was expected to be 2.7 percent, 2.4 percent and 2.3 percent during the periods 1996–2000, 2001–10 and 2011–15. For the developed market economies taken as a whole, the average annual increase was 1.1 percent during 1991–95 and was expected to maintain an average 1.4 percent, 1.0 percent and 0.6 percent in the periods 1996–2000, 2001–10 and 2011–15.

For the developing economies taken as a group, the average annual increase of CO_2 emissions was 4.4 percent during the first half of the 1990s and was expected to decrease to an average of 4.0 percent in the latter half of the 1990s. It was expected to maintain 3.9 percent and 3.7 percent in the later periods.

As for the economies in transition in Eastern Europe, the average annual increase in emission growth was expected to accelerate from –0.1 percent in 1991–95 to 2.8 percent in 1996–2000 and then to stabilize to at 1.3 percent and 1.2 percent for the periods 2001–10 and 2011–15. In the former USSR, the average annual increase was 1.5 percent in the 1980s and fell to –7.7 percent in the first half of the 1990s. It was expected to recover to 3.6 percent, 2.5 percent and 2.7 percent for the periods 1996–2000, 2001–10 and 2011–15.

The average annual increase in CO_2 emission for the developing economies in the Asia-Pacific region was expected to decrease from 5.7 percent during the period 1991–95 to 4.2 percent for the period 1996–2000 and slow to 4.1 percent and 3.9 percent in the following periods. As for the Southeast Asian group as whole, several indications suggest that the increasing rate of 5.8 percent in 1991–95 would tend to decrease to 1.1 percent in 1996–2000 and move to 2.9 percent and 2.7 percent for the periods 2001–10 and 2011–15. In contrast, the Chinese CO_2 emission recorded a high average annual increase of 5.7 percent during the period 1991–95 and it was expected to slow down to rates of 4.9 percent for the period 1996–2000 and 4.2 percent and 3.9 percent for the periods 2001–10 and 2011–15. It is worth noting that China will become the largest CO_2 emission country around the world, surpassing the US by the year 2015, although its *per capita* CO_2 emission is one quarter of that of the US.

Global Population and Employment

According to the FUGI model projections, the average annual growth rate of the global population was expected to be 1.7 percent and 1.6 percent during the periods 1996–2000 and 2001–15. For the developed market economies taken as a whole, the average annual population growth rate was 0.6 percent during the period 1991–95. It was expected to slightly decrease to an average 0.4 percent, 0.3 percent and 0.3 percent in the following periods. The Japanese population growth rate was expected to decrease from 0.3

percent for the period 1991–2000 to 0.1 percent and 0.0 percent during the periods 2001–10 and 2011–15.

In the developing economies, the annual average population growth rate of 2.0 percent in the second half of the 1990s was expected to decrease slightly to an average 1.9 percent for the period 2001–10 and sustain 1.8 percent for the period 2011–15.

The Chinese population growth rates estimated annual average 1.1 percent during the period 1991–2000 would be expected to slow down to rates of 0.9 percent and 0.8 percent for the periods 2001–10 and 2011–15. As a result the population growth rate of the Asia-Pacific region would be 1.7 percent, 1.5 percent and 1.4 percent for the three periods.

As for the Eastern European economies in transition, the annual average population growth rate was expected to increase from 0.3 percent for the first half of the 1990s to 0.7 percent for the period 1996–2000, and then decrease to 0.6 percent for the period 2000–15. In the former USSR, the average annual population growth rate was expected to recover to 0.9 percent from 0.4 percent in the first half of the 1990s and to fall to 0.8 percent and 0.7 percent for the periods 2001–10 and 2011–15.

The world population was estimated to grow at a rate of 1.6 percent per year for the period 1991–2015, while the ratio of urban population to total population should grow from 43 percent in 1990 to 67 percent in 2015. For the corresponding periods, the rate of population growth is only 0.4 to 0.3 percent per year in the developed market economies, although the urban population to total population ratio is likely to increase from 77 percent in 1990 to 82 percent in 2015. In contrast, in the developing economies, the urban population to total population ratio will grow from 35 percent in 1990 to 65 percent in 2015.

Although urban employment is on the increase, unemployment also seems likely to increase around the world. Civilian employment across the world will grow at a rate of 1.5 percent per year for the periods 1996–2015, while the unemployment rates to total civilian labor force should grow from 6.4 percent in 1995 to 7.0 percent in 2015. For the corresponding periods, the rate of civilian employment growth is estimated at only 0.3 percent per year in the developed market economies, while the unemployment rates should decrease from 8.3 percent in 1995 to 7.1 percent in 2015. In the developing economies, the civilian employment is expected to grow at a rate of 1.8 percent per year for the periods 1996–2015, while the unemployment rates grow from 5.8 percent in 1995 to 7.0 percent in

2015. As a result, unemployment will be a serious global issue in the 21st century. Global unemployment is expected to increase from 165 million in 1995 to 247 million in 2015.

In order to cope with unemployment issues, there is a need to promote employment opportunities while maintaining further cut-backs of labor days and working hours. On the one hand, the shortening of labor hours based on the improvement of labor productivity may provide an opportunity of improving the quality of life; on the other hand, it is hardly to be expected that there will be narrowing of the North–South *per capita* income gap and the developing world will face the serious problems relating to the quality of urban life.

Increasing International *Per Capita* Income Disparity

When we examine the results of the above baseline projections of global population and economy, we see that the future path of the global economy is still in some ways unstable because of increasing international *per capita* income disparity. The South IPCID (International *Per Capita* Income Disparity, in terms of average *per capita* income—at 1990 constant prices—of the whole world equal to 100) is expected to slightly improve from 23 in 1990 to 28 in 2000 and 33 in 2015, while the North IPCID increases more steadily: 502 in 1990 to 546 in 2000 and 603 in 2015. The IPCID of the US should increase from 540 in 1990 to 631 in 2015, while the Japanese IPCID increases from 591 in 1990 to 617 in 2000 and 736 in 2015. It is worth noting that the South–South *per capita* income disparities will be enlarged. Only Asia-Pacific will improve, from 13 in 1990 to 19 in 2000 and 27 in 2015; the rest of the South will hardly improve during these periods. In particular, Sub-Saharan Africa tends to decrease, from 13 in 1990 to 12 in 2000 and 9 in 2015.

Improving Life Expectancy at Birth

There is a hope that male life expectancy at birth for the whole world will increase from 62 in 1990 to 64 in 2000 and 67 in 2015. In the developed market economies, the male life expectancy at birth is expected to increase from 72 in 1990 to 74 in 2000 and 77 in 2015, but is much lower in the developing economies: 60 in 1990, 62 in 2000 and 65 in 2015.

It is interesting to note that female life expectancy at birth for the whole world will increase from 66 in 1990 to 68 in 2000 and 69 in 2015. In the developed market economies, female life expectancy at birth is expected to increase from 79 in 1990 to 81 in 2000 and 84 in 2015, but is much lower in the developing economies: 62 in 1990, 65 in 2000 and 67 in 2015. It is worth noting that the Japanese female has the longest life expectancy at birth, increasing from 81 in 1990 to 83 in 2000 and 87 in 2015. These trends seem likely to be positive impacts of urbanization and growing megacities, although it is reasonably expected that the burden of healthcare and social welfare improving the quality of life should be increased in the 21st century.

Selected Indicators of Quality of Life

Here we should like to consider the quality of life in the coming decades. The list of selected indicators for affecting quality of life was chosen as follows:

I. Environment
II. Sustainable development
III. Peace and security
IV. Human rights
V. Healthcare

Category I: Environment includes a number of sub-indicators:

(a) natural disasters (flood and earthquake, etc.);
(b) water pollution;
(c) air pollution;
(d) soil pollution;
(e) nuclear pollution;
(f) ecological imbalance (as caused, for example, by the missing green zone).

Category II: Sustainable development in the 21st century is very complex. We have included five sub-indicators as follows:

(a) poor infrastructure (needs for energy-saving housing, green zone, new traffic system with zero CO_2 emissions, safe water, clean air, removing harmful chemicals, recycling of urban waste, global multimedia communication networks, educational and cultural facilities, etc.);
(b) mass poverty and unequal income distribution;
(c) increased urban–rural and international *per capita* income disparity;
(d) higher domestic prices in terms of urban consumer price index (CPI); and

(e) increased unemployment and disguised unemployment.

Category III: Absence of peace and security consists of two major indicators:

(a) political conflicts; and
(b) increase in the crime rate.

Category IV: Violation of human rights includes;

(a) failure to meet basic human existence needs. This refers to very severe situations that are equivalent to the denial of the right to live as a human being. These would include severe problems having to do with such things as housing, public hygiene, and nutrition;
(b) ideological oppression against democratic popular movements;
(c) ethnic discrimination;
(d) religious conflicts;
(e) needs for educational expenditures; and
(f) needs for social welfare expenditure.

Category V: Lack of healthcare includes:

(a) lack of medical and healthcare expenditures;
(b) lack of nutrition and balanced diet;
(c) unhealthy foods due to harmful chemicals;
(d) lack of safe water and clean air; as well as
(e) lack of mental healthcare.

Monitoring and Early Warning for Quality of Life

The global QOL crisis has complex and interrelated causes. We have tried to look at these causes in a comprehensive way as involving the destruction of the environment, failures in development, lack of peace and security, violation of human rights and lack of healthcare.

As a countermeasure, we first of all prescribe economic development in either the developed or the developing countries and the economies in transition, carried out in such a way as to cope with urban environmental deterioration. As ingredients in effecting this purpose, we must no doubt have a sense of awareness of the spirit of common responsibility of the human race toward future generations.

The focus of QOL development strategies must surely be directed to the consideration of how to eradicate poverty among the increasing mass of the concentrated urban population. What, then, might comprehensive policies for that purpose be? Emphasis must be given both to self-reliant efforts on the part of the country in question and also to economic and technological cooperation from the developed countries.

Using the Global Early Warning System (GEWS) for risk management, we have first of all investigated the risks of large-scale concentrations of persons looking for employment opportunities in the megacities.

As earlier pointed out, a new generation FUGI global model 9.0 is already in the operational stage. This model classifies the world into 200/80 countries and regional units, thus making it possible to treat almost all countries at the individual country level. A prime characteristic of our global model is that it permits the study of how the individual country models are mutually interdependent, and especially the study of how the economic policies of the most powerful countries affect the developing countries.

Our research will not stop at the individual country level but can, by providing from a global vantage point information on issues affecting the potential risks of megacities, throw new and brighter light on possibilities for global adjustment and cooperation in our living human society.

Based on our findings, we have further studied the questions of how to alert people to potential dangers as early as possible, how to monitor human risks using FUGI-Global Early Warning System (GEWS) through global communication networks, and how to design counter measures. Building upon the already developed early warning system, we have tried to apply that system to all geographical regions of our globe.

Through advances in the life sciences, we now know something about the wisdom possessed by the human genome included in individual cells. It is because each cell of a living organism possesses information concerning the whole that there is the possibility of mutual adjustments and cooperation. This ought to suggest the possibility of closer cooperation in our global society, given the possession by each country of global information.

Beyond early warning and prevention mechanisms, it is worth noting that changes in human minds would also be needed to eliminate violent crime and conflicts in the high-density megacities through mental healthcare. According to Daniel Goleman, EQ—emotional intelligence—rather than IQ will be emphasized in our society (Goleman 1995). My own interpretation is that EQ means the following:

(a) Proper decision-making capability based on our own consciousness;
(b) Self-controlling capability of emotions inducing stress feelings such as uneasiness and anger;
(c) Self-controlling capability directed toward optimism even when facing failures in achieving targets; and
(d) Capability of sharing common sentiments with other persons and cooperative capability to maintain harmony in groups.

My views on progress in human minds and my suggestions for how to enhance EQ are given below:

(a) Humans seem to be robotics controlled by the genetic information of human genome.
(b) Human minds are controlled by non-genetic and basic information like imprinting up to the age of six.
(c) Human minds and EQ can be progressed and enhanced by the non-genetic information based upon humanistic cultures and education through creative simulations, gaming and virtual systems exercises.
(d) Global human society is progressing from the lower stages controlled by selfish existence emotions to the more advanced stages based on self-consciousness and cosmic minds.

Conclusions

In this way, we look forward to the establishment of a global early warning system that can help to eliminate the factors of unhealthy QOL situations, which are reflected in the appearance of risks, especially in the human minds. It can at the same time help to point to ways by which our human society can develop a better quality of life in the 21st century.

CHAPTER 14

Managing with Method: Information in Policy and Strategy for Innovation

Stuart Macdonald

Introduction

> 'The more modern thinking about empowerment as autonomy actually fits [this organization] very, very well ... I mean you just can't manage that matrix other than at local level. The principle by which we try to manage our business was the notion of global localization. Or was it local globalization?' (Interview with senior manager).

As much as English is the global language, the language of globalization is the language of management, which is also a form of English. The methods of management, which are expressed in this language, are the means by which globalization is to be achieved. Precisely what is meant by 'globalization' is uncertain, but then the language of management is not given to precision. Meaning and logic are sacrificed to belief and faith, much as they seem to be in the language of the Church. In consequence, it is difficult to use the language of management to question the methods of management. The result is that these methods survive unchallenged by those who rely on this language, and unconsidered by those who do not.

This chapter explores the world of management method and particularly the role of method in reducing the perceived uncertainty of the manager. It then considers the manager's ability to deal with uncertainty in the context of innovation. Examples are provided of policy and programs to capture the information critical for innovation, and the similarity between these and the corporate practice advocated by management method is explored. Speculation is provided on the link between these approaches to innovation and the external advice on which managers have come to rely for their method.

Management Language and Management Method

In the world of the manager—and managers are everywhere these days—language is fundamental: it helps determine discourse, placing conditions on what may be discussed and how it may be discussed (Jackall 1988, pp. 137–44). The very vocabulary of modern management, with its delayering, benchmarking, re-engineering, stakeholding, downsizing, best practice and total quality, is also restrictive, though mastering the argot need not take long (Pascale 1990, pp. 15–23). Quick fixes are available for the busy executive—'the latest management thinking in just sixteen pages a month,' (*Bulletpoint* 1996, p. 1) or a monthly update which 'packs into just eight easily absorbed pages, a mountain of business wisdom distilled down to just the purest essence,' guaranteed to contain 'not a single untested academic theory', (advertisement in the *Independent* 1994, p. 23). Confined to a very specific vocabulary with less specific meaning, the logic of new management methods can be frustratingly surreal. The report of the Inquiry into the Parkhurst Prison escape in the UK is illustrative:

> Any organization which boasts one Statement of Purpose, one Vision, five Values, six Goals, seven Strategic Priorities and eight Key Performance Indicators without any clear correlation between them is producing a recipe for confusion (Micklethwait and Wooldridge 1996, pp. 1–2).

Faith, not reason, supports the notion of the organization as an army led into battle by a messiah demanding total commitment to his mission and his vision. Debate and dissent are not encouraged.

The quality of thinking in management studies is the butt of many a joke, and causes concern among those with less sense of humor. The Economic and Social Research Council, the government funding body in the UK for academic research in the social sciences, recently took the unprecedented step of appointing a Commission to report on the quality of management research. Of 778 grants awarded by the ESRC, management studies had secured only nineteen (Caulkin 1994, p. 8). Even so, the great and the good of the subject did not seem to appreciate the severity of the problem. In customary management style, their report talks not about salvaging from disaster, but of sustaining and improving excellence by identifying and measuring quality. It concludes with a striking observation:

> Research can and does contribute to today's problems, but it has a greater contribution to make: it should also contribute to tomorrow's problems (Commission on Management Research 1994, p. 27).

Management studies is the study of what managers do. They are expected to do a great deal these days, in the public sector as well as the private (Macdonald and Simpson 1998). No longer need the manager rely on his own experience; much more can be achieved through the application of management method (*Economist* 1993, p. 81). The greater the academic and guru contribution to their armory, the more managers are expected to achieve, and the more corporate strategy and government policy depend on their ability to achieve. Indeed, much strategy and policy is now framed in terms of systems in which managers play the part of technical experts. Even innovation, that most fundamental and uncertain of organizational requirements, is now regarded as a process like any other part of production; and information, that most fundamental and nebulous of organizational resources, as something to be managed much like any other resource.

Method and Uncertainty

The mass of what is written on what managers do and should do is depressingly prescriptive and infuriatingly uncritical. There is, however, one school which offers a different and refreshing insight into the relationship between manager and management method (Alvesson 1993; Gill and Whittle 1992; Grint 1994; McGivern 1983). It hints darkly when it is not more explicit that there is collusion between managers and those who offer them method. To be sure, method is not self-taught. Method is derived from those who study managers and from those who advise them; from academics and consultants. While most seek to determine the value of this external advice in terms of improved organizational performance, a few reject this approach as missing the point. They observe, for example, the importance of fashion in the marketing and adoption of management method (Abrahamson 1996). The need to follow fashion—and rapidly changing fashion at that—would seem to be a consideration overriding both the infinite variety of circumstances in which managers find themselves and the continuity of the challenges they face. Moreover, there is a logical obstacle to the very easy assumption that managers know what their problems are and therefore what methods to apply. No more than anyone else can managers know what they do not know. All this is indication enough for some to suggest that the crucial relationship is not between method and problem at all, but between the manager and external advisers (Clark 1995). In short, there is collusion between the two, the manager providing the academic and consultant credibility (and money), while they offer the manager companionship and at least the illusion of certainty in a lonely and uncertain world (de Burgundy 1995; Sturdy 1997).

Despite the elevation of the manager to omnipotent status, there is much the manager cannot do, and should not be expected to do. This does not mean that the manager may not attempt these things, just that success should not be anticipated to follow from managerial method. In the study of innovation, the term 'serendipity' used to be frequently employed. It captured nicely the notion that change is influenced by factors beyond control and even prediction. The term is rarely used these days; uncertainty has been removed by confidence in method but with exceptions (Quintas and Guy 1995). Innovation is seen as process, and process is to be managed. Consequently, failure, which is inherent in innovation, is failure of manager or of management method. The latter can be readily replaced from an inexhaustible supply of new fads, the former just as readily with other managers more enthusiastic and less willing to contemplate the prospect of failure. Yet uncertainty is unavoidable in all the organization does and there is so much more to be learnt from failure than from success. Managers unable to cope with uncertainty and unprepared to learn from failure, or replaced as soon as they have learnt, contribute nothing to the understanding of innovation.

Method and Organizational Performance

How well organizations perform is commonly considered to be a function of how well their managers perform. Where organizational performance cannot be measured directly, it is measured by indicators. One consequence is the creation of a market in performance indicators in which managers have greater incentive to produce acceptable indicators than to produce whatever it is the indicators are supposed to indicate. In the academic world, a major indicator of research performance is number of papers published, which has generated a supply of published papers intended to be counted rather than read (Glass *et al.* 1996; Armstrong 1998). And thus it is in other organizations. We delude ourselves by assuming that we know from performance indicators how an organization is performing. We know only how well performance indicators are managed. Take the performance of the Sussex police force in 1998, exceeding by one percent a target of 90 percent of emergency calls answered within ten minutes in urban areas and within 20 minutes elsewhere. This performance was also associated with 873 accidents involving police cars, 39 injuries and three deaths (Bennetto 1999, p. 6).

Resources devoted to managing performance indicators are not available to manage anything else; in other words, there is an opportunity cost attached to the use of performance indicators. These resources are particularly unlikely to go anywhere near unmeasured and unmeasurable activities, and yet these are perhaps the most important of all (Tisdall 1982, p. 150–51). In the academic world, it is increasingly hard to find individuals who will referee papers or write book reviews. In organizations generally, managers not only have little incentive to tackle the unmeasurable, but little experience and training in how this might be done. It rapidly becomes hard for them to comprehend why anyone ever did anything which was not being measured, and measured immediately. To paraphrase Rebecca Boden, writing in the context of scientific laboratories, accounting has become synonymous with accountability (Boden 1998).

Method and Innovation

But this is not simply a diatribe against the triumph of market forces and the invisible hand. What is being questioned is the lack of questioning itself (Oliver 1998). This is a function not only of the force and enthusiasm with which methods of management are presented, but also of these methods having no place for adaptation and amendment. There is no partial business process re-engineering, no semi-delayering, nothing short of total and excellent. There is certainly rapid succession of management methods, but the old are replaced wholesale rather than improved through modification. There is no place for criticism (Baritz 1987). Indeed, debate in the language of management methods requires resort to a language and to mental processes which are themselves antagonistic to reasoning. As Jenny Stewart has noted, even ethics—surely an inherently debatable topic—is presented by management gurus as a sort of prophylactic against bad behavior (Stewart 1996). In the efficient organization, questioning is both wasteful of resources and disruptive.

Managers need to control, obviously so they can direct what the organization and its employees do, less obviously for the satisfaction of being in charge. Power is some compensation for responsibility. New management methods increase the control of managers. Even empowerment, in that it is instituted by managers, only increases the responsibility of employees without increasing their control (Collins 1997). The result is that the independence of thought and action, the individuality, the creativity which employees can bring to the organization are discouraged, and the task of managers, which was once to blend these characteristics to fit the circumstances and meet the needs of the organization, is now to eliminate them. They have no place in an efficient organization, they contribute nothing to immediate performance, and are unmeasured by performance indicators. Individuality has always struggled to survive in the organization; it has little chance when confronted by new management methods. A perverse example is the Swedish glass company, desperate to keep its designers creative and welcoming indicators of customer dissatisfaction as evidence that designers are still producing original work. More typical, perhaps, is the chief executive of the world's largest manufacturer of underwater ploughs (for burying submarine cables), thrown off a senior management course at Templeton College, Oxford—the very college which has held a course in new management methods for the entire Labour Cabinet—for insisting that the key to his company's success in innovation was that its engineers had fun. There is no place in new management methods for fun.

Fun is important, a serious matter. It is not just a question of employees receiving more from their employment and therefore putting more into their jobs in an exchange relationship; it is the nature of this psychic income. Fun is conducive to creativity. Fun is personal and individual, very different from the communal activities now organized by managers to encourage community spirit and teamwork—bread and circuses to compensate for the absence of fun. Bread and circuses encourage mass involvement and organizational loyalty, not individuality. Moreover, they undermine the professionalism which employees can take to their jobs, professionalism which drives individuals to do their jobs as well as they can because they perceive a social rather than an organizational responsibility. Frequently this means taking on tasks which are not dictated by the organization, and performing them in ways which do not fit existing systems. Such behavior is fundamental to innovation, especially the incremental innovation essential to the continuing prosperity of organizations. But such behavior is also inefficient and disruptive; it is beyond the control of managers determined that everyone should sing from the same hymnsheet and march to the same drumbeat, and it is not easily captured in performance indicators.

It is vital to accept that much of what the organization does cannot be managed by method and that attempts to do so are extremely damaging, certainly to the organization, but also to the economy and society of which the organization and its employees are parts. Concentration on what can be measured leads inevitably to the neglect of what cannot. Managers cannot manage fun, they cannot manage individuality and creativity—at least not as they manage production processes. The best they can do—and nothing tests the skills of a manager more—is create the conditions in which these characteristics and behavior can flourish. This means trusting employees, surrendering a large degree of control, tolerating (even encouraging) failure, accepting a degree of inefficiency for the sake of flexibility—and questioning new management methods. It means allocating resources to what cannot be measured, to activities which probably cannot be justified purely in terms of short-term gains and direct, private benefits. This sort of management requires real managerial skill, what Gunnar Eliasson, in the context of IT systems, calls the fundamental management resource—instinct (Eliasson 1999).

Nowhere are these attempts to manage by method more fatuous than in what is known as knowledge management, the attempt by organizations to capture and exploit all intellectual capital contained within the organization. While it is reassuring that organizations should recognize and value intellectual capital, much of the intellectual capital within the organization does not belong to the organization at all. It belongs to employees and it must remain their property if it is to benefit the organization. Employees' trading in information—the organization's as well as their own—is crucial to finding and acquiring the external information essential for the organization's innovation (Schrader 1991; von Hippel 1987). A regime in which this personal information exchange is forced into organizational systems or treated as industrial espionage is not conducive to innovation. Even internal information cannot be treated simply as corporate knowledge and managed by method as if it were just like any other resource. Much of this information is tacit, its use and exchange governed by complex conventions and subtle transactions. As new management methods seek to measure, knowledge management seeks to codify so that information can fit into organizational systems the better to be managed (Stewart 1994). With information, neglect of the unmeasurable is neglect of the uncodifiable. Moreover, because much of the knowledge within the organization belongs to employees, it is not the organization's to manage. This does not prevent the organization trying to appropriate the information, just as it seeks to appropriate, to own, to control, external information. The issue is captured nicely in the increasingly common requirement by universities that their academics register personal international networks so that university administrators can exploit these to develop the business of the organization. It would be hard to think of a procedure more likely to destroy essential networks which have taken years to construct, and more pointless in that, without the common experience and tacit knowledge which underlie these relationships, administrators can make little use of these contacts.

US Export Controls

On a grander level, the example of US export controls to prevent the loss of high technology to the Soviet Bloc in the 1980s is instructive. These were directed at 'dual use' technology, that works with both civilian and military applications (Macdonald 1990). By the mid-1970s, there was agreement that it was much more important to guard the information about how high technology was made than the equipment itself, and efforts were concentrated on preventing the flow of information to the Soviet Bloc.

> In theory, controlling the flow of 'know how' is a much more powerful defense than controlling product exports. But every time we make that decision, by classifying the knowledge, we pay a high price in slowed innovation rate (Branscomb 1988).

Preventing the transfer of know how proved to be much more difficult than preventing the transfer of hardware. Even if information could be stopped at the border, what was to prevent foreigners acquiring information in the US and then exporting it in their heads? And even if foreigners could be prevented from acquiring information in the US, what was to prevent Americans acquiring the information, exporting it in their heads, and then transferring it to foreigners overseas? And what if the equivalent information was already available overseas? What was the point then of preventing the same information leaving the US?

Through a succession of ever more desperate and draconian measures, the US government sought to control the flow of the world's high technology information. One immediate result was the Militarily Critical Technologies List (MCTL), an optimistic attempt to proscribe information by technological category.

> The MCTL is the size of the New York phone book and worth a lot less. It's a bastardization of the concept of critical technology. The bureaucrats have taken a clear concept and turned it into a two inch document that's absolutely worthless (Bucy, in Schatz 1983).

The inadequacy of the MCTL led to the classification of whole areas of academic study (such as cryptology), including information which had previously been unclassified; the imposition of veritable need-to-know regimes in companies, enforced through vicious penalties for those which did not comply; and the extraterritorial enforcement of US law throughout the world. Extreme as these measures were, they were ineffective in staunching the flow of technological information to the Soviet Bloc, not that the Soviet Bloc particularly needed this information anyway. It was already flooded with high technology information obtained from the West by legal means; its problem lay in its capacity to use this information. If US export controls had little impact on the Soviet Bloc, they may have had much more on the West itself. Innovation is highly dependent on ready information flow and particularly that achieved through personal networks. The very systems responsible for such hives of innovative activity as Silicon Valley were targeted for eradication.

> You have got to question about the validity of the firm you are dealing with, especially a foreign firm. Go to the FBI, ask questions. The FBI has recently sought to publicize their efforts in this problem in our particular area by putting up billboards similar to the World War Two type of thing about the walls having ears (Southard 1982, p. 53).

> Corporate executives and leaders of the business community must not only be understanding of the need for compliance and be supportive of the government's export control efforts, they must translate this state of mind into effective action by their company staff, managers and supervisors (Wu 1983, p. 107).

Just how much damage has been done to Western innovation is probably impossible to measure (National Academy of Sciences 1987 and 1991). It is also hard to be sure just how disingenuous were these attempts to prevent the flow of technological information. Certainly the Department of Defense, engaged in a turf battle with the Department of Commerce, relished its entitlement to control information and justified increasingly extreme measures in terms of the inevitable inadequacy of existing measures. Just as certainly, US confusion between military and economic strength allowed policy for the former to encapsulate the latter. In consequence, measures which damaged Japanese and European competitors were seen as making acceptable contributions to US national security. US export controls continue, most specifically in the Economic Espionage Act of 1996, intended to prevent the theft of information in the form of trade secrets, especially by foreigners (Nasheri and O'Hearn 1998).

Industrial Espionage

Growing concern about the importance of information, particularly its commercial value, has stimulated the growth of a considerable industry dedicated to countering industrial espionage (Macdonald 1993 and 1996). Though less dramatic than export controls, its approach to information and the impact of this approach on innovation are depressingly similar:

> Many businessmen fail to appreciate the extremely wide range of corporate data that could be useful to a competitor and thus harmful to their own company (Edwards 1987, 18–19).

> [Many managers] fail to appreciate the wide range of corporate data that could be useful to a competitor and, thus, harmful to their own companies (Carter 1989, 158–160).

The notion that information reaching a competitor inevitably damages the company whence the information came runs counter to all that is known about information exchange and all that is claimed for network organization. This is information mercantilism—the doctrine that wealth is derived from the mere possession of information, that more information is obviously better than less, that the totality of information is finite, and that information can be lost much like any other good. The doctrine is a nonsense, yet belief in it is widespread. This emanates from a failure to appreciate the nature of information, but more specifically from a conviction that the organization must contain and own the information its managers will control. Containing information which is not owned is unsatisfactory.

> The future trend is to limit the amount of people with security clearance and restrict classified information on a 'need to know' basis. If there is no clear reason for an individual to know a secret, access to the secret will not be allowed (Olney 1998, p. 28–32).

Even the information networks of Silicon Valley, long acknowledged as fundamental to the region's innovation, are to be silenced:

> There is no way to know who is listening... One experienced listener remarked about *The Lion and the Compass*, a popular Silicon Valley bar: 'If you really want to spy, just pull up a stool and listen' (Bronson 1987, pp. 173–78).

Intellectual Property Rights

The information mercantilism of export controls and of industrial espionage is equally evident in recent attitudes to intellectual property rights (IPR), and especially to patents. Patents are meant to encourage innovation for the benefit of all, the argument being that, without the patent system, inventors would not be able to make public their inventions for fear that they would be stolen. The patent system is a bargain between the inventor and society by which the latter grants the former a temporary monopoly in exchange for the inventor disclosing the information of his invention. Society may then use this information, with the inventor's permission, in its efforts to innovate. Increasingly, though, the bargain has been reinterpreted and seen as a monopoly given to the inventor so that the inventor—not society—can innovate. There is, then, little point in disseminating the information of invention and innovation is considered to be dependent on securing the monopoly rights of the inventor. Changes to the patent system in recent years have nearly all involved reinforcing the system by making the patent easier to defend (and hence more valuable) and by lengthening the monopoly term; there has been relatively little interest in the role of the patent system in encouraging innovation by disseminating the information of invention.

> ... an overemphasis on successful innovation, coupled with reduced attention to the presence or absence of a true invention, reinforces only one of the dual policy goals of the patent system: providing incentives to inventors. It ignores the goal of encouraging inventors to disclose technical information (Merges 1988, ref.6).

The value of a patent is now judged to be so great that many organizations do what they can to restrict indiscriminate information flow lest prior publication damage patent prospects.

> Our biggest competitors are not other agencies like ours [the British Technology Group]. They are researchers talking to industry or giving their ideas away at conferences and so on (Harvey 1989, pp. 121–22).

Patent considerations now influence resource allocation (Macdonald and Lefang 1997). These days, even universities direct resources towards areas of investigation which are likely to produce patentable results, and discourage staff from disclosing any information which may damage patent prospects. But even if a stronger patent system does encourage innovation in the patenting organization, restricted information flow from the organization may reduce innovation in the economy as a whole.

> A weak patent policy did not slow things down in the development of the integrated circuit and microprocessor. In fact, it sped things up. The legal environment of the 1970s allowed Fairchild, Intel and others to get their start, carrying the lesson that strong patents for every industry are not always good (Merges 1993, p. 62).

The patent system suits well the requirements of the pharmaceutical and chemical industries, which make disproportionate use of the system. The information of their invention is readily codified to fulfill the requirements of the patent specification, making subsequent patents easy to defend. The strategic interest of a few industries in stronger patents may well have produced a system which facilitates their own innovation, but which discourages innovation in other industries.

> . . . a very small group of large high technology firms and trade associations in the telecommunications, computer and pharmaceutical industries was essentially responsible for the creation of the CAFC [US Court of Appeals of the Federal Circuit]. The group believed that a court devoted to patent cases would better represent its interests (Silverman 1990, fn.62).

The patent system is also strikingly compatible with management methods requiring managers to control organizational resources for organizational benefit. There is no place in such methods for unmeasurable public benefit. In the global economy, the Agreement on Trade-Related Aspects of Intellectual Property Rights (TRIPS) would seem to encapsulate nicely the strategic method behind extending existing systems to capture the information of innovation (Drahos 1995).

Concluding Thoughts

Managers, of course, cannot be held entirely responsible for a policy approach to information which is inadequate and inappropriate. But this is policy for innovation, which is definitely the terrain of managers. Policy-makers look to managers for guidance in formulating innovation policy and, as we have seen, depend on them for its implementation. In market economies, government policy is expected to complement corporate strategy. In short, before there can be any prospect of changing policy towards information for innovation, managers must change their attitudes towards this information. This will not happen overnight. A new perspective is required and militating against the adoption of such a perspective is the advice management receives about how to change. Such advice now dominates the way managers manage. It focuses almost exclusively on achieving measurable criteria and is directed towards justifying the role of managers in achieving them. There is little consideration for the intangible, the unmeasurable, the indirect, the long term; flexibility is sacrificed to efficiency. Rather than reconciling themselves to living with uncertainty, managers are provided with the comfortable delusion that method will eliminate uncertainty.

Even in the bleakest of situations, there is always hope. In this case hope springs from the observations of a few consultants and fewer academics that the drive for efficiency has gone too far when there is no one left with the time, or indeed the incentive, to consider doing anything new (see, for example, De Nisi 1994). They argue that many organizations have lost the capacity to innovate and that this can be restored only by introducing some of the organizational fat, the organizational slack, which has been so mercilessly excised by management method. Extolling the counter-intuitive—the benefits of ignorance, failure, dissent—even accepting the inevitability of uncertainty, they face an uphill task. Bounded rationality is quite unrecognized in proactive team commitment to total excellence. This anti-method advice may, of course, shape itself into yet another temporary management fad; even so, it may just encourage managers to consider where their real skills and the real resources of the organization lie. Basically, the management of innovation requires that managers manage what they cannot control. The successful management of information for innovation is a real test of the manager's skills and is not to be achieved by simple method.

Acknowledgement

The author is grateful to the Economic and Social Research Council for its support (grants L325253021 and H52427500297) of some of the research underlying this paper.

CHAPTER 15

The Internationalization of R&D: Contents and Opportunities for Developing Countries

Jane Marceau

Introduction

This chapter examines some current trends in the internationalization of R&D that may or may not be of assistance to some developing countries in their quest for the economic growth which underpins higher standards of living. The chapter outlines some present trends and the motivations which seem to lie behind them. Much of the discussion will not be of direct relevance to the poorest of the underdeveloped nations: the very phenomenon of internationalization of research in its current form presupposes a degree of educational and scientific development.

For several decades now, developing countries have hosted manufacturing plants owned and operated by multinationals from the developed world. The internationalization of production had led to many debates about whether the presence of transnational corporations permits technology transfer such that the host nations can use them to improve their skills and economic chances.

The present chapter focuses not on manufacturing plants but on R&D laboratories and the conduct of R&D in specific overseas countries by foreign-owned transnational corporations. The implantation of R&D facilities may be the next stage of the internationalization process. Since Western countries are moving towards an economy based on innovation and increasing knowledge-intensity, it is sometimes argued that the presence of their R&D facilities may permit transfer of cutting edge technologies to the host nations. The spillover effects of knowledge-generation activities, for example, may mean that foreign-owned labs become the catalyst for local economic activity through the creation of new and high tech businesses by ex-employees. This chapter discusses present evidence.

The Growth of the Knowledge Economy

Recent international analysis of the drivers of economic growth has revealed the links between new technologies and economic growth. Work both within the OECD and elsewhere shows that innovation is increasingly the driver of growth in developed economies and that investment in the development and use of new technologies will be critical to success in coming decades. This prognosis suggests that both companies and governments in OECD countries should be investing heavily in the generation of new knowledge, in the R&D which is a critical part of innovation in knowledge-intensive industries, so more R&D is likely to be available to new locations.

There are several reasons why growth based on innovation may now be possible in the developing world. First, innovation and technological advance maximize higher skilled, higher paid employment and improved living standards by allowing businesses to build long-term advantage and hold strong market positions. The developing world may now have an opportunity to jump from very low to high technologies as part of development strategies since overseas firms are injecting high technology-related R&D.

Second, technological change can cause fundamental shifts in the competitive game, altering investment patterns to match new opportunities. Since new technologies usually need new organizational arrangements to work to best advantage firms may move to a new model and trajectory. The shift may allow room for organizational forms more advantageous to nations receiving foreign investment, since they often involve partnerships between firms of different sizes and competences through use of arrangements such as outsourcing and joint ventures. Some developing nations may have potential partner firms: as the UN *World Development Report* has stated:

> ... developing-country firms assumed a bigger role in strategic partnerships, (3 percent in 1989 to 13 per cent in 1995), suggesting that these firms may have attained sufficient technological sophistication and capacity to make them worth having as partners' (United Nations 1997, p. xvii).

Third, over the long run, a country's competitive advantage will lie in firms, industries and regions where rates of learning are higher than elsewhere. Building learning capability and generating of the knowledge underpinning innovation are thus critical to national development. Some underdeveloped nations may benefit from cooperation with companies creating within their borders. This could ensure higher rates of technological learning than were possible before.

The Drivers of Innovation

Recognition of the role of innovation in economic growth has prompted a search for the drivers of innovation itself. Recent conceptions emphasize interactions between different players in the innovation process. They demonstrate the feedback processes operating between scientific research, technical development and production, the simultaneity of R&D activities and the interaction among various actors in industrial R&D broadly defined. They emphasize the importance to innovating firms of working both with other firms and with a range of other organizations and institutions. If the R&D units in developing countries embed their activity in such innovative relationships at local level they may stimulate broader development.

Innovation patterns are greatly affected by the institutional framework in which innovation occurs. Acting within the institutional arrangements comprising 'national systems of innovation', firms take decisions about innovation. Factors affecting decisions include clients, intellectual property, design capability, machinery and equipment, materials, suppliers and a skilled labor force. The effectiveness of a national system of innovation to a large degree depends on its ability to assist firms to develop capability in each of these areas. National innovation policy thus remains an important determinant of the international competitiveness of nations, despite the globalization trend. Developing nations need to get that right since it is on this framework that the outcome for them—in terms of their capacity to use the new R&D conducted within their borders—depends.

Finally, here a Western economy's long-term capacity to produce jobs seems to be linked to its innovation capacity as measured even by R&D intensity alone. This may be the case for developing countries as well. A study by the OECD (1996) also found that industries with highly differentiated products and unfragmented markets (the kinds of industries typically requiring higher R&D intensity) were more likely to withstand the impact of rising import penetration than those in highly fragmented ones. This may allow countries to obtain long-term competitive advantage. Thus, a higher level of R&D, once translated into production, may enable a country to lever itself onto a new and more sustainable path than one which relies on low wages to attract investment. This could be a hope for developing countries that are host to technology-related FDI. The trick will be the translation into production of the new ideas generated.

Moreover, a move in the direction of high tech industries has important 'propulsive effects on economies'. One observer concludes that:

> ... technological spillover effects can widen and lengthen the wealth-producing properties of learning (both upstream and downstream, and horizontally into technologically complementary activities), while the quasi-rents earned from imperfect competition can be channeled through the producing economy in the form of wages, investment and cumulative change (Storper 1996: p. 25).

The Internationalization of R&D

Internationalization of economic activity is just about as old as trade itself. In recent years there has been much confusion about 'globalization', which was seen as different from internationalization and much more far-reaching in its consequences for national economies. It seems likely that 'true' globalization, that is the shift by companies to using a worldwide resource base without much preference for particular areas including their home bases, is still quite limited.

This section of the present chapter examines three questions—the amount of offshore R&D carried out, the reasons for such investments and the location of the investments in R&D of different types.

Offshore R&D investment

The late 1980s and early 1990s saw a considerable increase in the rate of internationalization. A spate of studies examined whether companies were 'globalizing' their R&D with the rest of their activity. The results are mixed.

Several studies of the internationalization of R&D by the world's largest companies were carried out by Patel and Pavitt at the Science Policy Research Unit at the University of Sussex in the early 1990s. Patel and Pavitt concluded that such firms were internationalizing much of their research and development activity but keeping their core R&D activities close to home, that indeed R&D was 'an important case of non-globalization', and that R&D was the last area of a firm's activities to move. Thus, although European and

US firms perhaps now conduct 15–20 percent of their R&D 'abroad', conduct of R&D offshore by other nations was negligible. Moreover, they found that European, Japanese and US firms were choosing only a very few non-home locations for R&D and these were essentially in the developed world.

In a recent paper (1998), the same analysts re-examined their earlier findings that R&D and patenting remains in great majority home-based. Using the activities of the Fortune 500 firms (of which 163 are European, 128 US and 95 Japanese), they show that even in the late 1990s most R&D remained at home.

Location of offshore R&D

This seems to be linked to motivations for conducting R&D. Several early studies showed that the most usual reason for conducting R&D overseas in the 1980s was adaptation of products for local markets or tastes and this perhaps remains so (OECD 1998, p. 17). Later analyses suggested that there were more diverse reasons for R&D investments in foreign countries and that several different motivations could be discerned, suggesting a quite complex picture. There are both 'push' and 'pull' factors.

One of the key push factors leading firms to invest in R&D overseas is emerging imbalances between what science has to offer and the demands of the technology system. These imbalances, said by Patel and Pavitt to put national innovation systems under strain, are the combined results of the liberalization of international exchanges, uneven rates of national technological development, the increasing range of fields of potentially useful technology and the increasing pressures of national competition and 'globalization' in some form. A second push factor is the shortage of skilled personnel in home countries (Reddy 1997).

A recent study by Kummerle (1997) published in the *Harvard Business Review* suggests that firms have two major types of R&D facility overseas: Home-Base-Exploiting and Home-Base-Augmenting. Firms have different expectations for each of these. The first is the well-known response to local markets' peculiarities: the firm selects a location for its proximity to a firm's existing manufacturing plants and markets so the overseas lab complements work done at home and uses mainly home-generated knowledge. In this case most information flows essentially from the home base outwards to the host country and encourages employees to interact primarily with other corporate units.

The second kind, Home-Base-Augmenting, is a response to the

increasing range of technologies available and the relatively low likelihood that all technological needs for new knowledge can be filled in the home country, whether by R&D inside the firm or via other organizations such as universities. The firm's lab is designed to send information back to the home base. In this case the company selects a location for its scientific excellence and promotes links between its own senior scientists and managers worldwide and active links with local scientific personnel.

In understanding trends in the location of R&D, Duysters and Haagedoorn suggest that the main question is whether companies are gradually becoming more international with respect to their foreign direct investment, their internal and external trade, their internal and external technology flows, their financial organization and their strategic alliances with other companies (1996). They suggest that there are many factors that affect decisions about where to conduct R&D. These are linked to broader issues of company strategy. Some of these push companies in the direction of concentrating their R&D while others favour dispersion.

The factors favouring concentration derive from the importance of economies of scale and scope in R&D that still exist within large facilities; the unstructured and intangible nature of R&D information, demanding personal interactions for its proper diffusion and understanding; the speed of decision-making needed for innovative projects; shortened product cycles requiring shorter interface distances; the need to protect and control product development as a major issue of corporate strategy close to the decision-making center of the company; and the potential to capitalize on accumulated experience in the home market and the technology networks with main suppliers.

In contrast, the factors encouraging dispersion—and hence the possibility of undertaking R&D in other countries—are also numerous. They include: potential interaction with high quality suppliers in innovative regions permitting benefit from technological advantages and regional agglomerative effects; the call for customization and adaptation to local needs mentioned above; host government pressures and incentives to conduct research locally or to maintain existing facilities; and reduction in the minimum size and divisibility of R&D facilities due to improved communication that allows for a more decentralized research capacity.

Mansfield and Lee (1996) have also examined company strategies in the internationalization of R&D. They have refined the analysis by looking at the different uses that firms make of new R&D overseas sites. They quote Florida (1997) who distinguishes between the use of R&D sites as 'strategic listening posts' designed to find out what is happening in new fields and to ensure that firms do not miss out on scientific breakthroughs early on, and their use as 'generating stations'. In the latter case, the R&D labs have a role in generating new information just as they would at home.

The question is whether there has been a fundamental change in the motivations for firms conducting offshore R&D in recent years. Patel and Pavitt (1998), using a subsample of 220 firms with the highest volume of patenting outside their home countries, concluded that firms locate their technology abroad in core fields where they are strong at home (more than 75 percent), not in order to exploit the technological advantages of the host country (only 10 percent). They do not seem to be 'pushed' by the factors emphasized by other analysts. Moreover, the largest increases in foreign technological activity, especially for chemical and pharmaceuticals, have been in technical fields where there are complementary strengths between the domestic activity of a firm and the host country. These results suggest that adapting products and processes and materials to suit foreign markets and providing technical support to offshore manufacturing plants remain major factors in the establishment of foreign R&D activities (Patel and Pavitt 1998, p. 13). There is very little evidence that firms routinely go abroad to compensate for their core weaknesses at home. This makes it seem likely that the internationalization of R&D follows that of other activities of the firm.

There are also cases where firms do indeed seem to go abroad to develop new technologies. These cases are of particular interest to developing countries because some of these decisions relate to the location of R&D in them, most notably in India and other parts of Asia. We now turn to look at these before drawing conclusions about the potential benefit of such overseas R&D to the host communities. Here we rely heavily on the work of Reddy and Sigurdson carried out in the early and mid 1990s. In a paper published in 1994, Reddy and Sigurdson indicate that since the mid 1980s, transnational corporations—especially those working in areas of new technologies—have started performing some of their R&D in selected developing countries (1994, p. 283). This strategic move, they say, has been facilitated by the availability of large pools of scientifically and technically trained manpower at substantially lower wages. Some of these countries also have an adequate industrial base so can ensure appropriate industrial experience where needed.

Cost is therefore clearly a factor in the wish by some firms to move to India, the developing country that has received both most Western R&D investment and the most analytical attention. Granstrand and his colleagues estimated (1992) that the cost of using Indian researchers with equivalent qualifications to those of research scientists working in the US and other industrialized countries was approximately one tenth when they worked in India.

Cost may not be the only issue, however. Reddy and Sigurdson (1994) suggest a second reason: that some OECD countries face a shortage of skilled personnel. They quote the case of Sweden, where, in the early 1990s, Asea and Ericsson were estimated to require 150 percent of all electronics graduates in Sweden while companies in biotechnology also faced a severe shortage of personnel (Hakanson 1990, quoted Reddy and Sigurdson 1994, p. 284). In contrast, some developing countries have a surplus of scientists. In addition to India, Brazil and Israel have pools of scientific talent which are not all utilized at home. South Korea, Singapore and other Pacific Rim countries are also said to be in this position, perhaps increasingly in the case of Korea after the currency collapse.

The net result, say Reddy and Sigurdson, is that TNCs, principally in pharmaceuticals, IT and chemicals, are making different decisions about where to locate their core R&D activities. Thus in India, Astra (a Swedish biotechnology firm), Hewlett Packard, Texas Instruments, Digital Equipment Corporation, Bull (France), Motorola and Siemens have all set up R&D facilities of varying kinds (Reddy and Sigurdson 1994, p. 285). TNCs in similar technologies have also set up in China, Taiwan, Singapore and Korea. In some cases the overseas investment has been in collaboration with local science institutions, for example, the Institute of Molecular and Cell Biology in Singapore.

The question here then is one of the extent of transfer of skills to host countries. In their paper, Reddy and Sigurdson conclude that, although the patterns of new investment in R&D in developing countries vary by firm, country and technology, 'TNCs are transferring advanced design tools, process technology and quality control know-how to developing host countries. Research personnel are being trained by TNCs locally and at their facilities in home countries' (1994, p. 286). They further quote a *Business Week* article which suggests that 'such human resource development will bring greater benefits to the host economy for decades to come.'

In a later paper, Reddy reports the results of a survey of sixteen overseas-owned R&D facilities focusing on conventional technologies and sixteen focusing on new technologies that he carried out in India in the mid 1990s. He points out that the two most important motives for investing in such facilities for conventional industries are proximity to manufacturing plants and to the Indian market. For new technologies, however, the reasons are different: access to trained personnel and the low cost of conducting R&D are paramount. Technology monitoring is important for all types of industry. In the case of the new technologies, it seems that R&D can be geographically delinked from manufacturing facilities (Reddy 1997, p. 1829). All the units are linked to the TNCs' corporate R&D in their home countries and worldwide.

Reddy concludes that his survey shows that:

> developing countries have now become locations not only for adaptation and product development for the local market types of R&D but also for R&D related to new products and processes. This performance of higher order R&D in India is a recent phenomenon ... The data also indicate that the primary driving force for locating R&D in India is technology-related (1997, p. 1831).

Most important of all, Reddy concludes that

> the countries that have an adequate supply of S&T personnel, even though they lack considerable industrial experience in conventional technology systems, can become locations for innovation activities in new technology systems. Moreover, the proximity of new technologies to basic science permits theoretically trained personnel with little industrial experience to be employed in R&D tasks (1997, p. 1831).

Some differences in links with local activities can be seen. In the case of the conventional technologies there are more links with local industries and the local university science base whereas in the newer technologies there are as yet few local links at all. Links are rather with the parent firms' world science and industry connections. This may be because there is little local high tech industry or because firms are nervous of allowing access to their material in an environment where property rights are not fully protected or because of the highly specialized nature of the work carried out.

Conclusions: Can Developing Countries Trap the Benefits of the Overseas-funded R&D Performed Inside their Borders?

This section addresses the critical question of the extent to which host nations may benefit from the location of R&D in new technologies on their territory. There are clearly some important issues that need discussion.

The first concerns the degree to which the new activities can be linked to the host countries' national systems of innovation considered more broadly. If it is true that it is well functioning systems of innovation which assist countries to develop, then the new technology development must be somehow integrated to the broader system. It is not at present clear how this would be done since the links of the R&D centers are with the rest of the world, not their local environment. Many do not have good links, it seems, with either industries or universities. Reddy, however, believes that the new facilities taken as a whole have developed closer links with local industry than have conventional technologies and hence stronger links with the local system of innovation. This, he claims, indicates that there is now greater diffusion of knowledge into the host country than before (1997, p. 1832). He suggests that such linkages will go on increasing because the new units are indeed new and are still exploring their local relationships. This, he says, implies that there is still scope for expanding and strengthening local linkages whereas the older R&D units have exhausted their contacts and are unlikely to make new ones.

In view of this, he suggests that the 'future prospects for some developing countries are bright'. In part this is because the new activities encourage local nationals trained in the USA who would not previously have returned home to do so, thus reducing the 'brain drain' through overseas education. Reddy also uses the example of the way in which TNCs' production activities in the NIEs have over time 'contributed immensely to the acquisition of production engineering related capabilities. Beginning with simple assembly activities, TNCs have increased the complexity and sophistication of their manufacturing activities in the NIEs in a short period of time. The successful assimilation of these skills by the NIEs gave the TNCs necessary confidence to locate critical design and product engineering tasks in these countries' (1997, p. 1832).

Dunning pointed out in 1992 that there are two opposing views regarding the impact of TNCs' R&D on host countries:

> One view considers inward R&D investments to be in general beneficial to economic growth, by providing technology and managerial skills which in turn create indirect positive effects for the host country at a lower cost. These positive effects include technical support to local suppliers and customers, contract jobs from foreign R&D units to local R&D organizations etc. [In contrast] the counterview argues that R&D activities by foreign firms

> tend to tap into unique local R&D resources with little or no benefit to the host country. Concentrating on problems of little or no relevance to the local economy, they may be little more than a disguised "braindrain", diverting scarce technical resources from more useful purposes' (quoted in Reddy 1997, p. 1833).

Reddy counters this negative view by noting that in the context of developing countries where S&T resources are underutilized, the benefits are larger and the cost marginal. He recognizes that such R&D may create 'high tech enclaves' with little diffusion of knowledge into the local economy, but claims that knowledge and skills cannot be isolated over the long term. Mobility of personnel, the need for local procurement of materials and other supplies are bound to diffuse the technologies throughout the economy, he suggests.

Much, it seems, depends on your point of view and on the strategies in practice of the firms concerned. These may vary by firm and by technology. On the more positive side, Reddy says that the evidence suggests that TNCs are not only adding new innovation capacity by making greenfield investments in creating R&D facilities, but are also bringing in new equipment and access to global knowledge networks. Through their linkages to the national systems of innovation in the host countries, these R&D activities are also contributing to the diffusion of new knowledge and technologies into the host economy. TNCs are also establishing chairs in local universities and adding new equipment to university labs. The most important benefit of all, in Reddy's eyes, is that the TNCs are inculcating a more commercial culture into local scientists. TNCs, he says, are contributing to the diffusion of application skills to researchers and encouraging them to go beyond just proving principles. He gives the example of Astra, which has been transferring the know how to produce by-products generated in its Indian R&D facilities to local firms, leading to the emergence of high tech spin-off enterprises. One such example is a firm called GENEI, which now exports recombinant DNA products to the US whereas before India had to import them all.

On the other hand, it seems likely that TNCs can dominate the labor market for highly skilled personnel, since they can offer both better pay and conditions and more advanced equipment and tasks, all of which are attractive to scientists. This may reduce the chances of local firms of being able to access their compatriots' skills in the shorter term. What happens in the longer term remains to be seen.

Much will depend on the strategies followed by the investing firms themselves. It may be that they will develop the kinds of research partnerships that are now becoming the norm in all countries as large labs give way to smaller, more specialist ones or to complete outsourcing or partnerships with centers of excellence worldwide. In some cases, developing countries are creating pools of expertise that may be greater than similar ones in other countries just because several firms have set up facilities and staff move between them. They have thus created clusters of skills and activities. This may lead to a situation similar to that in Denmark, where the firms in the radio-communications cluster near Aalborg are all owned by foreign multinationals but are left alone because their value lies in their participation in the cluster, not in their standing as individual firms (Dalum, personal communication).

What then can we learn about policy-making for host countries in this situation? Much will depend on the skills and understandings of local policy-makers. Some countries have shown the way. Singapore, for example, has long had in place a policy that ensures that TNCs investing must also transfer technology to the local community. It seems though it was this policy that enabled Singapore to be one of the first to become host to major transnational research facilities rather than just be a production site. This shift took place some time ago. Ensuring such a shift has to be the aim of all developing countries' governments if they are to ensure that the diffusion of knowledge to the local community is greater than the risk of what is otherwise effectively the export of carefully and expensively nurtured local science skills.

Similarly, nations need to give careful consideration to the ways in which their education system is linked to the local economy. In India the education system still retains some of the heritage of the British system. This values the pursuit of knowledge unlinked to local opportunities and incorporates few efforts to enshrine national priorities in the choices that students make both at undergraduate and postgraduate levels. Moreover, in many cases there is a discernible bias against engineering in favour of purer science. The existence of this bias is the cause of the pools of highly skilled and low cost but 'unapplied' scientists, which is what has attracted the TNCs to establish R&D facilities there in the first place. A new balance may be required.

It is also clear from the literature on national systems of innovation that there are many aspects of the system other than business and education that need to work together if development is to occur.

One of the most important is the financial system; another concerns the functioning of the labor market; yet another concerns the certainty of the public decision-making process and the protection of intellectual property. In many developing countries few or even none of the prerequisites are in place.

Moreover, there is no guarantee that all firms will respond to their situation in the same way and make the same contributions to the local economy. It is by no means clear, for example, that the behavior and impact of Astra in India will be the same as that of an IT firm investing in Africa. Astra is a Swedish firm. Swedish firms investing overseas are renowned for the independence of their overseas units and the degree to which they link with their local environment. Even in Australia there are, for example, very clear differences between Swedish car component manufacturers and US or Japanese ones in this respect. Governments in developing countries will need to take a very sophisticated look at the strategies normally followed by potential investors and may need to tailor local technology diffusion requirements to attitudes and practices of the different firms concerned.

In addition, WTO rules now make it harder for countries to bargain over technology transfer. This means that host governments will need to make very sophisticated judgements indeed about which policies to adopt to encourage, for instance, the geographical agglomeration of proposed R&D facilities to take advantage of what we know about the importance of agglomeration for technology diffusion and the creation of an 'innovative milieu' conducive to further business development. The developed world is still coming to grips with the new rules and has few clear policy recommendations to make that are based on successful local experience. Thus, for example, whereas there is very considerable policy interest in 'clusters,' however defined, very little is known about what makes effective policy in this field. One prerequisite for developing countries trying to maximize the advantage that they can gain from FDI in R&D is knowledge of the cutting policy edge in developed countries who face similar problems and are struggling with the solutions. If they cannot capture more of the benefit so that they can employ their local scientists in local industries, they run the risk of finding that their science education base has been pushed into specializations that suit the external investors but which may render the local economy vulnerable when TNCs develop new strategies or find that local cost differentials are no longer so favorable. Any apparent advantage based on cost is vulnerable.

Reddy indeed quotes a study which shows that some of these cost differentials are already eroding. Thus, by 1994 an article in *Business Week* indicated that while the salaries of engineers and department managers in India were US$2100–4300 and in Japan they were 20 times that, already the salaries of similar personnel in South Korea were approaching those of Italy and those of Brazil were one-half of those in the US. This suggests some short-term as well as long-term vulnerability in some countries to the erosion of cost differentials.

Political, economic or social instability which threatens expensive R&D investments and the lack of well developed intellectual property rights, for instance, may also combine to outweigh the lower salary costs of overseas R&D investments. It may transpire that TNCs are as footloose in these investments as they were in some others, notably the location of their manufacturing plants. Developing nations must take care that they do not get caught in a bidding war for the location of R&D facilities just as many poorer regions (including some in Europe) got caught in the race for manufacturing. If they do face such a war, they must at least have in place plans for capturing and embedding the benefits for which they may pay dearly. In particular, they must have local business development strategies well established.

The threat of distortion of education and R&D conduct at higher levels to suit TNC strategies is not an idle one. It is so serious that a publication by the OECD suggested that countries must ensure that they have an adequate domestic R&D system in place. If they do not, the OECD suggests,

> they may find that they spend considerably more on imports of patents and licenses than on their own research. In these countries, even in the developed world, more than one third of national R&D is carried out by foreign affiliates ... Massive imports of technology might then be expected to act as substitutes for domestic research and technology ... In the majority of countries, imported technology can obviously serve both to supplement and be a substitute for local R&D, even if it primarily serves foreign affiliates. However, when the bulk of the technology needed for industrial development and innovation is imported and foreign affiliates account for most of these imports, the technological base of the countries concerned could disintegrate in time unless the R&D effort by national firms can replace an increasing proportion of imported technology. This point is all the more important as the increasingly sophisticated new technologies can be assimilated only by firms which themselves conduct research and in their turn produce technology (OECD 1994, 72–3).

If this is the case for OECD nations such as Spain and Portugal, how much greater is the risk for developing ones whose industrial bases are far from having the capability to conduct research and absorb the new technologies developed within their boundaries.

A national innovation system includes public policies that encourage innovation, as well as the funds invested both in the public and private sectors and the inter relations between players and both sectors. A properly functioning national system of innovation underpins the innovative capacities of firms because the institutional structures provide collectively what firms cannot individually produce themselves. These factors include public good research and the development of expertise on a broad range of fronts which are necessary to firm innovation strategies but cannot be afforded by individual companies. This is especially true in small countries and for small firms which have too few resources to meet the cost of research of a more basic or promising but initially tangential kind.

Work by OECD and others has indicated that any national system of innovation is constrained by the underlying industrial structure of the economy. A 'patchy' industrial structure, for instance, where public sector research is linked only to a few companies or industries, breaks down the effectiveness of linkages within the national innovation system. Such a 'patchy' fabric is typical of many developing nations. The degree to which high level knowledge gained from R&D can compensate for the absence of the 'complementary assets' needed for transforming R&D into marketable products in developing countries is not clear.

Central to the analysis is the recognition that, despite increases in globalization, the nation remains the most important innovation arena. It is what happens inside national borders that largely determines the success of the national economic endeavor. It is still within the national arena, for example, that policies for research, for training, for the protection of intellectual property, for access to finance for development and so on are decided and local business skills developed.

It is not clear, therefore, that the new investments by TNCs in R&D facilities in developing countries are an unmixed blessing. The outcome will clearly depend on the skills with which policy-makers can ensure that there is maximum transfer of technology at minimum cost and that local industry can be brought to a level where it can absorb the new opportunities potentially available. This means not only ensuring that businesses are able to employ the skilled personnel that they need and are not priced out of the market by foreign competitors, but also that they have access to the necessary startup and expansion finance, the right export assistance and the right equipment—the latter being perhaps the hardest in nations as strapped for capital as most developing countries tend to be.

Like all overseas investments, investments in R&D, even in new technologies, have to be viewed judiciously and decided on in the light of the overall benefits to be gained. Specific diffusion policies need to be developed and the decisions set in the overall context of the nation's needs. This is just as daunting a task as the assessment of the benefits of all overseas investments, even in developed countries such as Australia. As in Australia, policies need to be developed which will embed the new investments and reduce the chances of footloose companies moving again in the near future, leaving little behind. The literature on the importance of well-integrated national systems of innovation for growth indicates some of the directions nations can take when considering such investments, but a successful outcome is likely to take both considerable vision and considerable toughness on the part of local decision-makers. It is not clear that all have the capacity to take advantage of an 'injection' of the technologies of the 21st century which the West will be using for the foreseeable future. If they can, this time the developing world may have a greater chance of co-developing rather than having to buy technologies if the policy cards can be played properly. This should be an urgent item on the policy agenda of the countries concerned.

References

Chapter 1

Arrow, K.J. 1974. *The Limits of Organization*. New York: Norton.

Arrow, K.J. 1987. "Oral history I: An interview". In *Arrow and the Ascent of Modern Economic Theory*, edited by G.R. Feiwell, pp. 191–242. London: Macmillan.

Boulding, K.E. 1966. "The economics of knowledge and the knowledge of economics". Reprinted in *Economics of Information and Knowledge*, ed. D.M. Lamberton, pp. 21–36. Harmondsworth UK: Penguin Books.

Boyle, J. 1992. "A theory of law and information: copyright, spleens, blackmail, and insider trading". *California Law Review*, 80:6, pp. 1413–1540.

Carter, A.P. 1996. "Measuring the performance of a knowledge-based economy". In OECD *Employment and Growth in the Knowledge-based Economy*, pp. 61–8. Paris: OECD.

Economist, The 1997. Telecommunications Survey: "A connected world", 13 September, pp. 3–4.

Economist, The 1999a. "Storm over globalisation", 27 November, pp. 13–14.

Economist, The 1999b. "Who needs the WTO?", 4 December, p. 82.

Economist, The 2000a. "Trade before the tariffs [Review of O'Rourke and Williamson]", 8 January, p. 84.

Economist, The 2000b. "The Net gets real", 15 January, pp. 20–5.

Economist, The 2000c. "The world's view of multinationals", 29 January, pp. 19–20.

Economist, The 2000d. "The record industry takes fright", 29 January, pp. 71–2.

Economist, The 2000e. "And the word is God", 29 January, p. 104.

Economist, The 2000f. "What is Europe", 12 February, p. 14.

Engels, F. "Letter to Bloch", In *Selected Correspondence*, quoted by V. Venable, *Human Nature; the Marxian View*. New York: A.A. Knopf, 1945, p. 31.

Enos, J. 1997. "Review of A.S. Bhalla, *Facing the Technological Challenge*: A study prepared for the International Labour Office". *Economic Journal* 107:442, pp. 808–10.

IMF 2000. *IMF Survey*, 24 January.

Johnston, H.J. 1991. *Dispelling the Myth of Globalization: The Case for Regionalization*. New York: Praeger.

Jowitt, K. 1992. *New World Disorder: The Leninist Extinction*. Berkeley: University of California Press.

Judt, T. 1999. "On Kosovo". *New York Review of Books* 46, 22 April, p. 16.

Kindleberger, C.P. 1994. "*The Great Disorder*: A review of the book of that title by Gerald D. Feldman", *Journal of Economic Literature* 32:3, pp. 1216–25.

Lamberton, D.M. 1993. "Globaloney: The impact of regions on the future of emerging markets in information technology and trade". *Pacific Telecommunications Review* 14:4, pp. 3–10.

Lamberton, D.M. 1995. "Organizational capital: An information-theoretic approach". *International Journal of New Ideas* 4, pp. 33–8.

Lamberton, D.M. 1997a. "Information economics research: Points of departure". *Information Economics and Policy* 10, pp. 325–30.

Lamberton, D.M. 1997b. "The knowledge-based economy: A Sisyphus Model". *Prometheus* 15:1, pp. 73–81.

Lamberton, D.M. 1999. "Information: Pieces, batches, or flows?". In eds S.C. Dow and P.E. Earl, *Economic Organization and Knowledge: Essays in Honour of Brian Loasby*, Cheltenham UK: Edward Elgar pp. 209–24.

Lamberton, D.M. 2000. 'A perspective on the information economy'. In eds E. Bohlin, K. Brodin, A. Lundgren and B.Thorngren *Convergence in Communications and Beyond*, Amsterdam: North-Holland, pp. 397–404.

Lucas, R.E. 1972 "Expectation and the neutrality of money". *Journal of Economic Theory* 4:2, pp. 103–24.

Machlup, F. 1962. *The Production and Distribution of Knowledge in the United States*. Princeton NJ: Princeton University Press.

Machlup, F. 1982. "Optimum utilization of knowledge". *Society, Knowledge, Information, and Decisions* 20:1, pp. 8–10.

Madden, G. 1999. "Asia-Pacific information flows and trade". In eds S. Macdonald and J. Nightingale, *Information and Organisation: A Tribute to the Work of Don Lamberton*, Amsterdam: North-Holland pp. 393–406.

Maddock, R. 1984. "Rational expectations macrotheory: A Lakatosian case study in program adjustment". *History of Political Economy* 16, pp. 291–309.

Nelson, R.R. 1981. "Assessing private enterprise: An exegesis of tangled doctrine". Reprinted in ed. Lamberton, D.M. *The Economics of Communication and Information*, pp. 59–77. Cheltenham UK: Edward Elgar.

O'Rourke, K. and J. Williamson, 1999. *Globalisation and History: The Evolution of a Nineteenth Century Atlantic Economy*. Cambridge, Mass.: MIT Press.

Parente, S.L. and E.C. Prescott. 1999. "Monopoly rights: A barrier to riches". *American Economic Review* 89:5, pp. 1216–33.

Pearson, K. 1892. *The Grammar of Science*. London: J.M. Dent.

Pelikan, P. 1969. "Language as a limiting factor for centralization". *American Economic Review* 59:4, pp. 625–31.

Penrose, E. 1992. "Economic liberalization: Openness and integration—but what kind?" *Development Policy Review*. Reprinted in *Prometheus* 11:1, pp. 30–44.

Ricardo, D. In R.M. Hartwell (ed.) 1971 *The Principles of Political Economy and Taxation*. Harmondsworth UK, Penguin Books.

Robbins, Lord. 1968. *The Theory of Economic Development in the History of Economic Thought.* London: Macmillan.

Romer, P. 1990. "Endogenous technical change". *Journal of Political Economy* 98, S71–S102.

Scarf, H.E. 1994. "The allocation of resources in the presence of indivisibilities". *Journal of Economic Perspectives* 8:4, pp. 111–28.

Sen, A. 1999. *Development is Freedom.* Oxford: Oxford University Press.

Shackle, G.L.S. 1967. *The Years of High Theory: Invention and Tradition in Economic Thought 1926–1939.* Cambridge: Cambridge University Press.

Shackle, G.L.S. 1972, *Epistemics & Economics: A Critique of Economic Doctrines.* Cambridge: Cambridge University Press.

Sobel, A.C. 1999. *State Institutions, Private Incentives, Global Capital.* Ann Arbor: University of Michigan Press.

Stiglitz, J.E. 1994. *Whither Socialism?* Cambridge, Mass.: MIT Press.

Stiglitz, J.E. 1999. *Public Policy for a Knowledge Economy.* Lecture at the UK Department for Trade and Industry, 27 January.

Toulmin, S. 1999. "The ambiguities of globalization". *Futures* 31, pp. 905–12.

Venable, V. 1945. *Human Nature: the Marxian View.* New York: A.A. Knopf.

Vines, D. and A. Stevenson 1991. *Information, Strategy and Public Policy.* Oxford: Blackwell.

Webster, E. 1999. *The Economics of Intangible Investment.* Cheltenham UK: Edward Elgar.

World Bank. 1996. *Global Economic Prospects and the Developing Countries.* Washington DC: World Bank.

Chapter 2

Amsden, A. 1989. *Asia's Next Giant: South Korea and Late Industrialization.* New York: Oxford University Press.

Bello, W. 1991. *Dragons in Distress: Asia's Miracle Economies in Crisis.* London: Penguin.

Bowring, P. 1998. Comments at seminar on Improving the Flow of Information in a Time of Crisis: The Challenge to the Southeast Asian Media. Subic, Philippines, 29–31 October.

Fallows, J. 1994. *Looking at the Sun.* New York: Pantheon.

Fischer, S. 1997. "Capital account liberalization and the role of the IMF". Paper presented at the Asia and the IMF Seminar, Hong Kong, 19 September.

Gapper, J. and N. Denton, 1997. *All That Glitters: The Fall of Barings.* London: Penguin.

Hughes, H. 1992. *East Asian Export Success.* Research School of Pacific Studies. Canberra: Australian National University.

Krueger, A. 1993. "East Asia: Lessons for growth theory". Paper presented at the Fourth Annual East Asian Seminar on Economics, National Bureau of Economic Research. San Francisco, California, 17–19 June.

Little, I.D. 1982. *Economic Development.* New York: Basic Books.

Pakorn Vichyanond. 1994. *Thailand's Financial System: Structure and Liberalization.* Bangkok: Thailand Development Research Institute.

Reuters. 1998. "Confidence returning to Asia, says report". 11 November.

Rubin, R. 1998a. "Strengthening the architecture of the international financial system". Speech delivered at Brookings Institution, Washington, DC, 14 April.

Rubin, R. 1998b. Remarks at the Sasin Institute of Business Administration, Chulalongkorn University. Bangkok, 30 June.

Saker, N. 1996. "Guest viewpoint: Thailand update: Market pessimism is overblown". *BOI Investment Review* 2, 31 December.

Summers, L. 1998. "The global economic situation and what it means for the United States". Remarks to the National Governors Association, Milwaukee, Wisconsin, 4 August.

Wade, R. 1990. *Governing the Market: Economic Theory and the Role of Government in East Asian Industrialization.* Princeton: Princeton University Press.

World Bank. 1993. *The East Asian Miracle.* New York: Oxford University Press.

Chapter 3

Bray, J.R. and W. Mudd 1998. *The Contribution of DSS Payments to Regional Income.* Australian Government, Department of Social Security, Technical Paper No. 2, July.

Bridges, W. 1996. *Jobshift.* London: Nicholas Brealey.

Bryan, D. and M. Rafferty 1999. *The Global Economy in Australia: Global Integration and National Economic Policy.* Sydney: Allen & Unwin.

Burbach, R., O. Nunez and B. Kagarlitsky 1997. *Globalization and its Discontents.* London: Pluto Press.

Burgess, J. and R. Green 1997. "A policy program for growth, jobs and the current account". *Journal of Australian Political Economy* 40, pp. 1–26.

Castles, F. 1985. *The Working Class and Welfare.* Wellington: Allen & Unwin.

Crockett, R. 1995. *Thinking the Unthinkable: Think-Tanks and the Economic Counter-Revolution 1931–1983.* London: HarperCollins.

Economist, The 1998, November pp. 14–20.

Gordon, D. 1996. *Fat and Mean: The Corporate Squeeze of Working Americans and the Myth of Managerial 'Downsizing'.* New York: The Free Press.

Gorz, A. 1985. *Paths to Paradise: On the Liberation from Work.* London: Pluto Press.

Hamilton, C., J. Quiggin and T. Hundloe 1997. *Ecological Tax Reform in Australia.* The Australia Institute, Discussion Paper No. 10, Canberra, April.

Heilbroner, R.L. 1995. "Preface". In J. Rifkin, *The End of Work.* London: Deep Books.

Hirst, P. and G. Thompson 1996. *Globalisation in Question.* Oxford: Polity Press.

Hutton, W. 1996. *The State We're In.* London: Vintage.

ILO. 1996. *World Employment 1996/97 National Policies in a Global Context.* Geneva: International Labour Office.

Jamieson House Employment Group. 1996. *Redistributing Work: Solutions to the Paradox of Overwork and Unemployment in Australia,* The Australia Institute, Discussion Paper No. 7. Canberra, June.

Jones, B. 1982. *Sleepers Wake! Technology and the Future of Work.* Melbourne: Oxford University Press.

Lane, R. 1991. *The Market Experience.* New York: Cambridge University Press.

Langmore, J. and J. Quiggin 1990. *Work for All: Full Employment in the Nineties.* Melbourne: Melbourne University Press.

Marceau, J., K. Manley and D. Sicklen 1997. *The High Road or the Low Road? Alternatives for Australia's Future.* Sydney: Australian Business Foundation Ltd.

Martin, H.P. and H. Schumann 1997. *The Global Trap: Globalisation and the Assault on Democracy and Prosperity.* London: Zed Books.

OECD 1977. *Structural Determinants of Employment and Unemployment,* Vol. 1. Paris: OECD.

Ohmae, K. 1996. *The End of the Nation State.* London: HarperCollins.

Parker, R. 1998. "Globalisation, political capacity and unemployment: a comparative analysis of 15 OECD countries 1974–1992". In *Unemployment: Economic Promise and Political Will,* eds. E. Carson, A. Jamrozik and T. Winefield. Brisbane: Australian Academic Press.

Reich, R. 1992. *The Work of Nations: Preparing Ourselves for 21st Century Capitalism.* New York: Random House.

Rifkin, J. 1995. *The End of Work.* London: Deep Books.

Robinson, J. 1973. *Collected Economic Papers.* Oxford: Basil Blackwell.

Russell, B. 1918. *Roads to Freedom.* London: Unwin.

Sanne, C. 1998. *The (Im)possibility of Sustainable Lifestyles—Can We Trust Public Opinion and Plan for Reduced Consumption?* Australian National University, Urban Research Program, Working Paper No. 63, August.

Schlemmer, L. 1998. Paper presented to TODA Conference on Globalisation, Employment and Quality of Life, University of Sydney, November.

Thurow, L. 1996. *The Future of Capitalism.* London: Nicholas Brealey.

Wolff. E.N. 1998. "Recent trends in the size distribution of household wealth". *Journal of Economic Perspectives* 12:3, pp. 131–50.

Chapter 4

Arthur, W.B. 1990. "Positive feedbacks in the economy". *Scientific American* 262(2), pp. 92–9.

Barnett, T.W. 1998. *Is the New Global Economy Leaving State-Local Tax Structures Behind?* National League of Cities, National Conference of State Legislatures, National Governors Association. Annapolis MD, USA.

Bootle, R. 1996. *The Death of Inflation: Surviving and Thriving in the Zero Era.* London: Nicholas Brealey.

Boulding, K.E. 1968. *Essays on Society, Religion and Ethics.* Ann Arbor: University of Michigan Press.

Burki, S.J. and G.E. Perry 1998. *Beyond the Washington Consensus: Institutions Matter.* Washington DC: World Bank.

Business Week. 1998. Editorial. 7 September, p. 122.

Daly, H. and J. Cobb 1989. *Toward the Common Good.* Boston: Beacon Press.

Dembinski, P.H. and A. Schoenenberger. 1998. "The safe landing of the financial balloon is not impossible", *Finance and the Common Good,* Observatoire de la Finance, 1, pp. 35–41.

Domini, A.L. and P.D. Kinder 1984. *Ethical Investing.* Reading, Mass.: Addison-Wesley.

Economist, The 1997a. "Thoroughly modern mercantilists". 1 February. 25.

Economist, The 1997b. "The disappearing taxpayer". 31 May. 15.

Economist, The 1997c. "Cleaning up dirty money". 26 July. 18.

Economist, The 1998a. "Hubble, bubble, inflation trouble?" 9 May. 90.

Economist, The 1998b. "Is the case for free financial flows as strong as that for free trade?" 23 May, p. 112.

Economist, The 1998c. "Japan, the yen and the dollar". 10 October. 18.

Epstein, J.M. & R. Axtell 1996. *Growing Artificial Societies—The 2050 Project of the Brookings Institution.* Boston: MIT Press.

Financial Times, 1998. 30 October. 1.

Fleming, M.J. 1962. "Domestic financial policies under fixed and floating exchange rates", *IMF Staff Papers* 9, pp. 369–79.

Georgescu-Roegen, N. 1971. *The Entropy Law and the Economic Process.* Cambridge, MA.: Harvard University Press.

Guerard Jr J.B. 1996. "Is there a cost to being socially responsible in investing?" New York: Vantage Global Advisors, Inc.

Henderson, H. 1971a. "Economists *versus* ecologists", *New York Times*, 24 October.

Henderson, H. 1971b. "Toward managing social conflict", *Harvard Business Review* 49:3, pp. 82–90.

Henderson, H. 1973. "Ecologist *versus* economists", *Harvard Business Review*, 51:4, pp. 28–36, pp. 152–157.

Henderson, H. 1978. *Creating Alternative Futures: The End of Economics.* New York: Putnam's Sons.

Henderson, H. 1981. *The Politics of the Solar Age.* New York: Doubleday.

Henderson, H. 1982. "The politics and ethics of the solar age", Horace Albright Lecture, University of California.

Henderson, H. 1990. "Introduce 'Green' taxes". *Christian Science Monitor* 6 July, 19.

Henderson, H. 1991. *Paradigms in Progress.* Indianapolis: Knowledge Systems, Inc.

Henderson, H. 1996a. *Building a Win-Win World.* San Francisco: Berrett-Koehler.

Henderson, H. 1996b. "Transnational corporations and global citizenship". Geneva: UN Research Institute for Social Development.

Henderson, H. 1998. "Economic lessons of the Asian meltdown", *World Business Academy Perspectives* 12(3).

Henderson, H. with H. Cleveland and I. Kaul 1995. *The United Nations: Policy and Financing Alternatives.* Elsevier: Futures; Washington DC: Global Commission to Fund the UN.

Henderson, H and A.F. Kay 1995. "A United Nations Security Insurance Agency", *Futures* 27:1, pp. 3–10.

Henderson, H. and A.F. Kay 1996. "Introducing competition to global currency markets", *Futures*, 28:4, pp. 305–24.

Huntington, S.P. 1991. *The Third Wave: Democratization in the Late Twentieth Century.* Norman, Ok.: University of Oklahoma Press.

Kapp, K.W. 1950. *The Social Costs of Private Enterprise.* Cambridge, MA.: Harvard University Press.

Kay, A.F. 1998. *Locating Consensus for Democracy.* American Talk Issues Foundation. See *www.publicinterestpolling.com*

Kelso, L.O. and P.H. Kelso 1967. *Two-Factor Theory: How to Turn 80 Million Workers into Capitalists on Borrowed Money.* New York: Vintage.

Lamberton, D.M. (ed.) 1971. *The Economics of Information and Knowledge.* Harmondsworth UK: Penguin.

Loye, D. 1998. *Evolutionary Outrider: The Impact of the Human Agent on Evolution.* Westport, CT: Praeger.

Mishan, E.J. 1969. *Growth: The Price We Pay.* London: Staples.

Mitchell, R.A. and N. Shafer 1984. *Standard Catalog of Depression Scrip of the US including Canada and Mexico.* San Jose, CA: Globe Print Co.

Müller, J.O. 1995. *The Future European Model.* Westport, CT: Praeger/Greenwood.

Mundell, R.A. 1962. "The appropriate use of monetary and fiscal policy for internal and external stability", IMF Staff Papers 9, pp. 70–7.

Prince Saddrudin Aga Khan *et al.* 1998. *Policing the Global Economy: Why, How, and For Whom?* Geneva.

Phillips, A.W. 1958. "The relation between unemployment and the rate of change of money wage rates in the United Kingdom, 1861–1957", *Economica* 25, pp. 283–99.

Romer, P.M. 1990. "Endogenous technical change", *Journal of Political Economy*, 98, S71–S102.

Rothschild, M. 1990. *Bionomics: The Inevitability of Capitalism.* New York: H. Holt.

Summers, V. and L. Summers 1989. "When financial markets work too well: A cautious case for a financial transactions tax". In *Regulating Reform of Stock and Futures Markets*, ed. F.R. Edwards, Special Issue, *Journal of Financial Services Research* 3, pp. 261–86.

Toohey, B. 1994. *Tumbling Dice: The Story of Modern Economic Policy.* Port Melbourne: William Heinemann.

Tobin, J. 1978. "A proposal for international monetary reform," *Eastern Economic Journal*, 4, pp. 153–9.

United Nations University. 1984. *The Science and Praxis of Complexity: Proceedings of the Montpellier Symposium.* Tokyo.

UNDP. 1995. *Human Development Report.* UN Development Programme. New York: Oxford University Press.

UTNE Reader. 1997.

Ward, B. and R. Dubos 1972. *Only One Earth: The Care and Maintenance of a Small Planet.* New York: Norton.

Weiss, L. 1998. *The Myth of the Powerless State: Governing the Economy in a Global Era.* Cambridge: Polity Press.

World Commission on Environment and Development. 1987. *Our Common Future.* New York: Oxford University Press.

Yergin, D. and J. Stanislaw 1998. *The Commanding Heights.* New York: Simon and Schuster.

Chapter 5

Albrow, M. 1990. "Introduction". In *Globalisation, Knowledge and Society: Readings from International Sociology*, ed. M. Albrow and E. King, pp. 3–13. London: Sage.

Brenner, N. 1997. "Global, fragmented, hierarchical: Henri Lefebvre's *Geographies of Globalisation*". *Public Culture* 6:1, Fall, pp. 135–67.

Clark, I. 1997. *Globalisation and Fragmentation: International Relations in the Twentieth Century*. Oxford: Oxford University Press.

Giddens, A. 1990. *The Consequences of Modernity*. Stanford: Stanford University Press.

Hirst, P. and G. Thompson 1996. *Globalization in Question: The International Economy and the Possibilities of Governance*. Cambridge, MA: Polity.

Holm, H-H. and G. Sorenson 1995. *Whose World Order?: Uneven Globalisation and the End of the Cold War*. Boulder, CO: Westview Press.

Holton, R. 1998. *Globalisation and the Nation State*. London: Macmillan.

Lubbers, R.F.M. 1998. *The Dynamic of Globalization*. Paper presented at Tilburg University, 26 November.

Robertson, R. 1992. *Globalisation: Social Theory and Global Culture*. London: Sage.

Robertson, R. 1990. "Mapping the global condition: Globalisation as the central concept". In *Global Culture: Nationalism, Globalisation and Modernity*, ed. M. Featherstone, pp. 15–30. London: Sage.

Walters, M. 1995. *Globalisation*. New York: Routledge.

Further Reading

The following references may be helpful in consideration of definitional issues.

Agnew, J. and S. Corbridge 1995. *Mastering Space: Hegemony, Territory and International Political Economy*. London: Routledge.

Albrow, M. 1997. *The Global Age: State and Security Beyond Modernity*. Stanford: Stanford University Press.

Amin, S. 1997. *Capitalism in the Age of Globalisation: The Management of Contemporary Society*. London: Zed Books Ltd.

Amin, A and N. Thrift (eds). 1995. *Globalization, Institutions, and Regional Development in Europe*. New York: Oxford University Press.

Axtmann, R. (ed.). 1998. *Globalisation and Europe: Theoretical and Empirical Investigations*. London: Pinter.

Baker, D., G. Epstein and R. Pollin (eds). 1998. *Globalisation and Progressive Economic Policy*. New York: Cambridge University Press.

Bauman, Z. 1998. *Globalization: The Human Consequences*. New York: Columbia University Press.

Baylis, J. and S. Smith (eds). 1997. *The Globalisation of World Politics*. Oxford: Oxford University Press.

Bell, S. 1997. "Globalisation, neoliberalism and the transformation of the Australian State", *Australian Journal of Political Science* 32:3, pp. 345–67.

Beyer, P. 1994. *Religion and Globalisation*. New York: Sage.

Boyer, R. and D. Drache (eds). 1996. *States Against Markets: The Limits of Globalisation*. London: Routledge.

Braman, S. and Sreberny-Hommadi (eds). 1996. *Globalisation, Communication and Transnational Civil Society*. Creskill, NJ: Hampton Press.

Bryan, D. and M. Rafferty 1999. *The Global Economy in Australia*. Sydney: Allen and Unwin.

Bull, H. 1977. *The Anarchical Society: A Study of Order in World Politics*. London: Macmillan.

Burbach, R., O. Nunez and B. Kagarlitsky 1997. *Globalization and its Discontents*. London: Pluto Press.

Cable, V. and A. Bressand 1998. *Globalisation: Rules and Standards for the World Economy*. London: Pinter.

Camilleri, J.A. and J. Falk 1992. *The End of Sovereignty*. Aldershot, UK: Edward Elgar.

Castells, M. 1998. *End of Millennium*. Oxford: Blackwell.

Castells, M. 1997. *The Power of Identity*. Oxford: Blackwell.

Cerny, P. 1996. "Globalisation and other stories: The search for a new paradigm for international relations", *International Journal* 51:4, pp. 617–37.

Cerny, P.G. 1995. "Globalisation and the changing logic of collective action", *International Organization* 49, pp. 595–625.

Chase-Dunn, C. 1989. *Global Formation: Structures of the World Economy*. Oxford: Basil Blackwell.

Commission on Global Governance. 1995. *Our Global Neighbourhood*. New York: Oxford University Press.

Cox, K.R. (ed.) 1997. *Spaces of Globalisation: Reasserting the Power of the Local*. New York: Guilford Press.

Currie, J. and J.A. Newson (eds). 1998. *Universities and Globalisation: Critical Perspectives*. Thousand Oaks. CA: Sage.

Daniels, J. L. and N.C. Daniels 1993. *Global Vision: Building New Models for the Corporation of the Future*. New York: McGraw Hill.

Davidson, A. and K. Weekley (eds). 1999. *Globalisation and Citizenship in the Asia Pacific*. Basingstoke, UK: Macmillan.

Dicken, P. 1992. *Global Shift: The Internationalisation of Economic Activity*, 2nd ed. London: Chapman and Hall.

Esping-Anderson, G. 1996. *Welfare States in Transition: National Adaptations in Global Economics*. London: Sage.

Fagan, R. and M. Webber 1994. *Global Restructuring: The Australian Experience*. Oxford: Oxford University Press.

Falconer, C. and P. Sauve 1996. "Globalisation, trade and competition", *OECD Observer* 201, pp. 6–9.

Falk, R. 1996. "An inquiry into the political economy of world order", *New Political Economy* 1:1, pp. 13–26.

Featherstone, M. (ed.) 1990. *Global Culture: Nationalism, Globalisation and Modernity*. London: Sage.

Garrett, G. 1998. *Partisan Politics in the Global Economy*. Cambridge: Cambridge University Press.

Germaine, R. (ed.). 1997. *Globalisation and Its Critics*. London: Macmillan.

Giddens, A. 1991. *Modernity and Self-Identity*. Stanford: Stanford University Press.

Gill, S.R. 1996. *Global Restructuring and New Multilateralism*. London: Macmillan.

Grant, W. 1997. "Perspectives on globalisation and economic coordination". In *Contemporary Capitalism: The Embeddedness of Institutions*, eds J. Rogers Hollingsworth and Robert Boyer, pp. 319–336. Cambridge: Cambridge University Press.

Green, A. 1997. *Education, Globalisation, and the Nation State*. New York: St Martin's Press.

Greider, W. 1997. *One World, Ready or Not: The Manic Logic of Global Capitalism*. New York: Simon and Schuster.

Guehenno, J-M. 1993. *La Fin de la Democratie*. Paris: Flammarion.

Guehenno, J-M.1995. *The End of the Nation-State*. Minneapolis: University of Minnesota Press.

Gummett, P. (ed.). 1996. *Globalisation and Public Policy*. Cheltenham, UK: Edward Elgar.

Gupta, S.D. and N.K. Choudhry (eds). 1997. *Dynamics of Globalisation and Development*. Lancaster, UK: Kluwer Academic Publishers.

Gwynne, R.N. and C. Kay (eds). 1999. *Latin America Transformed: Globalisation and Modernity*. New York: Oxford University Press.

Haynes, J. 1999. *Religion, Globalisation and Political Culture in the Third World*. New York: St Martin's Press.

Held, D. 1995. *Democracy and the Global Order*. Stanford: Stanford University Press.

Held, D. and A. McGrew 1993. "Globalization and the liberal democratic state", *Government and Opposition* 28:2, pp. 261–88.

Helleiner, E. 1995. "Explaining the globalization of financial markets: Bringing the State back in", *Review of International Political Economy* 2:2, pp. 315–41.

Helleiner, E. 1995. "Great transformations: A Polanyian perspective on the contemporary global financial order", *Studies in Political Economy* 48: Autumn, pp. 149–64.

Helleiner, E. 1994. *The Re-Emergence of Global Finance: From Bretton Woods to the 1990s*. Ithaca, NY: Cornell University Press.

Hettne, B. 1995. *Development Theory and the Three Worlds: Towards an International Political Economy of Development* 2nd ed. New York: Longman Scientific and Technical.

Hirst, P. 1997. "The Global Economy—myth and realities", *International Affairs* 73, pp. 409–25.

Howells, J. and M. Wood 1993. *The Globalisation of Production and Technology*. London: Belhaven.

Inoguchi, T. 1995. "Dialectics of world order: A view from Asia". In *Whose World Order?* eds. H-H. Holm and G. Sorensen, pp. 119–36. Boulder, CO: Westview Press.

Lawrence, R.Z., A. Bressand and T. Ito 1995. *A Vision for the World Economy: Openness, Diversity, and Cohesion*. Washington: The Brookings Institute.

McGrew, A. and P. Lewis 1992. *Global Politics: Globalisation and the Nation State*. Oxford: Polity.

Michie, J. and J.G. Smith (eds). 1998. *Globalisation, Growth and Governance*. Oxford: Oxford University Press.

Mittelman, J. H. (ed.). 1996. *Globalization: Critical Reflections*. London: Lynne Rienner.

Nadelmann, E. A. 1990. "Global prohibition regimes: The evolution of norms in international society", *International Organization* 44: 4, Autumn, pp. 479–526.

Nadelmann, E. A. 1993. "The internationalisation of US criminal law enforcement" and "Three models of transnational policing". In *Caps Across Borders: The Internationalisation of US Criminal Law Enforcement*. University Park, PA: Pennsylvania State University Press.

Ohmae, K. 1996. *The End of the Nation State*. London: HarperCollins.

Ostrom, E. 1990. *Governing the Commons*. Cambridge: Cambridge University Press.

Palan, R., J. Abbott and P. Deans 1996. *State Strategies in a Global Political Economy*. London: Pinter.

Pattnayak, S.R. (ed.). 1996. *Globalisation, Urbanisation, and the State: Selected Studies in Contemporary Latin America*. Lanham, MD: University Press of America.

Pollin, R. 1998. "Can domestic expansionary policy succeed in a globally integrated environment? An Examination of Alternatives". In *Globalisation and Progressive Economic Policy*, eds D. Baker, G. Epstein and R. Pollin, pp. 433–60. Cambridge: Cambridge University Press.

Probert, B. 1994. "Globalisation, economic restructuring and the state". In *State, Economy, and Public Policy in Australia*, eds S. Bell and B. Head, pp. 98–118. Oxford: Oxford University Press.

Probert, B. 1993. "Restructuring and Globalisation: What Do They Mean?", *Arena Magazine* 4: April–May, pp. 18–22.

Rogers Hollingsworth, J. and R. Boyer (eds). 1997. *Contemporary Capitalism: The Embeddedness of Institutions*. Cambridge: Cambridge University Press.

Rosenau, J.N. 1992. "Governance, order, and change in world politics". In *Governance Without Government: Order and Change in World Politics*, eds J. Rosenau and E. Czempiel, pp. 1–29. Cambridge: Cambridge University Press.

Rosenau, J.N. 1995. "Governance in the twenty-first Century", *Global Governance* 1:1, Winter, 13–43.

Rosenau, J.N. and E. Czempiel 1992. *Governance without Government: Order and Change in World Politics*. Cambridge: Cambridge University Press.

Sassen, S. 1991. *The Global City: New York, London, Tokyo*. Princeton: Princeton University Press.

Sassen, S. 1998. *Globalization and Its Discontents*. New York: The New Press.

Scott, A. (ed.). 1997. *The Limits of Globalisation: Cases and Arguments*. London: Routledge.

Schmidt, V.A. 1995. "*The New World Order incorporated: The rise of business and the decline of the nation state*", *Daedalus* 124: 2, pp. 75–106.

Simai, M. 1994. *The Future of Global Governance*. Washington, DC: United States Institute of Peace.

Strange, S. 1996. *The Retreat of the State: The Diffusion of Power in the World Economy*. New York: Cambridge University Press.

Strange, S. 1993. *States and Markets*, 2nd ed. London: Pinter.

Tomlinson, J. 1999. *Globalisation and Culture*. Chicago: University of Chicago Press, pp. 47–60.

Wade, R. 1996. "*Globalisation and its limits: Reports of the death of the national economy are greatly exaggerated*". In *National Diversity and Global Capitalism*, eds S. Berger and R. Dore, pp. 60–88. Ithaca, NY: Cornell University Press.

Wallace, I. 1990. *The Global Economic System*. London: Unwin Hyman.

Weiss, L. 1997. *The Myth of the Powerless State: Governing the Economy in a Global Era*. Cambridge: Polity.

Williamson, J.G. 1996. "Globalisation, convergence, and history", *Journal of Economic History* 56:2, pp. 277–306.

Wiseman, J. 1998. *Global Nation: Australia and the Politics of Globalisation*. Melbourne: Cambridge University Press.

World Bank. 1994. *Governance: The World Bank's Experience*. Washington DC: World Bank.

Chapter 6

Anderson, B. 1991. *Imagined Communities: Reflections on the Origin and Spread of Nationalism*. New York: Verso.

Appadurai, A. 1996. *Modernity at Large: Cultural Dimensions of Globalization*. Minneapolis: University of Minnesota Press.

Archibugi, D., D. Held and M. Kohler (eds). 1998. *Re-Imagining Political Community*. Cambridge: Polity.

Barber, B.R. 1995. *Jihad vs. McWorld*. New York: Times Books.

Camilleri, J.A. and J. Falk 1992. *The End of Sovereignty? The Politics of a Shrinking and Fragmenting World*. Aldershot, UK: Edward Elgar.

Ferguson, Y. and R.W. Mansbach 1996. *Polities: Authority, Identities, and Change*. Columbia: University of South Carolina Press.

Fleiner, T. 1994. "Nation state and autonomy for ethnic communities". *Peace and the Sciences*, December: pp. 1–10.

Frankenfeld, P.J. 1992. "Technological citizenship: A normative framework for risk studies". *Science, Technology and Human Values* 17, Autumn: pp. 459–84.

Gambles, I. 1995. "Lost time—The forgetting of the Cold War". *National Interest* 41, Fall: pp. 35.

Henningsen, M. 1989. "*Democracy: The future of a Western political formation*". *Alternatives* 14 , July: pp. 327–42.

Hill, G. 1995. "*Reason and will in contemporary social contract theory*". *Political Research Quarterly* 48, March: pp. 101–116.

Holm, H-H. and G. Sorenson (eds). 1995. *Whose World Order? Uneven Globalization and the End of the Cold War*. Boulder, CO: Westview Press.

Kuklinski, A. (ed.). 1990. *Globality versus Locality*. Warsaw: Institute of Space Economy, University of Warsaw.

Lipschutz, R.D. (ed.). 1995. *On Security*. New York: Columbia University Press.

Mlinar, Z. (ed.). 1992. *Globalization and Territorial Identities*. Aldershot, UK: Avebury.

Rosenau, J.N. 1983. "'Fragmegrative' challenges to national security". In *Understanding US Strategy: A Reader*, ed. T. Heyns, pp. 65–82. Washington DC: National Defense University.

Rosenau, J.N. 1990. *Turbulence in World Politics: A Theory of Change and Continuity*. Princeton: Princeton University Press.

Rosenau, J.N. 1997a. *Along the Domestic-Foreign Frontier: Exploring Governance in a Turbulent World.* New York: Cambridge University Press.

Rosenau, J.N. 1997b. "Material and imagined communities in globalized space". In *Globalization and Regional Communities: Geoeconomic, Sociocultural and Security Implications for Australia*, ed. D.H. McMillen, pp. 24–40. Toowomba, Australia: USQ Press.

Rosenau, J.N. 1998. "Disorder and order in a turbulent world: The emergence of globalized space". In *The Global Agenda*, 5th edn, eds C.W. Kegley, C.W. and E.R. Wittkopf, pp. 145–169. New York: McGraw Hill.

Rosenau, J.N., and W.M. Fagen 1997. "Increasingly skilful citizens: A new dynamism in world politics?" *International Studies Quarterly* 41, December: pp. 655–86.

Tamas, G.M. 1994. "A disquisition on civil society". *Social Research* 61, Summer: pp. 205–22.

Turner, B.S. 1993. "Outline of a theory of human rights". *Sociology* 27, August: pp. 489–512.

Zum, M. 1995. "The challenge of globalization and individualization: A view from Europe". In *Whose World Order? Uneven Globalization and the End of the Cold War*, ed. by H-H. Holm and G. Sorenson, pp. 137–64. Boulder, CO: Westview Press.

Chapter 7

Brecher, J. and T. Costello 1994. *Global Village or Global Pillage.* Boston: South End Press.

Cox, E. 1995. *A Truly Civil Society.* Sydney: ABC Books.

Daly, H. 1993. "The perils of free trade". *Scientific American* 269:5, pp. 50–7.

Daly, H. 1997. "Free trade: the perils of de-regulation". In *The Case Against the Global Economy*, eds J. Mander and E. Goldsmith, pp. 229–38. San Francisco: Sierra Club Books.

Elliot, L. 1999. "Third World debt relief gets world's attention". *Guardian Weekly*, May 2: p. 12.

Falk, R. 1993. "The making of global citizenship". In *Global Visions: Beyond the New World Order*, eds J. Brecher, J. Childs and J. Cutler, pp. 39–50. Boston: South End Press.

Freire, P. 1972. *Pedagogy of the Oppressed.* London: Penguin Books.

Hellyer, P. 1999. *Stop Think.* Toronto: Chimo Media.

Henderson, H. 1978. *Creating Alternative Futures: the End of Economics.* New York: Putnam's.

Henderson, H. 1996. *Building a Win-Win World: Life Beyond Global Economic Warfare.* San Francisco: Berrett-Kohler Publishers.

Hutton, W. 1993. "Choice does not pave the road to happiness". *Guardian Weekly*, 14 November, p. 21.

Hutton, W. 1994. "Markets threaten democracy's fabric". *Guardian Weekly*, 16 January, 21.

Hutton, W. 1995. *The State We're In.* London: Vintage.

Lane, R. 1993. *The Market Experience.* New York: Cambridge University Press.

Mander, J. and E. Goldsmith (eds) 1997. *The Case Against the Global Economy.* San Francisco: Sierra Club Books.

Martin, H-P. and H. Schumann 1997. *The Global Trap: Globalization and the Assault on Democracy and Prosperity*. Sydney: Pluto Press.

Putnam, R. 1993. *Making Democracy Work*. Princeton, NJ: Princeton University Press.

Ray, B. 1998. "Globalization and women in India: a women's studies perspective". Paper to Toda Institute Conference on Globalization, Employment, and Quality of Life, University of Sydney, November.

Robinson, M. 1998. *The Declaration of Human Rights: a Living Document*. Tokyo: The United Nations University.

Schlemmer, L. 1998. "Employment and quality of life: a South African perspective". Paper to Toda Institute Conference on Globalization, Employment and Quality of Life. University of Sydney, November.

Soros, G. 1998. *The Crisis of Global Capitalism*. Boston: Little Brown & Co.

Waring, M. 1988. *If Women Counted*. Auckland: Bridget Williams.

Wheelwright, E. 1995. "The complicity of economic think tanks". In *The Human Costs of Managerialism*, eds S. Rees and G. Rodley, pp. 29–37. Sydney: Pluto Press.

Chapter 8

Bell, D. 1981. "Models and reality in economic discourse". In *The Crisis of Economic Theory*, eds D. Bell and I. Kristol, pp. 46–80. New York: Basic Books.

Crozier, M.J., S.P. Huntington and J. Watanuki (eds.). 1975. *Crisis of Democracy: A Report on the Governability of Democracies to the Trilateral Commission*. New York: New York University Press.

Eckersley, R. 1998. *Measuring National Progress: Is Life Getting Better?* Australia: CSIRO Publishing.

Lane, R. 1991. *The Market Experience*. New York: Cambridge University Press.

OECD. 1997. *Final Report of the Project Group on Distressed Urban Areas*. Preliminary version (Doc DT/UA/LEED/RD(97)2). Paris: OECD.

Pusey, M. 1998. "Economic rationalism". In *International Encyclopedia of Public Policy and Administration*, vol. 2, ed. J. Shafritz, pp. 734–6. New York: Westview Press/Henry Holt & Co.

Rawls, J. 1984. "The right and the good contrasted". In *Liberalism and its Critics*, ed. M.J. Sandel, pp. 37–59. New York: New York University Press,

Veenhoven, R. 1996. "Happy life expectancy: A comprehensive measure of quality-of-life in nations". Paper presented to International Conference on Quality of Life, University of Northern Columbia, Prince George, Canada.

Vogel, J. 1998. "Coping with the European welfare mix: Welfare delivery institutions, family formation, and material inequality between types of families in the European Union". Paper to Siena Group Meeting on Families at the End of the Twentieth Century. Sydney, Australia, 7–9 December.

Chapter 9

Aurobindo, Sri 1972. *Social and Political Thought*. Pondicherry: Birth Centenary Library, vol.15.

Bannerjee, N. 1996. *Employment of Women and All That*. New Delhi: NCAER.

Bannerjee, N. and S. Mitter 1998. 'Women making a meaningful choice: Technology and the New Economic Order'. *Economic and Political Weekly* 33:52, 19 December, pp. 247–54.

Bello, W. 1998. "Globalisation and the Asian Financial Crisis". Paper presented at the Toda Conference on Globalization, Employment and the Quality of Life, University of Sydney, November.

Bhatt, E. 1998. "Towards second freedom". In *From Independence Towards Freedom: Indian Women Since 1947*, eds Bharati Ray and Aparna Basu, pp. 34–55. Delhi: Oxford University Press.

Chatterjee, M. 1996. "The nutritional challenge to health and development". In *Health, Poverty and Development in India*, eds M. Das Gupta, L. Chen and T. Krishnan, pp. 202–36. Delhi: Oxford University Press.

Chattopadhyaya, D.P. 1997, *Sociology, Ideology and Utopia: Socio-Political Philosophy of East and West*. New York: Brill.

Chattopadhyaya, D.P. 1988. *Sri Aurobindo and Karl Marx*. Delhi: Motilal Banarasidass.

Deshpande, S. and L. Deshpande. 1998. "Impact of liberalisation on labour market in India: What do facts from NSSO's 50th Round show?", *Economic and Political Weekly* 33:22, 30 May, L31–L39.

Ghosh, B. 1990. *The Indian Population Problem: A Household Economics Approach*. Delhi: Sage Publications.

Ghosh, B. and Mukhopadhyay, S. 1984. "Displacement of the female in the Indian labour force", *Economic and Political Weekly* 24 November, 1998–2002.

Government of India. 1996–97 and 1997–98. *Economic Survey*. New Delhi: Ministry of Finance.

Government of India. 1997. *Women in India: A Statistical Profile*. New Delhi: Ministry of Human Resource Development.

Gupta, C. and Chattopadhyaya, D.P. (eds). *Cultural Otherness and Beyond*. Boston: Brill.

Henderson, H. 1998. "Quality of life: Issues and questions". Paper presented at the Toda Conference on Globalization, Employment and Quality of Life, University of Sydney, November.

Hirway, I. 1996. "Economic reforms and gender issues in India", *Indian Journal of Labour Economics* 39:3, July/September, pp. 577–89.

Jhabvala, R. 1995. "Invisible workers reach international heights". *Economic and Political Weekly* 30:49, 9 December, pp. 3133–36.

Kurien, J. and T.R. Thankappan Achari 1994. "Overfishing the coastal commons: Causes and consequences". In *Social Ecology*, ed. R. Guha, pp. 218–44. Delhi: Oxford University Press.

Mallick, K. 1998. "Sex determination test in India: Reinforcing the bias against women". In *Cultural Otherness and Beyond*, eds C. Gupta and D.P. Chattopadhyaya, pp. 169–80 Boston: Brill.

Ray, R. 1999. *Fields of Protest: Women's Movements in India*. Minneapolis: University of Minnesota Press.

Roy, S. 1997. "Globalisation, structural change and poverty: Some conceptual and policy issues", *Economic and Political Weekly* 32:33–34, pp. 16–23 August, pp. 2117–35.

Schlemmer, L. 1998. "Globalisation, employment and the quality of life: Precis of my perspective". Paper presented at the Toda Conference on Globalisation, Employment and the Quality of Life, University of Sydney, November.

Sen, A.K. 1993. "Capability and well-being". In *The Quality of Life*, eds. M. Nussbaum and A.K. Sen, pp. 30–53. Oxford: Clarendon Press.

Somasekharappa, C.A. 1998. "Pepsitisation of society in India", Report, *The Hindu*, 23 December.

UNDP. 1998. *Human Development Report 1998*. New Delhi: Oxford University Press.

Chapter 11

Alston, P. 1984. "International law and the right to food". In *Food as a Human Right*, eds. A. Eide, W.B. Eide, S. Goonatilake, J. Gusson and Omawale, pp. 162–74 Tokyo: United Nations University.

CAFB (Canadian Association of Food Banks) 1999. *HungerCount 1999—A Growing Hunger for Change*, Canada's *Annual Survey of Emergency Food Programs*. Toronto: CAFB.

Esping-Andersen, G. 1990. *The Three Worlds of Welfare Capitalism*. Cambridge: Polity Press.

FAO. 1996. Rome Declaration on World Food Summit and World Food Summit Plan of Action, World Food Summit, Rome: Food and Agricultural Organization of the United Nations.

FAO/NGO. 1996. Consultation on the World Food Summit, E-mail communication, 19–21 September.

Houghton, J. and G. Riches 1997. "Food security in Prince George". In *Report on the Quality of Life in Prince George 1997*, ed. Alex Michalos. Prince George: University of Northern British Columbia.

Kneen, B. 1993. *From Land to Mouth: Understanding the Food System*. 2nd edn, Toronto: NC Press Ltd.

Lang, T. 1997. '*Food policy for the 21st century: can it be both radical and reasonable?*' Discussion Paper 4, Centre for Food Policy, Wolfson School of Health Sciences. London: Thames Valley University.

Macrae, R. 1997. "Does Canada have a food policy?" International Conference on Sustainable Urban Food Systems, Ryerson Polytechnic University, Toronto. 25 May.

Riches, G. 1999. "Advancing the Human Right to Food in Canada: Social Policy and the Politics of Hunger, Welfare and Food Security," *Agriculture and Human Values*, 16, 2, pp. 203–11.

Riches, G. (ed.). 1997. *First World Hunger: Food Security and Welfare Politics*. London: Macmillan/New York: St. Martin's Press.

Robertson, R.E. 1990. "The Right to Food—Canada's broken convenant". *Canadian Human Rights Yearbook, 1989–1990*: 6.

Winson, A. 1993. *The Intimate Commodity*. Toronto: Garamond Press.

Chapter 12

Crotty, J. and G. Epstein 1996. "In 'Defence of Capital Controls' ", *Socialist Register 1996.* London: Merlin Press, pp. 118–49

Daniels, R. 1996. *APEC—Human Rights and Development. Part 2—APEC Appeal Cases.* London: Amnesty International. November.

Kapstein, E. 1996. "Workers and the world economy", *Foreign Affairs* 75:3, pp. 16–37.

Kitney, G. 1999. "Light on in Davos, but nobody at home", *Sydney Morning Herald* 6 February, p. 26.

Kothari, S. 1994. "Global economic institutions and democracy: A view from India". In *Beyond Bretton Woods—Alternatives to the Global Economic Order*, eds J. Cananagh, D. Wysham and M. Arruda, pp. 39–54. London: Pluto Press.

Morrison, C.E. 1997. "Development cooperation in the 21st century: Implications for APEC". In *Building an Asia-Pacific community: Development cooperation within APEC*, ed. Andrew Elek. Brisbane: Foundation for Development Cooperation.

O'Neill, H. 1997. "Globalisation, competitiveness and human security: Challenges for development policy and institutional change". *The European Journal of Development Research* 9:1.

Sachs, J. 1997. "IMF is a power unto itself". See *www.stern.nyu.edu/ñroubini/asia/AsiaCrisisSachsViewFT1297.html*

Saul, J.R. 1999. "Globalization and Democracy". Lecture delivered at University of New South Wales, Sydney, 16 January.

Schwab, K. and C. Smadja 1996. "Start taking the backlash against globalization seriously", *International Herald Tribune* 1 February, p. 8.

Sewell, J.W. and M. McDowell 1998. "Birmingham and globalization—The missing players'. See *www.odc.org/birop.html*

Sheehan, P. 1999. "Why countries won't matter", *Sydney Morning Herald* January 9, p. 27.

Smillie, I. 1998. "Globalization, aid and the changing NGO world—The challenges ahead", Keynote address delivered at Australian Council for Overseas Aid Annual Conference, 29 August.

Soros, G. 1998. *The Crisis of Global Capitalism.* London: Little, Brown & Co.

Thurow, L. 1996. *The Future of Capitalism.* London: Nicholas Brealey.

UNCTAD. 1997. *Trade and Development Report, 1997.* United Nations, New York.

United Nations Development Program (UNDP). 1996. *Human Development Report 1996.* New York: Oxford University Press.

UNICEF. 1997. *The State of the World's Children 1997.* New York: Oxford University Press.

Watkins, K. 1997. "Fast route to poverty," *Guardian Weekly*, 16 February, p. 29.

Wolfensolm, J. 1998. "The other crisis" (Board of Governors Address, 6 October). (See http://www.worldbank.org/html/extdr/am98/jdw-sp/index.htm).

Wolfensolm, J. 1999. "Comparative development framework" (Remarks at the Symposium on Foundations for a Stable Global System, Tokyo, 1 March). (See http://www.worldbank.org/html/extdr/extme/jdwsp 030199.htm).

World Economic Forum (WEF). 1999. "World business, government and media leaders gather for talks on responsible management of globalization". 28 January. See *live99.weforum.org/press_releases.asp*

Chapter 13

Goleman, D. 1995. *Emotional Intelligence: Why It Can Matter More Than IQ.* New York: Bantam Books.

Chapter 14

Abrahamson, E. 1996. "Management fashion", *Academy of Management Review*, 21:1, pp. 254–85.

Advertisement for Business Now, *Independent*, Supplement, 29 October 1994.

Alvesson, M. 1993. "Organisations as rhetoric: Knowledge-intensive firms and the struggle with ambiguity", *Journal of Management Studies* 30:6, pp. 997–1015.

Armstrong, J.S. 1998. "Management science: What does it have to do with management or science?", *Marketing Bulletin*, 9, pp. 1–15.

Baritz, L. 1987. *The Servants of Power. A History of the Use of Social Science in American Industry*. New York: Wiley

Bennetto, J. 1999. "Police to scrap 999 call targets", *Independent* 20 February, p. 6.

Boden, R. 1998. "The 'Y-field thing'—Semantics, big science and accounting". Seminar given to PREST, Manchester University, October.

Branscomb, L. 1988. Testimony before Senate Judiciary Committee, Subcommittee on Technology and Law, Washington DC, 16 March.

Bronson, J.G. 1987. "Unfriendly eyes", *IEEE Transactions on Professional Communication* 30: 3, pp. 173–8.

Bucy, F. as quoted in Schatz, W. 1983. "The hitch in high tech trade", *Datamation* 29:10, pp. 148–59.

Bulletpoint. 1996, 34.

Carter, R. 1989. "Careless words cost business", *Accountancy*, 103:1147, pp. 158–60.

Caulkin, S. 1994. "Research into research", *Observer*, 27 February, p. 8.

Clark, T. 1995. *Managing Consultants. Consultancy as the Management of Impressions.* Buckingham. Open University Press.

Collins, D. 1997. "Two cheers for empowerment: Some critical reflections", *Leadership and Organization Development Journal* 18:1, pp. 23–8.

Commission on Management Research. 1994. *Building Partnerships: Enhancing the Quality of Management Research.* Swindon: ESRC.

de Burgundy, J. 1995. "Working daze: Uncertainty and ambiguity in consulting", *Management Decision* 33:8, pp. 51–5.

DeNisi, A. 1994. "Is relevant research irrelevant?: On evaluating the contribution of research to management practice", *Journal of Management Issues* 6:2, pp. 145–59.

Drahos, P. 1995. "Global property rights in information: the story of TRIPS at the GATT", *Prometheus* 13:1, pp. 6–19.

Economist. 1993. "Quacks and coaches", 17 April, 81.

Edwards, E. 1987. "Corporate espionage: Legal but usually dishonest", *Management Accounting* 65:10, pp. 18–19.

Eliasson, G. 1999. "Communication, information technology and firm performance". In *Information and Organisation: A Tribute to the Work of Don Lamberton* eds S. Macdonald and J. Nightingale, pp. 285–304. Amsterdam: North-Holland.

Gill, J. and S. Whittle 1992. "Management by panacea: Accounting for transience", *Journal of Management Studies* 30:2, pp. 281–95.

Glass, C., N. Hyndman and D. McKillop 1996. "UK universities: A time series study of economies of scale and scope in the context of the research assessment exercises", *Public Money and Management* October–December, pp. 59–64.

Grint, K. 1994. "Reengineering history: Social resonances and business process reengineering", *Organization* 1:1, pp. 179–201.

Harvey, I. 1989. as quoted in Harvey, D. 1989. "BTG: The mother of invention", *Director* September, pp. 121–2.

Jackall, R. 1988. *Moral Mazes. The World of Corporate Managers*. Oxford: Oxford University Press.

Macdonald, S. 1990. *Technology and the Tyranny of Export Controls. Whisper Who Dares.* London: Macmillan.

Macdonald, S. 1993. "Nothing either good or bad: Industrial espionage and technology transfer", *International Journal of Technology Management* 8:1/2, pp. 95–105.

Macdonald, S. 1996. "Industrial espionage and innovation", *Interdisciplinary Science Reviews* 21: 3, pp. 209–14.

Macdonald, S. and B. Lefang 1997. "Innovation and the patent attorney", *Prometheus* 15:3, pp. 329–43.

Macdonald, S. and M. Simpson 1998. "Keeping a healthy distance: Management research and managers", *Clinician in Management* 7, pp. 221–33.

McGivern, C. 1983. "Some facets of the relationship between consultants and clients in organizations", *Journal of Management Studies* 20:3, pp. 367–86.

Merges, R. 1988. "Commercial success and patent standards: Economic perspectives on innovation", *California Law Review* 76, pp. 805–76 (ref. 6).

Merges, R. as quoted in "Patent plague", *Forbes ASAP Supplement* 1993, p. 62.

Micklethwait, J. and A. Wooldridge 1996. "Gurus of gobbledygook", *Sunday Telegraph Review* 27 October, pp. 1–2.

Nasheri, H. and T. O'Hearn 1998. "Crime and technology: New rules in a new world", *Information and Communications Technology Law* 7:2, pp. 145–57.

National Academy of Sciences. 1987. *Balancing the National Interest.* Washington DC: National Academy Press.

National Academy Press. 1991. *Finding Common Ground.* Washington DC: National Academy Press.

Oliver, N. 1998. "Rational choice or leap of faith? The creation and defence of a management orthodoxy", *Iconoclastic Papers* 1, 2. See: *www.solent.ac.uk/sbs/iconoclastic/index.html*

Olney, C.W. 1988. "The secret world of the industrial spy", *Business and Society Review* 64, pp. 28–32.

Pascale, R. 1990. *Managing on the Edge. How the Smartest Companies Use Conflict to Stay Ahead.* New York: Simon and Schuster.

Quintas, P. and K. Ken Guy 1995. "Collaborative, pre-competitive R&D and the firm", *Research Policy* 24, pp. 325–48.

Schrader, S. 1991. "Informal technology transfer between firms in cooperation through information trading", *Research Policy* 20, 1991, pp. 153–70.

Silverman, A. 1990. "Intellectual property law and the venture capital process", *High Technology Law Journal* 5:1, pp. 157–92 (fn.62).

Southard, D. 1982. In Permanent Subcommittee on Investigations, Committee on Government Affairs, Senate Hearings, Transfer of United States High Technology to the Soviet Union and Soviet Bloc Nations, Washington DC: USGPO.

Stewart, J. 1996. "Management", *Qantas Club* September, pp. 29–33.

Stewart, T. 1994. "Your company's most valuable asset: Intellectual capital", *Fortune* 30 October, pp. 28–33.

Sturdy, A. 1997. "The consultancy process—an insecure business?", *Journal of Management Studies* 34:3, pp. 389–413.

Tisdall, P. 1982. *Agents of Change. The Development and Practice of Management Consultancy.* London: Heinemann.

von Hippel, E. 1987. "Cooperation between rivals: Informal know-how trading", *Research Policy* 16, pp. 291–302.

Wu, T. 1983. "The citizen partner: A key force in effective strategic export control", *Signal* August, pp. 106–8.

Chapter 15

Dalum, B. 1998 (IKE Group, University of Aalborg), Personal communication.

Duysters, G. and J. Haagedoorn 1996. "Internationalization of corporate technology through strategic partnering: an empirical investigation", *Research Policy* 25, pp. 1–12.

Florida, R. 1997. "The globalization of R&D: results of a survey of foreign-affiliated R&D laboratories in the USA", *Research Policy* 26, pp. 85–103.

Freeman, C. 1995. "The 'National Systems of Innovation' in historical perspective", *Cambridge Journal of Economics* 19:1, pp. 5–24.

Granstrand, O., L. Hakanson and S. Sjolander 1992. *Technology Management and International Business: Internationalization of R&D and Technology*. Chichester, UK: Wiley.

Kummerle, W. 1997. "Building effective R&D capabilities abroad", *Harvard Business Review* March–April: pp. 61–70.

Mansfield, E. and J-Y. Lee. 1996. "The modern university: contributor to industrial innovation and recipient of industrial R&D support", *Research Policy* 25: pp. 1047–58.

OECD. 1994. *The Performance of Foreign Affiliates in OECD Countries.* Paris: OECD.

OECD. 1996. *Employment and Growth in the Knowledge-based Economy*. Paris: OECD.

OECD. 1998. *The Internationalisation of Industrial R&D: Patterns and Trends.* Paris: OECD.

Patel, P. and K. Pavitt 1998. *National Systems of Innovation under Strain: The Internationalisation of Corporate R and D* Science Policy Research Unit Electronic Working Paper Series, Paper No. 22.

Patel, P. and K. Pavitt 1991. "Large firms in the production of the world's technology: an important case of non-globalisation", Journal of International Business Studies 22, pp. 1–21.

Patel, P. and K. Pavitt 1994. "National Innovation Systems: Why are they important and how might they be measured and compared?", *Economics of Innovation and New Technology* 3, pp. 77–95.

Reddy, P. 1997. "New trends in globalization of corporate R&D and implications for innovation capability in host countries: a survey from India", *World Development* 25:11, pp. 1821–37.

Reddy, P. and J. Sigurdson 1994. "Emerging patterns of globalisation of corporate R&D and scope for innovative capability building in developing countries?" *Science and Public Policy* October: pp. 283–94.

Storper, M. 1996. "Institutions in the knowledge-based economy". In OECD, *Employment and Growth in the Knowledge-Based Economy*, pp. 255–89. Paris: OECD

United Nations. 1997. *World Development Report.* New York: United Nations.

Author Index

Subject Index